Cyber-Proletariat

Digital Barricades:
Interventions in Digital Culture and Politics

Series editors:
Professor Jodi Dean, Hobart and William Smith Colleges
Dr Joss Hands, Anglia Ruskin University
Professor Tim Jordan, University of Sussex

Also available

Information Politics:
Liberation and Exploitation in the Digital Society
Tim Jordan

Cyber-Proletariat

Global Labour in the Digital Vortex

Nick Dyer-Witheford

 PLUTO PRESS Between the Lines
TORONTO

First published 2015 by Pluto Press
345 Archway Road, London N6 5AA
www.plutobooks.com

First published in Canada in 2015 by Between the Lines
401 Richmond Street West, Studio 277, Toronto, Ontario M5V 3A8 Canada
1-800-718-7201
www.btlbooks.com

British Library Cataloguing in Publication Data
A catalogue record for this book is available from the British Library

ISBN 978 0 7453 3404 2   Hardback
ISBN 978 0 7453 3403 5   Pluto Press paperback
ISBN 978 1 77113 221 3   Between the Lines paperback
ISBN 978 1 7837 1278 6   Pluto Press PDF eBook
ISBN 978 1 77113 223 7   Between the Lines PDF eBook
ISBN 978 1 7837 1280 9   Kindle eBook
ISBN 978 1 7837 1279 3   Pluto Press epub
ISBN 978 1 77113 222 0   Between the Lines epub

Library and Archives Canada Cataloguing in Publication
Dyer-Witheford, Nick, 1951-, author
    Cyber-proletariat : global labour in the digital vortex / Nick Dyer-Witheford.
Co-published by: Pluto Press, London.
Includes bibliographical references and index.
Issued in print and electronic formats.
ISBN 978-1-77113-221-3 (bound).--ISBN 978-1-77113-222-0 (epub).--ISBN 978-1-77113-223-7 (pdf)
    1. Information technology--Social aspects. 2. Electronic industry workers--Social conditions. 3. Digital divide. 4. Computers--Social aspects. I. Title.
HM851.D94 2015   303.48'33   C2015-901312-7
                                C2015-901313-5

This book is printed on paper suitable for recycling and made from fully managed and sustained forest sources. Logging, pulping and manufacturing processes are expected to conform to the environmental standards of the country of origin.

Between the Lines gratefully acknowledges assistance for its publishing activities from the Canada Council for the Arts, the Ontario Arts Council, the Government of Ontario through the Ontario Book Publishers Tax Credit program, and the Government of Canada through the Canada Book Fund.

10   9   8   7   6   5   4   3   2   1

Typeset by Stanford DTP Services, Northampton, England Text
design by Melanie Patrick

Contents

Series Preface

Crisis and conflict open up opportunities for liberation. In the early twenty-first century, these moments are marked by struggles enacted over and across the boundaries of the virtual, the digital, the actual and the real. Digital cultures and politics connect people even as they simultaneously place them under surveillance and allow their lives to be mined for advertising. This series aims to intervene in such cultural and political conjunctures. It will feature critical explorations of the new terrains and practices of resistance, producing critical and informed explorations of the possibilities for revolt and liberation.

Emerging research on digital cultures and politics investigates the effects of the widespread digitisation of increasing numbers of cultural objects, the new channels of communication swirling around us and the changing means of producing, remixing and distributing digital objects. This research tends to oscillate between agendas of hope, that make remarkable claims for increased participation, and agendas of fear, that assume expanded repression and commodification. To avoid the opposites of hope and fear, the books in this series aggregate around the idea of the barricade. As sources of enclosure as well as defences for liberated space, barricades are erected where struggles are fierce and the stakes are high. They are necessarily partisan divides, different politicisations and deployments of a common surface. In this sense, new media objects, their networked circuits and settings, as well as their material, informational, and biological carriers all act as digital barricades.

Jodi Dean, Joss Hands and Tim Jordan

Acknowledgements

I thank my wife Anne for her companionship as this book was written, while we were both working on different but related academic projects, which made life together even more complex, interesting and enjoyable.

Cyber-Proletariat owes a special debt to a group of young scholars who are or were recently doctoral students at the University of Western Ontario's Faculty of Information and Media Studies and at the Centre for the Study of Theory and Criticism. Their work is reflected in various ways in these pages. Thanks to Svitlana Matviyenko, for insightful editorial assistance and an education in the politics of Ukraine and Lacan's cybernetics; to Atle Kjøsen and Vincent Manzerolle, for their exciting new materialist analyses of circulation and automation; to Elise Thorburn, for her inspiring analysis of assemblies, assemblages and social reproduction; to Indranil Chakaraborty, for sharing his intrepid fieldwork on service work in India's IT industry; to Rafael Alarcón, for his visit from Mexico and all the resultant debates and conversations; to Brian Brown, for wonderful talks about unpaid labours on Flickr; to Eric Lohman, for help over offshored office work; and to Emmanuel Leonardi, whose research contributed to the early stages of the book, even though he may not recognize the form it now takes.

Thanks also to Greig de Peuter and Enda Brophy, for allowing me to make extensive use of their work on the circuits of cell phone exploitation; to Tony Weis, for advice on land-grabs, enclosures and primitive accumulation; to Tobias Nagl, for translations of the work of Karl Heinz Roth; to Warren Steele, for conversations on Jünger, Ballard and weather machines; to Kane Faucher, for vortical discussions; to Sarah T. Roberts, for permission to cite her forthcoming work on commercial content moderation; to my friend Gil Warren, for help finding a few bright political glimmers in a generally dark scene; to two long-time comrades and colleagues, Dorothy Kidd and Santiago Valles, for the example of their scholarly work and political engagements; to the editors of the Digital Barricades series, for helpful revision suggestions; to Tim Clark, for incisive copy editing; and to David Castle at Pluto Press, for his great editorial patience.

Thanks, finally, to all who have over the years accused me of being 'too optimistic'; this book is for you.

1

Proletariat

Deep Knowledge Ventures

On 13 May 2014, a press release from Deep Knowledge Ventures, a Hong Kong-based venture capital fund specializing in biotechnology, age-related disease drugs and regenerative medicine projects, announced that it 'formally acknowledges VITAL, a crucial Artificial Intelligence instrument for investment decision-making, as an equal member of its Board of Directors'.

VITAL was the product of Aging Analytics UK, a provider of health-sector market intelligence to pension funds, insurers and governments. Developed by 'a team of programmers, several of which have theoretical physics backgrounds', the system 'uses machine learning to analyze financing trends in a database of life science companies and predict successful investments'. VITAL 1.0 was a 'basic algorithm', but the goal was 'through iterative releases and updates ... to create a piece of software that is capable of making autonomous investment decisions' (Fontaine 2014). Apparently, however, Deep Knowledge Ventures thought VITAL was already pretty good: it told reporters the program would 'vote on whether to invest in a specific company or not' (BBC 2014).

All this sounded very futuristic. As commentators quickly pointed out, however, it was really 'publicity hype' (BBC 2014). This was not because decision-making algorithms are impossible, but, on the contrary, because their use, often in forms far more complex than VITAL, is commonplace in today's capitalism. Such programs are, for example, central to the operations of the financial sector, whose high-speed multi-billion trades are entirely dependent on algorithms – and whose bad decisions brought the world economy to its knees in the great Wall Street crash of 2008. The press release was a stunt because the future to which it seemed to point exists now.

Whatever interest VITAL's debut may have stirred was immediately eclipsed by more sombre news. On the same day 301 workers died in a massive explosion at Turkey's Soma coal mine. The mine, once publicly owned, had been privatized in 2007. The disaster was caused by neglect of safety equipment generally attributed to profit-boosting cost-cutting. The miners' charred and choked bodies were pulled to the surface from two miles underground: they would not be needing regenerative medicine and anti-aging treatments, to which, of course, they would never have had access anyway.

Turkish trade unions declared a one-day general strike. At the same time, street protests burst out in Istanbul, Ankara, Izmir and other cities across Turkey. Students calling on the government to resign wore hard hats to show solidarity with the miners. They were met with tear gas and rubber bullets. These protests were a continuation of the social turmoil that had raged intermittently since the occupation of Gezi Park in Istanbul's Taksim Square in May of 2013. That occupation, started to protect a grove of trees from the construction of an Ottoman-barrack themed shopping mall, had rapidly become a focus for discontent with the religiously conservative neoliberal capitalism of President Erdogan's regime. It lasted for 17 days. In some 5,000 related demonstrations across Turkey, 11 people were killed and more than 8,000 injured, many seriously.

Throughout the unrests, protests and criticism of the government had been mobilized through social media, provoking a farcical attempt by the Erdogan regime to ban Twitter and YouTube. This ban, though universally violated, had only been formally rescinded six weeks before the Soma disaster. Now, social media again disseminated news, first of the scale of the catastrophe, initially minimized by the government, and then of the fresh protests: a photograph of an advisor to President Erdogan savagely drop-kicking a demonstrator held down by security forces in the streets of Soma circulated widely (Saul 2014).

The same-day news of the algorithmic boss-entity and the mine disaster was coincidence. Yet it condenses paradoxes and contradictions central to this book. For a start, it starkly highlights the coexistence within contemporary capitalism of extraordinary high-technologies and workers who live and die in brutal conditions often imagined to belong in some antediluvian past. This coexistence is also a connection. Mines and artificial intelligences seem to belong to different worlds, but they are strongly linked. Although only a small part of production at Soma went to power plants, similar coal mines around the planet provide – at appalling, biosphere-endangering environmental cost – the basic energy source on which all digital technologies depend: electricity. Other mines, for columbite tantalite, gold, platinum, copper rare earths and other minerals, many with working conditions as or more dangerous than those at Soma, provide the materials from which computers are made.

At the same time, computers are being applied not just to the creation of artificial bosses but even more strenuously to the cost-cutting automation of work. From West Virginia to South Africa mining is on the front lines in a new wave of robotization that could wipe away whole tranches of manual labour. The automation of hard and hazardous work underground by drones, driverless trucks and robot drills might seem an unqualified good. Yet for communities with no other source of waged work it does not necessarily appear so simple, for it places them at risk of joining a deepening pool of unemployed populations no longer required by digital capital. This, however, is an issue not just for manual workers, such as miners, but also for intellectual workers, such as the students who donned hard hats in the support of the Soma community. These students might, hypothetically, one day themselves be building artificial intelligences or designing new pharmaceuticals. Yet they too face the possibility that the professional and technical careers for which they train may suddenly be automated out of existence.

In recent years a complex array of revolts around the world against exploitative work, the misery of worklessness, and ecological disasters – revolts sometimes closely allied, sometimes distant from or even hostile to one another – have all thrown into question the basic structures and processes of advanced capitalism. In yet another apparent paradox, such uprisings themselves increasingly use digital technologies. The Twitter-storm of Turkey's demonstrators is just one example of this insurgent use of networked social media, even as such movements also put people bodily into city streets and squares, conversing with each other in popular assemblies and in physical confrontation with security forces. Both in terms of the crises that cause them and the weapons they take up, such unrests are thus situated within capitalism's whirlwind of technological change.

What then is the relation between cybernetic capitalism and its increasingly disposable working class? What are the interactions between segments of that class with different, yet also sometimes shared, relations to information technologies, such as miners and students, extremes of manual and mental labour? And what is the significance of the networked circulation of the revolts which, beyond Turkey, have so widely disturbed today's algorithmic capital? These are the questions that impel our own 'deep knowledge venture'.

Facebook Revolutions?

Our theoretical point of departure lies in the tradition of autonomist Marxism, so called because of its emphasis on workers' power to challenge and break their subordination to capital (Cleaver 1979; Dyer-Witheford 1999; Eden 2012). In this tradition analysis starts with class struggles, 'their content, their direction, how they develop and how they circulate' (Zerowork Collective 1975).

The revolts at Soma and Gezi Park were only part of a much wider sequence of protests, riots, strikes and occupations that towards the end of the first decade of the twenty-first century had begun to circle the planet. In 2008, Wall Street's sub-prime mortgage crisis, relayed at light-speeds from one financial centre to another by some of the most advanced computer networks in existence, had brought the world economy to the brink of collapse. Immediately, states locked-down into emergency measures – bank bailouts, austerity budgets – to save global capital. Responses from below took time to emerge and were shaped by how the crisis affected specific zones of the system. For if the 'global slump' (McNally 2011) touched the entire planet, it did not everywhere do so in the same way. Some areas fell into economic decline, others stagnated, yet others grew even faster than before but with increased social polarization. Thus the rebellions that sprung up in the wake of the crisis did so in regional clusters, simultaneous or serial, some clearly interlinked, some more apart: Eurozone anti-austerity revolts; a strike wave in China; an Arab Spring and an American Fall; later, in a Winter of emergent markets, uprisings in Brazil, Turkey and Ukraine, yet all together marking a widespread intensification in social antagonisms. A new cycle of struggles had begun.

No aspect of these revolts attracted more attention than their use of digital networks. Reportage of 'Facebook' 'Twitter' or 'YouTube Revolutions' focused on protestors' use of social media and mobile communication. Andrew Sullivan's 'The Revolution will be Twittered' (2009) set the tone, with its allusive repudiation of the anti-media radicalism of Gil Scott-Heron's 'The Revolution Will Not Be Televised' (1971). There was no shortage of examples: the internet relay of news of the self-immolation of Mohamed Bouazizi, the impoverished street vendor whose death catalyzed popular revolt in Tunisia in 2011; the similar role of the 'We are all Khalid Said' blog, commemorating a young man beaten to death by security forces outside a cybercafé, in the Egyptian revolution; the Mubarak regime's failed and back-firing attempt to shut down internet service as battles raged in Cairo's Tahrir Square; the outwitting of police by smartphone coordinated riots that sent smoke rising over London and other UK cities; the digital circulation of photos of anti-suicide nets hanging outside the Foxconn factories where iPhones rolled off the production lines; the popular assemblies live-streamed between occupiers of Madrid's Puerta de Sol and Athen's Syntagma Square; the internet call to 'Occupy Wall Street' and the Tumblr origin of the slogan 'We are the 99%'; the hacker exploits of Wikileaks and Anonymous; the Facebook message from Ukrainian journalist Mustafa Nayyem – 'Come on, seriously. Tell me, who is ready to come out on Maidan before midnight?' – that sparked revolt in Kiev; the Turkish government's failed attempt to quell street protest by banning Twitter – all these became defining moments of a global ferment stirred with new means of communication.

A graphic instance of this journalistic depiction is provided by the cover of the 29 June 2013 issue of *The Economist*. Titled 'The March of Protest', it shows four revolutionary figures: a tricolor-brandishing woman, based on Delacroix's famous *The Spirit of Liberty*, labelled '1848 Europe'; a yippie, Molotov cocktail in one hand, flowers in another for '1968 America & Europe'; a Lech Walesa-type East European worker-intellectual, with a candle for vigils and a spanner, for '1989 Soviet Empire', and an ethnically indeterminate young woman, with a takeout coffee in her left hand and a cell phone in the right, the iconic Guy Fawkes mask of Anonymous at her feet, and behind her a police van water-cannoning crowds with signs reading 'Cairo', 'Istanbul', 'Rio'; her label is '2013 Everywhere'.

This theme is expanded in several longer accounts of the 2011 revolts. Paul Mason's (2012: 130) study of 'global revolution' (itself originally a blog post) suggests the protests reflect the emergence of forms of 'networked individualism'; Manuel Castells (2012) has tracked the 'networks of rage and hope'; and Paolo Gerbaudo (2012) argues that 'tweets in the streets' were critical for the organization of protests; several more regional studies, particularly on the Arab Spring, echo these themes (Faris 2013; Howard and Hussain 2013; Herrera 2014).

Others, however, are critical of this network-centric optic on the unrests. They claim it underestimates the importance of more traditional, on-the-ground organizing methods (Aouragh and Alexander 2011; Therborn 2012); misses the continuing importance of older media forms (Kidd 2012a; Nunes 2008); and, most importantly, obscures the underlying grievances that drove people to streets and squares. Jodi Dean characterizes the 'Facebook revolution' trope as 'reactionary', a recuperation of radical politics by focusing on the high-tech gadgetry and networked chatter integral to 'communicative capitalism' (cited in Arria 2012). Philip Mirowski (2013) attributes the success of neoliberalism in withstanding dissent partly to the trivializing effect of journalists' focus on social media.

Arguments about the *tactical* role of digital platforms are important, especially for activists who want to learn from the 2011 revolts and also learn what their opponents are learning: we will return to them later. Behind the contending claims about social media empowerment and digital distraction there is, however, another issue – that of the *strategic* role of computers and networks in shaping the forces that clashed in squares and streets around the world. In North America, the slogan of Occupy – 'we are the 99%' – contrasted the fortunes of a 'one per cent' corporate elite controlling the most advanced digital systems on the planet with the fate of precarious workers and unemployed, for whom networked outsourcing and automation meant the loss of jobs and workplace bargaining power. Elsewhere around the world, movements challenging plutocratic elites combined, in varying mixes and alignments, the urban poor and homeless, waged industrial and service labour, students facing unemployment and anxious professionals – all groups whose conditions of work, or worklessness, had within a generation been drastically changed by the diffusion of computers and networks across a global capitalist economy. Within and beyond the 'Facebook revolution' controversy is, therefore, a wider question, that of the relation of cybernetics to class.

Vampires with Smartphones

Cybernetics and class are both old terms. 'Cybernetics' (Wiener 1948) was coined in the 1940s to describe issues of control and communication that lie at the root of early electronic computer development. Though the term dates from the days of giant mainframe computers, big as bungalows, it has given its name to all the cybernetic technologies – desktops, laptops, tablets, smartphones – that followed. Since then, however, there have also been many other names to designate these technologies, and their social consequences and dimensions: 'post-industrialism', 'information society', 'knowledge society' (Bell 1973). And these include not just names given by the friends and apologists of capital, but also by critical theorists, speaking of 'information capitalism' (Mosco and Wasko 1988), 'digital capitalism' (Schiller 1999), 'cognitive capitalism' (Vercellone 2006), and other variants on the same theme.

So, again, why 'cybernetics'? In part *because* it is old; understanding processes involves seeing directions, vectors and lines of movement, and this requires glimpsing from whence ideas come, before they arrive crashing into one's cranium like a brick through a window or a military robot demolishing a door – and from that point of view an old word is good. Indeed, it is from accounts close to origins and points of conflict, not so obscured by the layers of mystification and self-congratulation built up by the victors of those battles, that some of the best accounts of the machinic processes we analyze here come. Specifically, it is the historical connotations of command, control and communication carried by the term 'cybernetics' – a name which originates in the Greek *kybernetes* for rulership – that recommends so pointedly the concept of 'cybernetic capitalism' (Robins and Webster 1988; Peters et al. 2009; Tiqqun 2001) for the study of computers and class.

Class is an even more ancient, blood-encrusted term. A Marxist concept of class designates the division of members of society according to their place in a system of production: today, as capitalists, various fluid intermediate strata or 'middle classes', and proletarians. But this is not a mere observation that societies are divided into economically in-equal strata, a bland sociological truism. The point is that a dominant stratum exploits all the others. Since the concept of class identifies a process of predation, it is unsurprising that no message is more frequently transmitted through the intellectual organs of society than that class does not exist. Or that it once existed, but has now passed away. Or that in so far as it exists, it is entirely innocuous. Thus it is suggested that the polarity between workers and owners has dissipated into infinite, negotiable gradations of income and status; that because working-class communities no longer have the close knit solidarity they did in the industrial city, class is no longer important; that ethnic and gender relations have replaced class in providing the coordinates of social life; that because living standards have risen, exploitation has been replaced by consumerism; and that, if class is to be mentioned at all, it should only be to affirm that we are all, every last one of us, 'middle class'. To name class in an any more critical sense is to be condemned as, at best, reductionist, inhumanly insensitive to the rich textures of everyday life, committed to unearthly clinical abstraction, and, at worst, actively hostile towards social harmony, if not inciting civil war.

And it is indeed in such a spirit, let us confess, that we insist on class analysis, as that instrument required to recognize the inhuman, abstract and unearthly reductions forced onto people and planet by an economic system founded on a constitutive state of civil war, even if, today, this is a class war waged effectively only from above – by capital, for which the denial of class, the insistence that the world be understood only as a set of individual projects, is one of the most powerful and destructive weapons in that war. Yes, class does not today present itself in the same way as it did in Marx's era. But there is a difference, a world of difference, between saying that something has ceased to exist, and saying that it has mutated, become more complex, enlarged its scope on a worldwide basis. Today some computer scientists speculate that the entire universe is an artifact fabricated from the simple, binary on-off alternations of simple cellular automata (Wolfram 2002). We think much the same about the fabrication of society from the binary antagonisms of class. Class has become ontologically not less, but more real, more extended, entangled, ramified and differentiated – and yet without abolishing the opposition of exploiter and exploited on which it is posited, which is generative of countless intermediate forms, and yet preserves its simple, brutal algorithm. Who can doubt, seeing the difference in the condition of financier super-yacht owners and immigrant *sans papiers*, of the social media billionaire and the minimum-wage fast-food worker, that class exists?

Yet our ability to understand or even perceive class *has* been diminishing, and not only because of the restructuring of the global economy and its propagandist representation by free market ideologues, but also because of the numbing jargon of academic discussions, including discussion by Marxists. So, as inoculation, let us resurrect one of Marx's most vivid metaphors: he writes that capital, 'vampire-like, only lives by sucking living labour, and lives the more, the more labour it sucks' (1977: 342). Let's say straight out: class is a vampire relationship. It is a transfer of energy, time and consciousness – *aka* the extraction of surplus value – from one section of a species to another, in a process that makes the recipients increasingly alien to the coerced donors. In what follows, we will try to describe this process with a scholarly exactitude and terminological rigor that does not lose sight of its bloody, toxic nature. Nevertheless, if the

reader at any point feels her or his eyes glazing over, we recor
thought experiment: for class read 'position in the vampire food c
class struggle read 'the battle against vampires'; for class and cybernetics,
'vampires – but perhaps also vampire-slayers – with smartphones'.

Since the discovery of the microchip, promoters of the information
revolution have argued that it dissolves class. Personal computers,
laptops or smartphones place the 'means of production' in the hands of
the working class, permitting the upward mobility of those who educate
themselves sufficiently in new skills and literacies to leave the ranks of
manual labour, transform into white-collar knowledge workers (Bell
1973) or digital artisans in electronic cottages (Toffler 1980), enter an
ever-rising 'creative class' (Florida 2002), and become geek-inventors
or, best of all, multi-billionaire digital entrepreneurs. After the collapse
of the Soviet Union in 1989 – widely attributed to the West's ascendancy
in information technologies – and the disappearance of any apparent
alternative to worldwide market society, this techno-triumphalism rose
to a crescendo. Digital technology promised a 'long boom' (Schwartz et
al. 2000) of endless growth as antagonism to the existing order dissolved
in a 'friction-free capitalism' (Gates 1995: 197). Communism's utopian
aspirations could, it was claimed, be realized without conflict, within
the boundaries of capitalism through social media self-organization
(Shirky 2008) and online collectivism (Kelly 2009); cybernetics would
abolish class.

There was always dissent from this happy diagnosis. Harry Braverman's
(1974) account of the 'degradation of work' proposed that computers, far
from being liberatory, extended the 'deskilling' of labour commenced in
the factory assembly-line to the office-cubicle. Several similar studies
argued that computerization intensified industrial capitalism's processes
of rationalization, routinization and redundancy (Noble 1984; Shaiken
1984; Webster and Robins 1986). Socialist-feminist theory both deepened
and complicated this analysis by addressing the interaction of class with
gender in digitizing workplaces; computerization could undermine the
patriarchal privileges of male skilled workers, yet also subject the female
labour that might replace them to high levels of exploitation (Cockburn
1983 and 1985).

Amongst the fiercest critics of the new technologies were members of
the 'workerist' or '*operaismo*' tendency, forerunner of what would later
become known as 'autonomist Marxism'. Observing the assembly-line car
factories of Northern Italy theorists of this school such as Raniero Panzieri

(1980) had in 1963 described how technological development became part of capitalist planning to disempower workers. In the same year, Romano Alquati analyzed how in the plants of Olivetti, a manufacturer of typewriters and calculators, computerized automation was beginning to be used to control a new generation of information workers; he concluded that 'the universal diffusion of capitalist despotism ... realizes itself above all through its technology, its "science"', and suggested that 'Cybernetics recomposes globally and organically the functions of the general worker that are pulverised into individual micro-decisions: the Bit links up the atomised worker to the figures of the [economic] Plan' (Alquati 2013; Pasquinelli 2014a).

It was therefore a surprise when in 2000 one of the leading *operaismo* theorists, Antonio Negri, with co-author Michael Hardt, proposed a dramatic reinterpretation of social conflict in a digital era. Their *Empire* (2000) suggested that a fully global capital now confronted not so much a working class as a 'multitude' immersed in 'immaterial labour' involving the communicational and affective dimensions of networked production. Attuned to the excitement of the World Wide Web, open source software, and music piracy, and echoing the earlier work of Donna Haraway (1985), who had shaken feminist techno-pessimism by insisting on radical 'cyborg' potentials, Hardt and Negri, rather than emphasizing capital's cybernetic domination, declared the possibility of its digital subversion and supersession.

Their work appeared just as capital experienced its first major outburst of networked resistance. Youthful alter-globalist protestors were not only taking to tear-gas drenched streets from Seattle to Genoa, but also experimenting with indie-media centres; Zapatismo in cyberspace and electronic civil disobedience. In this context, Empire, and its two subsequent volumes, *Multitude* (2004) and *Commonwealth* (2009), struck a chord. Its ideas, further developed by authors such as Tiziana Terranova (2004), Maurizio Lazzarato (2004), Paolo Virno (2004), Andrea Fumagalli (2007) and Yves Moulier Boutang (2011), became the basis of a 'post-*operaismo*' analysis of 'cognitive capitalism' (Vercellone 2006) in which control of knowledge is understood as the main site for contesting capitalism and networks present an opportunity for multitude.

Hardt and Negri's work was an iconoclastic challenge to Marxism's attachment to the class configurations of an industrial era. It met with fierce scepticism (Dean and Passavant 2003; Balakrishnan 2003; Camfield 2007). Critics found 'multitude' frustratingly vague. 'Immaterial labour' seemed to deny the persistence of hard, corporeal, and all too material toil. The image of a 'smooth' global Empire airbrushed jagged gulfs between planetary North and South. Enthusiasm for the radical potentialities of networks skipped too quickly over the dull, disciplinary actualities of information work. Hardt and Negri were accused of 'downgrading the negative' (Noys 2010: 125) in a way that uncannily mirrored capital's own digital prophets.

My work has been involved in these debates; *Cyber-Marx* (1999) argued for the importance of autonomist Marxism to the politics of a digital age. When *Empire* appeared I was inspired by its radical experimentalism and critical of some of its propositions (Dyer-Witheford 2001; 2005; 2008). Writing *Games of Empire* (2009) with Greig de Peuter uncovered in the global video games industry an exemplary site of 'immaterial labour', complete with exciting cybernetic subversions, but also disclosed the recuperation of digital commons by the new forms of Web 2.0 capitalism, and supply chains extending from game studios to electronic assembly lines, conflict mineral mines and digital waste dumps, with all this revealing the continuing existence of material toil and deep divisions within the planetary multitude.

These problems in post-*operaismo* analysis were intensified by the 2008 financial meltdown. The abrupt transition from alter-globalism's 'another world is possible' to the 'no future' aftermath of the crash seemed to repudiate the optimism of *Empire* like a slap to the face. Youthful 'immaterial labour' found itself out of a job and without prospects; networked commons were overtaken by the immiseration of austerity; any idea that digital winds were filling the sails of progressive politics suddenly revealed itself as a reflex of capital's 1990s boom, and, like that bubble, burst.

Yet the social movements that eventually emerged in response to the crisis, with their mix of on-the-ground occupations and digital media mobilizations, pose again the question of the forms of resistance generated within cybernetic capital. Hardt and Negri responded with a *Declaration* (2012) identifying four main 'subjective figures' involved in such uprisings: the *indebted*, revolting against financial institutions; the *mediatized*, rising against corporate control of information and networks; the *securitized*, seeking protection from state violence; and the *represented*, rejecting the corruptions of electoral democracy. This is descriptively quite compelling. However, like the authors' earlier concept of 'multitude', it doesn't give much sense of the systemic relations of these groups, of why and how they would have commonalities in struggle, or the difficulties and conflicts they might encounter in working together. Tellingly, where *Declaration* does address these issues, it returns to older categories of class – the very language 'multitude' once sought to terminologically escape, but is now apparently unable to do without. This book therefore re-examines the relation of cybernetics and class in the stark light of the great crash of 2008 and the fiery uprisings on 2011, proposing a 'post-post-*operaismo*' analysis of cybernetic capital, taking as its starting point neither 'worker' nor 'multitude', but 'proletariat'.

Cyber-Proletariat

'Proletariat' derives from the ancient Roman term for the urban poor who possessed nothing but the capability of biologically reproducing themselves. Marx used it to describe the class within capitalist society that must live by labour. Writing of the factory labourers of the early industrial revolution, he describes them as 'free' in 'a double sense' – free to sell their labour for a wage, but also free to starve if this sale fails, as they have no other commodity to exchange (Marx 1977: 272). In this context to be proletarian is to be deprived of control over one's work process and what is produced, separated from other people by competitive market relations and dispossessed of connection to the natural environment (Marx 1964: 106–119). These shared conditions made the proletariat a potential revolutionary force.

Subsequently 'working class' and 'proletariat' were often used synonymously by Marxists to mean simply wage-labour. Proletariat can, however, convey a wider provenance. For, as *Endnotes* (2010: 33) reminds us, Marx wrote that '"Proletarian" must be understood to mean, economically speaking, nothing other than "wage-laborer", the man who produces and valorizes "capital", *and is thrown out onto the street as soon as he becomes superfluous to the need for valorization*' (Marx 1977: 764, emphasis added). Others have elaborated on the final, crucial phrase. For example, Ramin Ramtin's prescient work on capitalism and automation, which seems increasingly relevant to post-2008 conditions, defines the proletariat as 'the class that has nothing but its labour power to sell and which has no decision-making control over either its operational or allocative use of material productive forces and the labour of itself' (1991: 129). He too makes a distinction between 'wage labour' and the 'proletariat': for 'although a proletarian needs to sell his/her labour power, this necessity does not mean that such a sale has actually taken place'. While the term 'working class' clearly includes all wage labourers, 'proletariat' opens to the explicit inclusion of the unemployed and paupers.

Using proletariat, rather than worker, acknowledges that today, as the weak joke has it, capitalism isn't working; a large proportion of the working class is workless. Proletariat encompasses not only the assembly-line electronics worker or the call centre operative but also the former peasant populations plucked off the land without necessarily being able to find employment, or labour ejected from production by cybernetic automation and communication. Now, as in Marx's era, proletariat denotes the incessant phasing in and out of work and workless-ness, the inherent precarity, of the class that must live by labour, a condition raised to a new peak by global cybernetics.

This book's title shows an evident debt to Ursula Huws' concept of a 'cybertariat' (2003; 2014). Huws particularly emphasizes how digital value chains have intensified capital's dependence on a female and globalized labour force performing routine and neo-Taylorized clerical, data entry and office work, work that perpetually crosses with the demands of unpaid labour in the home, and sharply contrasts with the glamorized, 'cooler' and often masculinized high-end forms of so-called 'immaterial labour'. My argument attempts to maintain this important perspective, but draws mainly on lines of thought within the broad school of autonomist Marxism but less well known than Hardt and Negri's. The work of George Caffentzis (2013) and Silvia Federici (2012), whose analysis of primitive accumulation in the global South and female work in the home and factory showing how networked capital demand both 'cyborgs' and 'slaves' has been particularly important.

So too has that of Karl Heinz Roth on 'global proletarianization' (Roth 2012). His work with labour historian Marc van der Linden (2014) insists that the conventional Marxist definition of the proletarian as a 'doubly-free wage labourer' misses much of the underside of twenty-first-century capital. Instead, they delineate a proletarian 'multiverse' made up of diverse waged and unwaged labours, emphasizing how much the global economy depends on forms of dependent, informal, bonded or slave labour, and other forms of shadow work, many of which, we would add, now occur on digital networks (see also Denning 2010). Roth also sketches a dynamic process by which certain workers can become 'de-proletarianized', emerging out of sheer poverty and disempowerment by virtue of strong organization or special skills to make gains that give them a stake in capitalism, only to potentially face 're-proletarianization' as technological change or new labour sources roll back such advances, kicking the floor out from beneath apparently secure and well-rewarded jobs (2010: 219).

Roth and van der Linden emphasize that in the violent sifting and sorting of these layers of proletarianization, gender and race as well as class play a major part. We understand this process not just as an intersection of pre-given categories, but as one of mutual determination. Thus, in the global North to be of the 'working class' – rather than some other indefinite labouring category – was for decades to be white and male. Conversely, however, the very content and significance of what it means today, within capital, to be 'woman' rather than 'man', is not just an anatomical designation but is shaped by the historical and current occupation of positions of unpaid reproductive labour vis-à-vis wage labour. To be 'black', 'brown', 'yellow' or some other shade of 'non-white' is not just a matter of colour but of how skin encodes a legacy of slavery, indentured and bonded labour and other forms of super-exploitation in the one-time colonies and peripheral zones of capital. That is why so much of the new intensification of exploitation required and enabled by cybernetic accumulation is borne by women and non-European populations, even as this digitization reworks both the organization of the home and the geopolitical division of labour.

Beyond this book's autonomist sources, it has, however, been significantly shaped by the 'communisation' theory that emerged strongly after 2008 (see Cunningham 2009; Noys 2011). This current is in fact highly critical of autonomist Marxism's 'workerist' tendencies but nevertheless shares with it a problematic of 'class composition' and 'cycles of struggles' (two concepts described in the next chapter). Especially important for the analysis of cybernetics and class struggle is Theorie Communiste's discussion of the growing disjunctions between capital's requirements for its own reproduction and those of its proletariat (Simon 2011), and Endnotes' (2010; 2013) revival of Marx's concept of 'surplus populations'. It is probably fair to say that the pages that follow begin on an autonomist note, show an increasing communisation influence, and end by subscribing fully to neither position, thereby ensuring a general dissatisfaction.

Beyond and behind these theoretical perspectives the analysis draws heavily on the concrete investigations into class conflicts in and out of the workplace conducted by various forms of worker's inquiry. These include, in the global North, those of the German groups Wildcat and Kolinko, and in the South, the Gurganon News collective, working from the industrial satellites of New Delhi, and the Asia Monitor Resource Centre, whose reports are especially important to understanding information industry supply chains. It is also heavily indebted to the many individual researchers delving, sometimes at personal risk, into the on-the-ground conditions of today's cybernetic struggles.

What follows argues that the conjunction of automation and globalization enabled by information technology raises to a new intensity a fundamental dynamic of capitalism – its drive to simultaneously draw people into waged labour and expel them as superfluous un- or under-employed. This 'moving contradiction' (Marx 1973: 106) now manifests as, on the one hand, the encompassing of the global population by networked supply chains and agile production systems, making labour available to capital on a planetary scale, and, on the other, as a drive towards the development of adept automata and algorithmic software that render such labour redundant. This book is about digital capital's making of a planetary working class tasked with working itself out of a job, toiling relentlessly to develop a system of robots and networks, networked robots and robot networks, for which the human is ultimately surplus to requirements, on a fatal trajectory at once dramatized and protested in the self-immolation of Bouazizi, the death leaps of Foxconn workers and other political suicides in the revolts of 2008 to 2014. It is about a global proletariat caught up in a cybernetic vortex.

Chapter 2 lays down theoretical foundations. Drawing on Marx and Engels' famous description of the world market as a system in which 'all that is solid melts into air', it thinks of capitalism as a vortex; a whirlwind, hurricane or tornado, made up by the triple processes of production, circulation and financialization. In the dynamics of this vortex, two factors are crucial. One is the composition of capital: the ratio between technology and humans involved in commodity production. The other is the composition of the working class or proletariat: the relation between technical conditions of work (or worklessness) and the forms of political organization to which it gives rise. Using these two concepts, we see how the digital revolution has enabled capital both to eject dangerously powerful workers from work and globally recruit new sources of cheapened labour while relentlessly ramping up the speed and scope of its commodity circuits.

Chapter 3 opens a historical perspective on the cybernetic transformations of class composition. Starting in 1949 with a famous exchange between Norbert Wiener, founder of the science of cybernetics, and Walter Reuther, the President of the United Autoworkers' Union, about the effects of computers on employment, it reviews the Cold War origins of cybernetics, its place in the development of computing, and its theories of automata and networks. It then returns to Wiener's predictions, and examines how in the US automobile industry cybernetic innovations of robotization and just-in-time networks disintegrated the power of the mass industrial worker in what was once its strongest bastion, in a trajectory that ends amidst the ruins of contemporary Detroit.

Chapter 4 goes from bankrupt rustbelts on one side of North America to billionaire palaces on the other. In the last decades of the twentieth century, the computer industry was founded in Silicon Valley. Its bifurcated and poisoned workplaces, divided between high-skilled 'hacker' professionals, and low-paid industrial and service proletarians, circled by venture capital and reigned over by hip information entrepreneurs, prefigured class divisions that would spread across the planet. We follow this global dissemination to three sites – the electronic assembly factories in the Mexican city of Ciudad Juárez, the software parks of Hyderabad in India, and the gigantic semiconductor fabricators of Hsinchu, Taiwan. The chapter then returns to today's Silicon Valley, where the buses carrying software engineers from newly gentrified San Francisco to the Googleplex meet the rage of the urban poor.

Chapter 5 travels on 'from Silicon Valley to Shenzhen' (Lüthje et al. 2013). It examines how cybernetic technologies constructed the main axis of capitalist globalization in the 1990s and early 2000s – the perverse connection of the working classes of China and America. We examine this relationship in three dimensions. First is the production of cheap digital devices by a migrant proletariat in China's assembly-line factories at the end of electronic supply chains. Second is the increasing use of the internet, in North America and beyond, to circulate commodities, with free online labour emerging as a source for the swelling profits of Web 2.0 capitalism. Third is the rise of a financial capital dependent on high-speed trading and artificial intelligence, pumped with profits from cheap labour in China and free labour online, whose sub-prime mortgage crisis brought catastrophe to North American proletarians and drove the world economy to the brink of collapse.

Chapter 6 turns to mobile technologies, and the rapid spread of the cell phone in some of the poorest regions of Asia, Africa and Latin America. Contesting euphoric predictions of mobile-based economic development, it argues that the 'universal intercourse' of wireless communication provides the basis for a new intensity in capital's domination of world-labour (Marx 1970: 56). Drawing on the work of Enda Brophy and Greig de Peuter (2014) it first examines the circuit of cell phone production as its winds through South American coltan mines, Indonesian assembly plants, India's call centres, and Africa's e-waste dumps. It then turns to the proletarian use of mobiles – to search for work, handle emergencies, communicate in migration, remit moneys and survive by crime. These are ways to individually cope with and adapt to, rather than collectively change, the conditions of precarious proletarianization amongst the world's 'surplus populations' (Marx 1973: 608).

Chapter 7 takes stock of the argument so far with a synoptic overview of the global class composition of early twenty-first-century cybernetic capital. It scans the world-historical exodus of agrarian populations from the land, as automation and biotechnologies disintegrate peasant cultures; the consequent formation of vast surplus populations engaged in informal and subsistence labour; the supply-chain enabled transfer of manufacturing work from the global north-west to Asia; the growth of a diffuse 'service sector' involving wage labour in the spheres of circulation and social reproduction; the mobilization of women both for wage work and unpaid domestic labour; the escalation of unpaid, insecure and under-employment; the expansion of professional and technical intermediate strata, and of capital's managerial sector, both of which in turn fuel the creation of university 'edu-factories' (Edu-Factory Collective 2009); and the vertiginous ascent of capital's info-tech-armed '1 per cent'.

Chapter 8 returns to the tumults resulting from the financial crash of 2008, and the role of social media and mobile technologies in these struggles. It discusses this issue via the autonomist concept of the 'circulation of struggles', but argues that this circulatory model needs to be modulated by an understanding of what communisation theorists term the 'uneven dynamics' of class conflict (Rocamadur 2014). The cycle that reached a crescendo in 2011 comprised riots, wage struggles, assembly-based occupations, and hacker and whistleblower exploits. While all involve omnipresent digital media, they do so in very different ways. The resulting 'cascade of struggles' moves with extraordinary speed but also with jagged striations and interruptions, in both connecting and dividing the various fractions of a segmented proletariat. The chapter concludes by discussing how far either the successes or failures of the 2011 revolts can be ascribed to digital networks.

Chapter 9 looks at the aftermath of the crash. Although the immediate job-loss effects of the meltdown were dramatic, even more telling are the problems of the so-called recovery, in which employment in key wage zones refuses to return to pre-recession levels. The globalized search for cheap labour is being followed by its accelerated ejection from work, via a new wave of robotization, app- and big-data enhanced social media, and the restoration of a financial sector whose algorithmic processes generate profits on a scale dwarfing labour. While establishment economists and scientists acknowledge that the 'rise of the robots' now threatens the very basis of waged work, and proposes a variety of reformist solutions, some echoed from the left, the actual practices of global capital suggest these are unlikely to be adopted, and that an emergent regime of futuristic accumulation may expel proletarians from the wage-relation even faster than it inducts them.

We conclude with a look in Chapter 10 at prospects for the collapse of the cybernetic vortex. In his 'Fragment on Machines' Marx (1973: 690–712) predicted a horizon on which capital would automate itself out of existence. Today, some of capital's contemporary seers refuse to consider this an end-game scenario. The suggestions of nihilist philosopher Nick Land (2011) that the commodity-form's cyclonic processes will metamorphosize into a machinic system in which humanity is utterly surplus to requirements are only a dark-side version of ruminations by intellectual courtiers of Sergei Brin, Larry Page and other information sovereigns. In this context, two opposed views on the relation of cybernetics to class struggle are considered: the rejection of the 'cybernetic hypothesis' by the anarchist collective Tiqqun (2001), and 'accelerationism's' left appropriation of Land's vision (Williams and Srnicek 2013). We suggest that both refusal and recapture will be aspects of movements against cybernetic capital. The necessity and the difficulty of organizing these dual tactics will be heightened by the conditions of renewed financial meltdowns, ecological chaos, and, ultimately, war, under which such proletarian struggles are likely to be waged.

2

Vortex

Turbulent System

In a too-familiar passage of *The Communist Manifesto*, Karl Marx and Friedrich Engels describe capitalist globalism as 'uninterrupted disturbance ... everlasting uncertainty and agitation' in which 'all fixed, fast-frozen relations ... are swept away' and 'all that is solid melts into air' (1964: 63). Yet however many times this description is cited, it remains mysterious; the exact nature of the titanic agitating, melting and sweeping-away process with which capital is identified remains enigmatic – although today it sounds like a meteorological convulsion arising from global warming. To some readers it suggests a 'maelstrom' or whirlpool (Berman 1982: 15) or a cyclone (Land 1992: 106); following their lead, we will describe capital as a vortex.

What is a vortex? It is 'the rotating motion of a multitude of material particles around a common center': the 'vorticity' of matter is given by its rate of rotation around an axis or 'angular velocity' (Lugt 1983: 2–3). Vortices do not, however, just move in circles, but also often have a vertical dimension: the downward suction of a whirlpool, the upward pull of a tornado's funnel. In nature, vortex phenomena are ubiquitous. The 'spectrum of vortices' includes 'sub-microscopic eddies in liquid helium', 'vortices generated by insects', 'vortices behind leaves', 'vortex rings of squids', 'dust whirls on the street', 'whirlpools in tidal currents', 'dust devils', 'vortex rings in volcanic eruptions', 'vortices shed from the Gulf Stream', 'high and low pressure systems', 'ocean circulations', 'planetary atmospheres', the 'Great Red Spot of Jupiter', 'the rings of Saturn', 'sun spots', the 'rotation inside of stars' and the movement of galaxies scaled in an 'order of light years' (Lugt 1983: 26–7).

The vortices that attract most human attention are, however, storms, such as those in the US Midwest's tornado alley, tracked not just by storm chasers, but also by satellites 20,000 miles over the equator and Doppler radar that spot tornados in formation, 'seeing' their rotating winds, the fastest on earth, as they begin to turn (Reiss 2001: 10). Cold air collides with warm air. The hot air tries to rise, but the cold air above contains it 'in the same way as an iron lid keeps steam in a boiling pot' (Reiss 2001: 8). The pressure of the rising warm air 'pushing steadily upward in a spiraling helix' threatens to 'smash through the cold air and break outward' so that an observer watching from earth would see:

> a huge dark anvil shape above, a monstrously high cloud that at its uppermost levels contains ice ... Inside this huge cloud or 'supercell thunderstorm', warmer and cooler air would form a violently rotating tube of air, invisible from the ground. High-altitude winds would spin the whole air mass, the rotation accelerated even further by more winds below ... a floating mass of supercharged energy or dark 'wall cloud' ... as wide as a mile across begins rotating like a UFO in a Spielberg movie. (Reiss 2001: 8)

This wall cloud can 'take on a greenish tinge, as if pumping itself up with energy' (Reiss 2001: 9). Suddenly a small 'nipple shape' will form at the bottom of the bowl, then 'elongate and descend in a tube'; rising to meet it comes 'a swirl of dust and debris as the tornado's strength and intensity becomes visible and the funnel cloud links sky to earth' (Reiss 2001: 8). Such a giant vortical storm appears as a hostile, alien, utterly inhuman power.

Since the *Manifesto*, weather systems have provided metaphors for capitalism to its opponents; Walter Benjamin wrote of 'a storm ... blowing in from Paradise' (1969: 257) that blasted a stunned observing angel backwards into the future, and the radical anti-Vietnam War movement, the Weather Underground, borrowed its name from Bob Dylan's 'you don't need a weatherman to tell which way the wind is blowing'. But the image also served capital's friends; in 1942 the economist Joseph Schumpeter revised Marx and Engels' account of global markets' 'everlasting disturbance' to produce a celebratory account of capital's perennial 'gale of creative destruction' (1942: 139).

It was, however, in the financial markets of the early twenty-first century that the idea of capital as a storm attained practical consequence. The crucial concept is 'turbulence', the apparently chaotic but actually only 'fiendishly complex' (Bonta and Protevi 2004: 28) flows that occur in rotating vortical systems. For most of the twentieth century turbulence was a specialized concept in the engineering field of fluid mechanics, dealing with problems such as water flow in confined spaces. In the 1980s, however, the mathematician Benoit Mandelbrot applied it to wilder open systems, such as storms and earthquakes (see Cooper 2010: 186–7). He also suggested that financial markets displayed turbulence. This was a matter not of metaphor but mathematics. The statistical patterns detectable in turbulent weather – fractal scaling, intermittence, discontinuity, bursts of activity, long-term dependence on small shifts in condition, and sudden extreme variations from bell curve norms – could also be found in markets; their violent fluctuations were 'blowing in the wind' (Mandelbrot and Hudson 2004: 112).

Appearing amidst the booming deregulated financial markets of the Reagan era Mandelbrot's ideas attracted attention after Wall Street's 1987 Black Monday, in which it lost and then regained half its value in two days. What fully vindicated his emphasis on chaotic volatility, however, was the Wall Street crash of 2008. As the markets tumbled, turbulence was invoked everywhere to explain the sudden, destructive cascade of events: Alan Greenspan, Chair of the Federal Reserve Board, titled his memoirs *The Age of Turbulence: Adventures in a New World* (2008). Since then assumptions about the stability, equilibrium and security of capitalism as a global system have gone out the window. The idea that 'the normal state of the market' is 'something more akin to the ever-shifting patterns of global weather in which new disturbances, storms and patterns emerge in ... highly irregular and unpredictable ways', and are 'inherently prone to stormy chaos' comparable to that which periodically sweeps 'tornado alley' has become a commonplace in business literature advising how to profit from crises, disruptions and runaway change (Buchanan 2013: 18, 8).

We therefore apply to capital its own self-understanding of its processes as those of a vast vortical storm, using as our 'Doppler radar' to track its motion Marx's three volumes of *Capital* (1977; 1981a; 1981b) and his notebook *Grundrisse* (1973). These texts can be read as modelling a system that sucks up human and natural energies, transforms them into commodities bought and sold in a circulatory process that accelerates in speed and expands in scope until its super-storm engulfs the entire planet. Thinking of capital as a very big storm, of the type created by anthropogenic climate change, is a way to suggest the magnitude and dynamism of a system, created by human labour, but which now detaches from human scale and human purpose.

Whirlwind Machine

The capitalist vortex is self-expanding value: money making money. The entities and activities hurtling around in the vortex, including the activities of human beings, take the form of commodities, ex-changed into money, then re-coalescing as new objects and actions to be in turn volatilized into yet more money. This system starts to turn in the historical moment of 'primitive accumulation' in Europe from the sixteenth century to the eighteenth, as early agribusiness and mercantile trading tears feudal peasant populations away from subsistence on the land, and into the factory to labour in exchange for a wage (Marx 1977: 873–927). The transfer of the work of dispossessed proletarians into capitalist profit is the basic dynamic – the 'energy gradient' (see DeLanda 2011: 7–22) – powering the vortex. As this system picks up strength, it passes from the initial moment of primitive accumulation to a circular process of capitalist reproduction, in which waged labour and commodity consumption, each requiring the other, sustain a whirlwind of growth and profit that extends around the globe.

There are three main moments in this vortex: production, circulation and financialization. Production is the funnel of the storm; circulation its rotational motion; financialization its crashing turbulence. Marx's 'Doppler radar' read-out explains the process in algebraic symbols. In production, the vortex seizes hold of the human capacity to work: labour power (LP). This is thrown into combination with machines and raw materials, the means of production (MP), to generate commodities (C), which can potentially be exchanged for more money than it costs to produce them. This pumping-out, sucking-up and siphoning-off of surplus value is the core of the vortex, around which all its other processes orbit.

In circulation, commodities are bought and sold. This can be considered in two moments. In the first, labour power and means of production are purchased by capital with money for use in the production process (M – LP + MP): proletarians sell their capacity to labour for a wage, as 'workers'. In the second moment, commodities coming out of production are exchanged for more money than they cost to make (C – M'). Here the human caught up in the production moment of the vortex as 'worker' reappears as 'consumer'. If the circulation process is completed (it is always subject to failure or interruption) the surplus value created in production is realized in exchange: part is retained as profit, part thrown back into production to activate further labour power, machines and raw materials, so that the circular process of the vortex renews and expands, eventually becoming a 'world market' (Marx 1973: 408).

The vertical and horizontal vectors of production and circulation provide the basic dynamic of the value vortex. Its moving force field is, however, unstable. In production, the upward siphoning off of value tends to a downward pressure on wages, but in circulation, holding down wages limits consumption. At the same time, as we will discuss at greater length in a moment, the machinic intensification of value extraction reduces the quantities of living labour transformed into surplus value, undoing the basic energy transfer that forms the vortex. Thus the suction and rotation of value precipitates within itself refluxes and counter-flows that interrupt the value vortex's self-reproduction and even threaten to collapse it entirely.

In response to these instabilities, the self-perpetuating dynamics of the vortex generate what is today known as financialization – an ever greater reliance on credit and debt, leading into ever more elaborate speculative attempts to overleap production and consumption, jumping directly from money to money magnified ($M - M'$). This pumps up vast speculative bubbles whose collapse throws whole societies into crisis. This is the turbulence of capital, with all the characteristics that Mandelbrot and others have seen as paralleling the violent tumults of the vortical storm.

Our diagrammatic radar read-out of the dynamics for capital's vortex can thus be given as $M - (LP + MP) - C - M'$, with production comprising $LP + MP - C'$, circulation as $C - M'$, and finance as the attempted direct leap from $M - M'$. This vortex is machinic. As a storm subjects water particles in the atmosphere to phase changes, from vapour to liquid to solid, the whirlwind of capital transforms living labour into a technological crystallization.

This process is paradoxical. In the vortex it is the amount of 'socially necessary labour time' involved in producing a commodity that determines its 'value', the attractor around which its market price probabilistically fluctuates (Cockshott et al. 2009: 136). But both competition between rival enterprises and attempts by proletarians to improve their wages pressure capitalists to drive down the cost of labour by replacing it with machines. Thus although the basic process of the vortex is the suction from human activity of surplus value, the results of this transfer are translated into metal or transcribed to silicon. The vortex mobilizes human labour, but also eliminates it. This 'moving contradiction' (Marx 1973: 106) is not, however, a static equilibrium, but rather precipitates more and more machine elements, spiralling towards ever higher automation.

Marx refers to capital's 'human material' (1977: 517, 600, 784, 814) – that is, proletarians – as 'variable capital' and to machines and raw materials as 'fixed capital'. The ratio of variable to fixed capital is the 'organic composition' of capital. This ratio can be estimated two different ways. A rough descriptive estimate of the physical mix of machinery, materials and humans gives capital's 'technical composition'. Measuring each of these elements' monetary worth – wages for humans and costs for machines and materials – gives the 'value composition' (see Mohun 1983). However it is calculated, the concept of the 'organic' composition of capital has spooky implications. 'Organic' suggests the natural, the biological; if a growth in the machine side of capital increases its 'organic composition', the body of capital, its organic nature, is machinic.

Machine use intensifies historically as capital engulfs or 'subsumes' labour (Marx 1977: 1019–25). In the early phase of 'formal subsumption' workers using traditional pre-industrial craft tools are drawn into commodity production. The extraction of surplus value depends on the 'absolute exploitation' of extending the working day to the limits of human endurance. The social disintegration such brutal discipline causes in the pandemonium of new factory cities threatens to collapse capital. The vortex re-stabilizes itself through 'real subsumption', condensing scientific knowledge and technology into a system of 'machinofacture'. In real subsumption, value extraction does not need to depend entirely on lengthening the hours of work. Rather, it proceeds by adding machines to labour, raising workers' productivity, so that in this 'relative exploitation', wages can rise even as capital continues to siphon-up surplus value as profit.

The cyclonic path of capital thus comes to depend on the acceleration of throughputs made possible by the industrial revolution. In particular, James Watt's invention of the steam engine marks the onset of an entirely new phase of machinic intensification:

This universal machine (uncanny harbinger of the computer, an even more general machine) could be connected to vast assemblages of other machines to supply their motive power, thus giving rise to the assemblages of assemblages that turn the industrial age into a weird cybernetic system, a primitive artificial intelligence of a sort – to wit, industrial capitalism, with the vampire like downward causality of the emergent machine level, with its related machine like qualities of abstract values, sucking away at the humans on the levels beneath. (Morton 2013: 5–6)

The offspring of the steam engine include the early automation of the cotton jenny and self-acting mule, which transform the production process, and then the railway and coal-burning ship, which similarly alter the nature of circulation, and in turn lay the basis for new heavy industries. Every gyration of capital intensifies this mechanizing process as it progresses to the electrification and chemical innovations of the nineteenth century's second industrial revolution. The vortex becomes a machinic whirlwind. Ernst Jünger (2004), who saw the eventual military results of this process on the battlefields of the First World War, called it a 'storm of steel', but as Dirk Leach (1986: np), who worked in a late twentieth-century assembly line, observed, this phrase could also be applied to what is endured by a worker in a car factory.

The Rate of Profit

Both capitalism's early economists, and their critic, Marx, predicted that the system's machinic drive was potentially self-destructive. They described this in terms of the 'law' or 'tendency' to a falling rate of profit (Marx 1981: 317–75), today often simply referred to by the acronym 'FROP'. If the basic dynamic of the value vortex is the transfer of human labour into commodities, then an increase in capital's organic composition, i.e. ongoing mechanization, undercuts this process. This idea warrants some explanation, as it is counter-intuitive; what follows draws heavily on Guglielmo Carchedi (1997), one of the most lucid of contemporary FROP theorists.

Increased application of technology increases productivity: more 'stuff' is made per unit of capital invested. Because less human labour is involved, however, the value of each unit of output – and hence, ultimately, its purchasing price – declines. An innovating capitalist may gain significant competitive advantage with a new technology; this provides the incentive for ongoing automation. But as the invention is widely adopted, prices within the entire system re-set at the lower level. Growth in the scale of industrial operations might maintain the *mass* of profits, but the return on any given amount of investment declines, resulting in long-term stasis and crisis.

In terms of our vortex metaphor, the tendency to the falling rate of profit can be thought of as broadly similar to the self-cancelling process that occurs inside the circulatory atmospheric flows of storms. Manuel DeLanda (2011: 11) provides a vivid account of these dynamics in a tornadic thunderstorm: upward drafts of warm, water-vapour carrying air (in our analogy, the siphoning up of living labour) at a certain altitude encounter colder temperatures (the imperative to cut labour costs). The water vapour then undergoes a phase transition, condensing into rain or even freezing as ice (the crystallization of increasingly technological means of production). The latent heat released in this transition temporarily increases the upward velocity of the air mass (short-term competitive advantage), but as the ascent continues into yet colder regions the rising air mass becomes saturated with larger water drops and ice crystals (generalized technological adoption): their weight eventually reaches a 'tipping point' and they begin to fall as rain and hail, dragging air down with them, 'stealing energy from the updraft and eventually destroying the internal machinery of the storm' (DeLanda 2011: 11).

The FROP hypothesis thus suggests that the vortex of capital, which at its outset seems to sweep away all 'fast frozen relationships', will itself become an ice storm, freezing out its living energy source, leaving a calcifying and collapsing cathedral of mechanical automata, dead monuments to a self-defeating pursuit of surplus value. However, sophisticated variants of the theory suggest this outcome is interrupted or delayed in a cyclical pattern (see Carchedi 1997; Kliman 2012). Recurrent crises of the most violent sort – recessions or wars – destroy or deeply reduce the value of machinic assets, and eliminate many firms. This temporarily smashes the sclerosis of capital's increasing organic composition, and enables the profit rate to rejuvenate – until a new wave of technological innovation set the process in motion again.

As with many weather forecasts, predictions about the FROP are beset with uncertainty. The chapters of *Capital* (Marx 1981: 317–75) which discuss the FROP also acknowledge 'counteracting factors' that may slow or even 'suspend' its operation. These include the intensified exploitation of labour, such as that arising from the use of 'slaves and coolies' in colonies; establishing new labour-intensive industries of low organic composition; early forms of financialization; and reductions in the costs of machines and raw materials. This last point poses a particularly serious challenge to FROP theory. If automation lowers the prices of commodities, it can presumably also lower the price of automating machinery. This would permit an increase in the technical composition of capital – more machines relative to workers – while leaving the value composition unchanged or even diminishing its cheapened machinic component. These qualifying factors seem to make the FROP merely one vector in a complex matrix of dynamic forces.

It is therefore not surprising that the FROP is amongst the most contentious aspects of Marx's thought, dividing theorists who see its action as the major determinant of capital's crises (Kliman 2011) from others who find the logic of the 'law' flawed. These critics tend to emphasize other crisis dynamics. In particular, they focus on the way capital's contradictory imperative to lower wages and to simultaneously raise consumption creates gigantic imbalances of over-production and under-consumption. These disproportions can be temporarily covered over by the expansion of debit, credit, and speculative activities, but eventually trigger financial crises (Heinrich 2012). This version of crisis theory is also, however, related to capital's machinic drive, as one of the main forces for reducing wages is the technological replacement or cheapening of labour; put in an over-simplified form it poses the obvious question: 'if no one has a job, who is going to buy the stuff?'

Marx (1981: 352) regarded these two versions of crisis theory as compatible, a perspective which some of the most interesting work in the field attempts to restore (Simon 2011). But the dispute between FROP and over-accumulation/under-consumption theorists is both intense and arcane. Its conceptual difficulties are intensified by contested methodologies for empirical measurement of the profit rate, the movement of which, even if agreed on, can be accounted for in different ways by different theories. The debate does have political implications, both in terms of explaining why capital is a crisis-prone system and of envisaging alternatives to it; FROP theorists accuse under-consumptionists of being disguised Keynesians, who hope to merely reform capitalism by raising wages, rather than abolishing it, a charge that the under-consumptionists hotly repudiate.

Nonetheless, the argument is in many ways an intellectual sand-trap for militants. This is because the factors it invokes – the balance between capital's investment in its fixed and variable components – is, by virtue of capital's own class structure, completely out of the control of the majority of people. The falling rate of profit is, one might say, capital's problem, with which its owners, managers and political representatives must deal – even if that dealing is at the expense of the rest of us. For those who suffer the consequences of these manoeuvres, however, the more immediate problem and opportunity is that posed not by the composition of capital and the rate of profit but by the composition of class, on which depends the rise or fall in what could be termed 'the rate of struggle'.

The Rate of Struggle

The human material in the capitalist vortex is sifted into layers, all themselves internally striated and fractioned, all moving in relation to one another. These are classes. The concept of class is not primarily an enumerative device, a means of pigeon-holing individual subjects, any more than identifying an atmospheric current in a tornado is a census of air-molecules. It is rather a concept of powers. DeLanda (2011: 12) observes that the atmospheric layers from which storms arise have to be understood in terms of 'capacities', 'tendencies' and 'emergent properties' that interact with one another, often with violent consequences: lightning that starts forest fires, rains that result in floods, winds that flatten cities. Similarly, the class layers of the capitalist vortex should be thought of in terms of capacities, tendencies and collisions. Class is a force.

Following Marx's incompletion of his chapter defining class in the third volume of *Capital* (1983: 1025–6), no issue has been more hotly debated in Marxian circles than the identification of classes (see Przeworski 1977; Draper 1978). As we are interested here in the relation between class and cybernetics, we will define class in relation to machines, and then describe some lines of theory that examine this relation through the concepts of 'class composition' and 'cycles of struggle'.

The class of capitalists owns, and is the personified representative of, fixed capital, the large machine-systems that, in combination with the raw materials that feed them, drive production. The proletariat, dispossessed by such systems from direct access to the means of its reproduction, attempts to sell its labour for a wage and builds, runs and is replaced by these machines: it is 'a living appendage of the machine' (Marx 1977: 614). As the value vortex expands, there emerges between capitalists and proletarians various 'intermediate strata' of managers, professionals and technician workers (aka 'the middle-class') who design machines and supervise, train and educate those who work with machines (Nicolaus

1967). Within the proletariat itself various fractions appear. Relatively secure wage workers separate from the chronically unemployed and immiserated. A layer of female unwaged labour – almost invisible to Marx and many male Marxists, but not to generations of Marxist-feminists – underlies and sustains all the other strata, bearing and caring for the humans that tend or own machines.

It is the separation and interaction of these strata that sets the value vortex in motion, and keeps it spinning. The class struggle, the struggle that continues, always, is the friction and fluctuation at the border of these bands. The motion of the capital vortex also, however, incessantly alters the strata of which it is composed. That not only capital but its human workforce has a changing 'composition' was the insight of *operaismo*, or workerism, a grouping centred in Italy around the mid twentieth-century factory conflicts (see Wright 2002). *Operaismo* theorists inverted Marx's concept of capital's organic composition. Instead, they looked at the ratio of constant capital (machines and raw materials) to variable capital (workers) as it affected the capacities of the working class (since *operaismo* texts usually refer to 'the working class', rather than 'proletariat', we will maintain this terminology in discussing their texts).

To this end, *operaismo* thinkers and those who later followed in their footsteps distinguish the technical and political elements of class composition. 'Technical composition' is the organization of the working class by capital; this includes both its 'conditions in the immediate process of production' – the division of labour, management practices, and, of particular interest here, the use of machinery, and also, in some accounts, the 'forms of reproduction', such as community and family structures, through which the class relation is perpetuated (Kolinko 2002: 3). 'Political composition', is the organizational capacity of the working class to fight for its own needs and development: the individual and collective actions of refusal, resistance and re-appropriation of surplus value. The political composition of the working class determines its capacity to subvert or go beyond the organization of society around capitalist value: to destroy the vortex from within.

Changes in the composition of capital and the composition of the working class chase one another in a 'cycle of struggles' (Zerowork 1975). As Raniero Panzieri (1980) argued, the increase in capital's organic composition is not the outcome of a neutral, purely scientific process of technological progress, but rather of a historically prolonged machinic offensive aimed at 'decomposing' working-class counter-power. Thus the resistances of skilled workers to early industrial capital were slowly broken down first by the time and motion studies of Taylorism and then by the mechanized assembly lines of the Fordist factory. However, such changes could become the basis for working class 're-composition'. The increase in the organic composition of capital which creates the Fordist factory also generates a new technical composition of the working class whose political power lies in its ability to 'stop the line', halting the huge machinic apparatus in which it is implanted, paralyzing a vast fixed overhead whose profitability rests on continuous operation. The result of reducing work to the homogeneity and monotony of the assembly line was to produce the 'mass worker' organizations that terrified mid twentieth-century capital, and provided the base within which *operaismo* thought grew.

Operaismo made other innovations in class theory. One was the identification of a 'circulation of struggles' (Alquati 1974; Bell and Cleaver 1982), paralleling but subverting the circulation of capital. The circulation of capital involves the market realization of surplus value in commodity exchange, processes in which transportation and communications are vital. The circulation of struggles, however, entailed the connection of resistances against the extraction of surplus value, which, either by inadvertent knock-on effects of strikes and other actions or by intentional solidarity builds an ever greater mass of opposition to capitalist accumulation. Ramono Alquati (1974) wrote of the way workers learned of struggles at other sites 'as if by telecommunication' and of the emergence of a 'network' made up of the 'combined vertical-horizontal articulation' of struggles.

Some branches of *operaismo* suggested capital could be fought not just at the immediate point of production, but also throughout the whole 'social factory' which surrounded and serviced it. These ideas were especially important for a feminist wing of *operaismo* that eventually detached itself from the original grouping. This 'wages for housework' movement proposed that women's work in the home made an invisible and unrewarded contribution to capitalist value creation by its unpaid labour of care for children and families (Dalla Costa and James 1972; Fortunati 1995). Such offshoots of *operaismo* made not only the workplace but also the sites where labour power was reproduced – that is, where people are raised, trained, educated and socialized for work in households, schools and welfare offices – into points of struggle.

What became known as 'autonomist Marxism' thus mapped a scenario in which the spiralling enlargement of the capitalist vortex multiplied the chances of its rupture, destabilization and destruction. But despite, or because of, this, *operaismo* and its autonomist offshoot have been intensely controversial within the Marxist tradition. Although tactical and organizational issues are at stake in these disagreements, at root are major theoretical divergences. One major criticism of *operaismo* is that it had too 'pure' a view of the working class, leading to unrealistic, not to say dangerously romantic, strategies of struggle. A famous *operaismo* aphorism declared workers 'in and against' capital. This acknowledges the envelopment of labour within the value vortex. It also, however, suggests an essential core of working-class identity that is 'against' capital – an innate tendency to resist.

Many critics argue that this does not adequately recognize the degree to which 'labour' as such is caught up in the commodity system. Workers are themselves the sellers of a commodity – their own labour power, exchanged for a wage. They are thus engaged in a commercial transaction that may be more or less intensely bargained but is not in itself inconsistent with general commodification. The very subject-position 'worker' is not 'autonomous', but rather defined by capital; it thus cannot spontaneously provide an adequate basis from which to oppose it. This criticism comes from a variety of theoretical perspectives, including orthodox Marxisms, for whom the critique of romanticism validates vanguard party organization. It is also, however, delivered in a very different style by other 'ultra-left' groupings sharing *operaismo*'s scepticism about programmatic, top-down party organization.

One of these is the group Theorie Communiste (TC), whose work informs recent communisation theory. Like *operaismo*, TC had its origins in the 1960s and '70s, though in France not Italy. TC shares with it the concept of the 'cycle of struggles' (Simon 2011), but seeks to explain not so much worker movements' moments of strength as their repeated failures. These, TC argues, cannot be accounted for merely in terms of mistakes, or betrayals, but are intrinsic to the 'reciprocal implication' of capital and proletariat, which, rather than being simply antagonistic are also integrated as two poles of a single system (Endnotes 2008: 215).

This integration, TC argues, has intensified historically. In early capitalism, the proletariat is very much outside capital, a hostile and unruly force to be coercively subdued. As capital subsumes production an increasingly formalized working class is absorbed into capital, through the mediation of institutions such as trade unions, political parties and the welfare state. The very factors that strengthen the mass worker also give it a place within capital, as a bargaining interlocutor: the reproduction of capital and its workers mesh together. All the programmatic reforms to capital that are proposed on the basis of working-class power, from state planning to self-management, and various autonomist alternatives, can in fact be digested by capital as ways of improving value-extraction. However, TC argues, capital's own compulsive drive to integrate the proletariat as a factor of production to be used or ejected at will eventually breaks down any appearance of a social contract. This begins to occur from the 1970s on with what is colloquially called 'neoliberal' globalization, privatization and technological assault on the organized working class. TC (2011) makes a Pascalian 'wager' that facing this no-holds barred offensive, reformist compromise will become impossible; the proletariat will have to throw into question its own existence as one pole of the capitalism that attacks it.

Communisation theory seems to stand at an opposite extreme from the revolutionary optimism of autonomism. It is very critical of Hardt and Negri's post-*operaismo* line and its concept of a spontaneously unified multitude. It insists that, on the contrary, the proletariat's implication in capital results in an endless series of divisions and conflicts between its more and less favoured segments. At the same time, communisation theory's insistence that such divisions ride towards a revolutionary *denouement* seems highly implausible absent the active circulation of struggles to overcome such divisions theorized by autonomists. We therefore read autonomist and communisation theory with and against each other, taking up those lines of autonomist thought that deal not with multitude, but with proletarianization, and understanding this as a contradictory process both *of* and *against* capital, a current within the vortex than can twist back on itself to collapse the very storm of which it is an intrinsic part.

Silicon Cyclone

The intensification of the machinic element in the value vortex occurs in bursts and abrupt condensations precipitated by wars and economic crisis. The most recent of these sudden machinic injections, the cybernetic revolution, was occasioned by the Second World War and by the Cold War. The digital computer and the digital network, developed for use against capital's external enemies, was incubated within the US national security state. They then rapidly migrated to form the basis of commercial industries (still subsidized by military contracts) selling computers first to other capitalist enterprises, who deployed them as weapons of automation and outsourcing in internal class conflicts, and then, as processing power rose and cost and size fell, as successive generations of consumer goods – PCs, laptops, notebooks, tablets, smartphones – making the very texture of everyday life in advanced capitalist society cybernetic.

This 'digital capitalism' (Schiller 1999), initiated in the United States, and then transferring to Europe and Japan, continues to be largely headquartered in these advanced zones. It has nevertheless spread out from the centre of the capitalist world system on a runaway trajectory transforming the relation of its core and peripheral regions. Following a path marked out in earlier studies (Robins and Webster 1988; Garnham 1990; Manzerolle and Kjøsen 2012), the consequences of this cybernetic revolution can be charted across the three moments of capital's vortex – production, circulation and finance.

In production, cybernetics appears as a new intensity of automation, transforming the labour process with a new type of fixed capital. This occurs first in manufacturing, with the arrival of numerically controlled machine tools, industrial robotics and systematized assemblages of computer-guided flexible production, accompanied by new forms of workplace organization, comprehensive systems of total management control, and demands for new types of labour subjectivity quite different from those of the mass worker (see Roth 2010: 210–11). These industrial applications are soon followed by the increasing computerization of office work and the emergence of whole new forms of cultural production – websites, video games, chat rooms – based in digital technologies and closely linked with the cybernetic transformation of circulation.

In circulation, cybernetics makes its entrance as the network, or rather the network of networks, the internet. In the part of the circulation process that leads commodities *out* of production into the market, it manifests in an acceleration in capital's sales effort as the possibilities of the networked computer are appropriated for advertising and shopping, moving from primitive forms of e-marketing such as pop-up ads and commercial portals to the intensities of tracking and prediction made possible on Web 2.0 where social media and search engines enlist the free labour and personal data of millions of users.

In the circulation *into* production phase, where the commodities of labour power and raw materials are purchased in order to make more commodities, networks are a matter of supply chains, electronically connecting geographically separated but functionally integrated business operations. Telecommunications infrastructures, modularized interfaces, bar codes and RFIDs enable a logistical revolution which allows capital to reach out to global labour and resource pools. This is the aspect of cybernetics that, rather than replacing labour, expands it globally, but at the lowest possible rate, and with maximum disposability in a savage labour arbitrage. Here too, in a vast remaking of the international division of labour, cybernetics activates new subjectivities, most basically those of the millions of migrant workers pouring off the land into new industrial zones that are the end points of the electronic supply chains, and then in successive levels of cultural and economic change arising from this transplantation.

In this globalization process cybernetics is increasingly called upon in the third moment of the vortex, that of finance. US banks were early cybernetic adopters of ATD machines, automated banking services, and credit card networks, components of the 'financialization of daily life' (Martin 2002). Where cybernetics meeting with finance is especially fateful, however, is in the worldwide digitalization of stock exchanges, and in the development of exotic financial instruments such as derivatives and futures that originate as a way of defensively hedging foreign investments against currency fluctuations, but rapidly morph into offensive speculative activities dependent on arcane risk modelling and high-frequency trading (see McNally 2011).

Electronic computers did not exist before the 1940s, and computer networks until the late 1960s. The realm of Information and Communication Technologies (ICTs) thus grew *ex nihilo* over half a century. The value of ICT industries for the world economy, defined as including communications services, computer and related services, communications goods and semiconductors, and computers and office machinery, measured in constant current dollars, rose from $800,349 million 1990, to $1.5 trillion in 2000, to $2.8 trillion in 2010. The US share was $257,503 million in 1990, $517,907 in 2000, $729,169 million in 2010 (NSB 2012). Since the late 1990s ICTs have accounted for about one-third of private investment in US economy, and between 10 and 25 per cent of that in other advanced economies. Today the ICT sector's share of the GDP of the global economy as a whole, and of most major economies (including China), is about 6 per cent (OECD 2013a).

However, these figures understate the importance of cybernetic technologies because they do not include digital devices incorporated in other products, such as motor vehicles or machine tools. According to the OECD (2013a) ICTs were 'the most dynamic component of investment in the late 1990s and early 2000s'. Many economists claim their importance cannot be assessed sectorally because they act as a 'general-purpose platform technology' that 'fundamentally changes how and where economic activity is carried out ... much as earlier general-purpose technologies (e.g., the steam engine, automatic machinery) propelled growth during the Industrial Revolution', facilitating broad development of new markets and providing an 'infrastructure' that is 'as or more important than the physical cities, roads and harbors' (NSB 2012).

Although there is neatness in dividing the effects of cybernetics amongst the moments of the vortex – automation in production, networks in circulation, their algorithmic fusion in finance, this is of course false. Production is itself a circulation process, as the commodity must move through the labour (or robot) process, so it too involves networks (e.g. the supply chain linkage of dispersed facilities); circulation entails production, involving its own enterprises of advertising and logistics, exploiting their own workers, and then automating them out of existence; and because, ultimately, money rules all these activities, everything becomes algorithmic. Thus, the most recent 'mobile' phase of cybernation makes the smartphone capital's Star Trek-like 'universal communicator' a device for work, purchases and money transfers alike (Manzerolle & Kjøsen 2014). It is the common medium of cybernetics, bits and bytes, which enables the integration and acceleration of capital's circuit, and by merging its apparently discrete sectors makes ever clearer its singular, vortical process.

Compositions and Decompositions

This cybernetic transformation has complex, contradictory effects on the organic composition of capital. Marx in his era noted a recursive process in industrial innovation, as machinery created the processes for manufacturing new 'cyclopean' machines, such as steamships and railways (1977: 506). Computerized advance itself followed a similar path of positive feedback, generating the means to accelerate its own development. But in the case of computers and networks this bootstrapping process proceeded faster than in previous technological revolutions.

The captains of digital industry explain this to themselves in terms of two great 'laws'. Moore's Law, attributed to Gordon Moore, founder of

Intel, specifies that the computer power available at a given price doubles approximately every 18 months: this is the process that yields contemporary laptops with more power than the supercomputers of 40 years ago. Metcalfe's Law, formulated by John Metcalfe, the inventor of Ethernet, declares that the value of a network increases as the square of its nodes, a principle that encourages investment in wired and wireless connections.

In Chapter 3 we will examine how the fulfilment of Moore's Law arises from the semiconductor industry's success in applying cybernetic technologies – capable of increasingly microscopic operations and made with escalating quantities of toxic chemicals – to its own manufacturing processes, while globally relocating them towards the cheapest sources of labour, which it then automates nearly out of existence. The kind of 'value' that Metcalfe's 'Law' promises will grow exponentially with network expansion was never fully defined in its original formulation, but by implication, and in what has become its normalized usage, it is commercial value; hence the value expansion of networks depends, as we will see in Chapter 4, on a deepening commodification of communication, and the extraction of increasing quantities of free labour from network users.

By lowering the costs of its own elementary component, the microchip, the computer industry enabled a cheapening of machinery that, in principle, would permit capital's technical composition to rise without activating a fall in the rate of profit. It allowed the development of a new set of machinery to counteract the fixed costs of industrial investment: machines to make other machines, machines to speed up yet more machines, machines to capture cheap labour, machines to utterly replace labour – a meta-machinery turning the calcifying cathedral of industrialism into a scuttling hive of artificial intelligences. Jünger's 'storm of steel' is seemingly transformed into what, in a prophetic account written in the 1950s of an Apple-like information company manufacturing flying mini-robots on a secret campus, he saw as a 'swarm of glass bees' (Jünger 2000). The iron tornado becomes a 'crystal world' (Ballard 1966), a vortex of robots and networks, robot networks, and networked robots.

However, the very cheapening of cybernetic technology invites its omnipresent adoption and elaboration into increasingly comprehensive systems. Marx in his age saw this process in relation to industrial machinery: 'What becomes cheaper is the individual machine and its component parts, but a system of machinery develops; the tool is not simply replaced by a single machine but by a whole system ... Despite the cheapening of individual elements, the price of the whole aggregate increases enormously' (2000: 366). As computerization proceeds from the level of a few big mainframes at corporate headquarters or a handful of robots on the industrial shop floor to work stations throughout factories and offices, and then to satellite-connected manufacturing, logistics and point-of-sale platforms, its costs become immense. To give only one example, in 2004 Hewlett Packard, following its takeover of Compaq, initiated a new business management computing system. The project, originally priced at a mere $30 million, ran into problems integrating legacy components, and cost the corporation some $160 million (CIO 2007). Indeed, in a 'perpetual innovation economy', routine updating of software becomes a massive expense (Morris-Suzuki 1997: 25). The cost-saving effects of Moore's Law therefore race against the scope, complexity, renewal and fragility of the systems it creates, all of which tend to raise the value composition of capital.

This increase in capital's organic composition is to some degree offset by the application of cybernetic systems to give capital new sources of low-wage labour, via electronically coordinated supply chains, outsourcing systems, and the activation of unpaid virtual work. Caffentzis argues that what he terms the 'law of increasing dispersion of organic composition' decrees that 'every increase in the introduction of science and technology ... will lead to an equivalent introduction of low organic composition production in other branches of industry' (2013: 280). Following Marx's comments on the world market in the third volume of capital, he proposes that, globally, markets transfer value from sectors with a low organic composition (lots of labour, less machines) towards sectors with high organic composition (high-tech sectors). A mechanism for this process (which remains somewhat mysterious in both Caffentzis' and Marx's accounts) can be seen in the supply chains which relay value extracted from the production of, say, iPhones in Foxconn factories with thousands of low-wage workers into profits for companies such as Apple who directly employ only a small number of knowledge workers.

Later in this book we will question Caffentzis' assumption that increases in and abatements of capital's organic composition necessarily balance out symmetrically, but for the moment we can say that the addition of cybernetics to the value vortex powers up *both* aspects of capital's 'moving contradiction', the double dynamic by which on the one hand it expels labour through automation, and on the other absorbs new, cheapened labour, all the while trying to abridge the consequent contradictions between production and consumption by increased reliance on debt and speculation.

What does this do to class composition? From the 1970s on capital's 'cybernetic offensive' (Tiqqun 2001) relentlessly destroyed the factory bases of the mass worker, reducing their workforce by automation, relocating them from the north-western quadrant of the globe to the former periphery of the world system via container transportation and electronic networks, and, in the core, shifting from industrial jobs to service and technical work. By 1989 cybernetics had enabled capital to defeat the state socialist USSR through a high-technology 'Star Wars' arms race that forced its opponent into bankruptcy, with all that followed in political dissent and popular defection, culminating in the symbolic fall of the Berlin Wall. With these transformations, a whole culture of industrial class struggle, including both the technical composition on which it was based and its political composition in political parties, trade unions, community solidarity and militant cadres, was effectively annihilated. Not just working-class power, but the very concept of class itself seemed erased as a triumphant capitalism announced social existence to be a mere sum of privatized market choices.

Writing in the early 1980s as this class decomposition gained momentum, Marshall Berman, author of one of the most extended discussions of Marx's vision of whirlwind change, suggested that what was being swept away was the entire revolutionary tradition to which *The Communist Manifesto* was foundational:

Marx [wrote] of the industrial worker as 'new-fangled men ... as much an invention of modern times as machinery itself'. But if this is so, then their solidarity, however impressive at any given moment, may turn out to be as transient as the machines they operate or the products they turn out ... The workers may sustain each other today on the assembly line or the picket lines, only to find themselves scattered tomorrow among different collectivities with different conditions, different processes and products, different needs and interests ... Ironically, then, we can see Marx's dialectic of modernity re-enacting the fate of the society it describes, generating energies and ideas that melt it down into its own air (1982: 104–5).

To see what such class decomposition means we now travel to a city that the cybernetic vortex struck with extraordinary violence: Detroit.

3

Cybernetic

A Letter to Detroit

It is 1949, the Second World War just ended, the Cold War newly begun. Norbert Wiener, professor at the Massachusetts Institute of Technology, pioneer of the new discipline of 'cybernetics', writes to Walter Reuther, President of the United Auto Workers (UAW), headquartered in Detroit, world centre of car production. In what David Noble (1984: 75) calls 'one of the most remarkable letters in the annals of twentieth century science', Wiener (1949) tells Reuther he has been asked by 'a leading industrial corporation' to help them develop 'an inexpensive small scale, high speed computing machine'. Technically, Wiener believes, the project is relatively simple. Socially, the implications are momentous, for it will 'undoubtedly lead to the factory without employees; as for example, the automatic automobile assembly line'. Under the control of 'the present industrial set-up', i.e. corporate capitalism, the unemployment 'can only be disastrous'. A 'critical situation' will arise in 'ten to twenty years', sooner if war with the Soviet Union requires full-scale mobilization of industrial resources. Wiener tells Reuther he has declined the corporate request but warns that in future it will not be enough to take a 'passive' attitude. Trade unions should acquire the rights to computer technologies or campaign for their suppression. The scientist sends the trade unionist a copy of his forthcoming book, *Human Use of Human Beings* (1950), actually a denunciation of the *inhuman* potentials of computerization, and asks to meet with him.

As a young man Reuther had entered the automobile factories of Henry Ford, where mass production methods redefined industry in the twentieth century. Later, as a trade union leader, Reuther represented the power won by the workers within 'Fordist' capital. Before Ford, car manufacture was a craft business, employing skilled workers making carefully customized, very expensive, automobiles. Fordism broke this craft tradition. The means came from various sources. Francis Winslow Taylor's management techniques, dividing mental from manual work and reducing the latter to repetitive timed operations, originated in the US steel industry. The mechanized line moving products for processing past stationary workers had been invented in the carcass 'chain' of Chicago slaughterhouses. But Taylorism and mechanization came together in the vast industrial mega-complexes of Ford's Detroit auto plants, where workers produced cars through the performance of routinized tasks using standardized parts in a process whose rhythms and sequence were determined by the assembly line.

Work was exhausting, monotonous, noisy and dangerous. Ford became famous for the '5 dollar day', enabling workers to purchase the cars they made, setting in motion the virtuous circle of mass labour and mass consumption that by the mid twentieth century boosted advanced capitalism to extraordinary prosperity. But these wages were a concession forced on Ford by his early workforce of farm-boys and immigrants, who quickly learned a hatred of the assembly line that resulted in massive labour turnover. Increased pay fixed this problem, but at a price – literally. Exchanged for work that offered no other reward, the wage became the focus of ongoing industrial conflict. Because auto factories concentrated many workers in one place, large-scale trade union organizing was possible. Ford tried to prevent it by surveillance, intimidation and the outright violence of goon squads (see Gambino and Sacchetto 2014). However, because any interruption of production immobilized millions of dollars of machinery and inventory, work stoppage was a formidable weapon. In 1936–7 car workers at the General Motors plant in Flint, Michigan paralyzed assembly lines with sit-down strikes, making the auto industry a bastion of the mass worker.

Workplace solidarity backed by strike power also characterized mass worker organization in the steel, shipbuilding, mining and transportation industries in the US and Europe. Similar organization spread to clerical, administrative and public sector jobs. Not all workers had such strength. Ethnic minorities tended to be employed in more vulnerable sectors; it took black Americans decades to break into the car industry in Detroit in the face of fierce opposition from white workers (Georgakas 1975). Moreover, mass worker formations often depended on the gendered division between male workers, who went to factories as 'breadwinners', and housewives, who cared for children and dealt with the physical and psychological damage inflicted on their men by the assembly line. Women worked in the auto industry, but in low-wage office and 'detail' jobs, such as upholstery sewing; during the war they joined the assembly line, only to be pushed out afterwards by the return of male workers. Nonetheless the mass worker was a form of class composition that won unprecedented gains in wages, social benefits and living standards for North American proletarians.

Autoworkers remained the paradigm example. By 1949 the car was becoming central to North America's culture and economy, a symbol of personal freedom and prosperity, the crucial commodity in a nexus linking vehicle ownership, highway construction, suburban homes, and fossil fuel consumption. In the 1950s, General Motors, the biggest manufacturing company on the planet, would alone generate 3 per cent of the US GDP. The UAW too benefited from this prosperity, and, as it gained power, became increasingly integrated with US capital. Reuther typified this process. His reputation was as a labour firebrand, yet as UAW President he purged communist militants, held the union under tight bureaucratic control, and bargained hard, but for limited objectives (Moody 1988; Davis 1986). Auto factories might be sweatshops, he allowed, but they would be 'gold plated sweatshops' (quoted in Mann 1987: 56).

At the end of the Second World War the metropolitan area of Detroit – 'Motor City' – had the highest median income and home ownership of any sizeable US city (Schifferers 2007; Reich 1992: 46). In the city's Institute of Arts the great murals of the Mexican Marxist artist Diego Rivera, commissioned by Edsel Ford – son of Henry, and president of his father's company – celebrated the dynamism of humans and machines in assembly-line production and the paradoxical combination of industrial capitalism and worker power that Detroit represented. Jobs in the car industry placed 'the American dream' within reach not just of the middle managers who oversaw Fordist factories but of the workers who everyday watched their life vanish down the assembly line in return for reliable, rising pay checks that created the possibility of good nutrition and clothing, buying a house – perhaps eventually even a cottage on the Great Lakes – and sending kids to college. Now Wiener told Reuther the mass worker was threatened by cybernetic automata.

Control

'Cybernetics' has two meanings. The first designates a school of scientific thought that emerged during the 1930s and '40s, amongst researchers working on radar, ballistics, crypto-analysis and atomic weapons for the US and British war effort. The second, broader sense refers to the computer systems, from mainframes to mobiles, in whose evolution this school played a part. This book uses the term in both senses, taking the ideas of cybernetic thinkers as a guide to how computers in general have altered the technological processes of capital.

As John Johnston (2008: 28) observes, the cyberneticists' crucial insight was to see machines not as 'heat engines' generating energy by consuming fuels, but rather as entities governed by information control. Crucial to Wiener's wartime work on improving the accuracy of anti-aircraft fire was the concept of the 'feedback loop' that enables a machine to measure the effect of its action on its surroundings and adjust accordingly. Machines that use feedback processes to cancel out the effects of disturbances on their operations are known as 'servomechanisms'. An early servomechanism was the mechanical 'governor', a device that registered and regulated the operating speed of nineteenth-century steam engines. This example suggested to Wiener the term 'cybernetics', derived from the Greek for 'governor', 'ruler' or 'steersman'.

Wiener's ideas were core to the ten interdisciplinary Macy Conferences held in New York from 1946 to 1953 which brought together computer scientists, psychologists and biologists and established cybernetics as a body of thought with radical implications for the relation between humans and machines. Behind discussions of feedback and servomechanisms there was, however, a broader principle of cybernetics that makes clearer why it was so important to the development of computing. This was the idea that information is not about *knowing* but *doing* (Pickering 2010: 6). As another early cyberneticist, the psychologist Ross Ashby, put it: 'the brain is not a thinking machine, it is an *acting* machine; it gets information and then it does something about it' (Ashby 1948: 379).

What an 'acting machine' could do with information was dramatic. At 7.15 a.m. on the morning of 1 November 1952, the Pacific island of Elugelab literally 'melted into air'. Where it had been, there burst a deep-orange fireball 3.5 miles wide. A churning grey-brown pillar of water, dust and ash lofted into a mushroom cloud rising about 27 miles into the sky, seething with lurid colours and surrounded by lightning flashes. An observer plane flew into the vortex, spun out of control, burst into flames and crashed into the sea. As the cloud billowed outward, its colours faded to pastel shades, it formed a 100-mile-wide cauliflower that drifted away, carrying the vaporized remains of 800 million tons of solid material that fell to ground around the world as radioactive waste; 'all that remained of little Elugelab was a circular crater filled with seawater, more than a mile in diameter and fifteen stories deep' (Schlosser 2013: 129). It had been the test site for the first hydrogen bomb, nicknamed 'Mike', with an explosive yield of 10.4 megatons, about 500 times that of the atomic bombs that had destroyed Nagasaki and Hiroshima.

There would have been no Mike without MANIAC, the ironically named Mathematical Analyzer, Numeric Integration and Computer. Making nuclear weapons depends on engineering an initial explosive blast to set off fission or fusion in the uranium or plutonium at their core. Calculating the trajectories of the necessary shockwaves in the midst of a compounding furnace of atomic and subatomic mayhem posed complex mathematical problems. MANIAC was created to solve these problems faster than the human 'computers' whose laborious adding-machine-assisted calculations were far too slow for the doomsday schedule of the arms race. The overseer of MANIAC was John von Neumann, who alongside Wiener, with whom he would clash over the ethics of nuclear weapon research, was one of the founders of cybernetics.

MANIAC was not the first computer; that title could be claimed by mechanical devices in the nineteenth century, such as Charles Babbage's Difference Engine. It was not even the first electronic computer; it had been preceded by other Second World War military machines – ENIAC, the Electronic Numeral Integrator and Computer, which had calculated firing tables for artillery pieces, and Colossus, the British crypto-analytic code-breaking machine. But as George Dyson argues, MANIAC was the first computer to make use of a stored random access memory, containing both data and instructions; it thus decisively 'broke the distinction between numbers that *mean* things and numbers that *do* things'. As a cybernetic device – one the made information actionable – it was also the computer 'whose coding was most widely replicated and whose logical architecture was most widely reproduced' (Dyson 2012: ix). MANIAC ran on vacuum tubes, and like other pioneering machines was of a size that made it a 'very personal computer, not one you carry around with you, but rather lived inside' (Dyson 2012: ix), but it was a prototype for all the subsequent mainframes, minicomputers, PCs, laptops and tablets, that would become collectively known as cybernetic technologies.

Automata and Networks

Cybernetics left its legacy in two distinct but related fields – automata and networks. Automata encompass robots and other autonomous technologies, and, more broadly, artificial life. Key works include Wiener's *Cybernetics, or, Control and Communication in the Animal and the Machine* (1948), which developed the idea of the 'feedback loop' that allows an entity, biologic or machinic, to negotiate its environment, and von Neumann's *Theory of Self-Reproducing Automata* (1966), which envisaged self-reproducing robots programmed to build themselves. In network theory the crucial cybernetic contribution was Claude Shannon's *A Mathematical Theory of Communication* (1949) which, by defining information in purely quantitative terms, opened the way to consideration not only of how human communication might be augmented by computers, but also of communication as a process that may occur solely between machines.

Ramtin's (1991) history of capitalist machinery succinctly explains the significance of the automata strand. Machines consist of three elements: power transmission, motion transformation, and control of direction and speed. In the steam-driven machinery of the industrial revolution these three elements were built into one another. Machines were bulky and limited in tasks, repeating only a single action, even if at far greater speed and for much longer than a human. They were 'self-acting' in principle but inflexible in practice (Ramtin 1991: 3). Such machines enabled early factory-owners to stop the absolute exploitation of endlessly extending working hours and still profit from relative exploitation by taking a major share of productivity gains. Steam machines also forced workers to comply with their rhythm, setting the basis for more mechanization. But their rigidities seriously limited their capacities and made their 'dead labour' seem clearly secondary to and derivative of the vitality of living workers.

In the late nineteenth century the electrical motors of the second industrial revolution separated a machine's power source from its motion. One machine could have several motors or many machines could be run from a common motor. This significantly increased the efficiency of industrial machines. However, the issue of control continued to limit technological capacities. Although it became possible to alter how a specific machine functioned, with cams, stops, slides or gearing, this was time consuming, and required human skill. Even though industrial machinery routinized and deskilled large sections of manual labour it intensified capital's dependence on specific sectors of the working class, such as skilled machinists. Overall, mechanical automation still demanded the combination of human and machine. Philosophically, the ontological difference between machines and humans still seemed intact. Politically, workers could still stop the machine – the basis, as we have seen, of mass worker power.

The cybernetic feedback loop revolutionized machine control. If a machine has sensors that can measure and correct its own performance, adjusting input to output, it usurps the function that had seemed to remain irreducibly human in earlier industrial technology – the steering of the system. Feedback loops gave machines qualities thought to be specific to living labour: flexibility, adaptability, primitive learning and self-sensing (Ramtin 1991: 45). As we have seen, cyberneticists considered brain functions, and thought itself, as a sort of feedback loop. Humans and machines thus differ only quantitatively, in level of complexity, not qualitatively, in the very nature of their being. Stanley Ulam, one of von Neumann's collaborators on MANIAC, jotted succinct, chilling notes on artificial life: 'An organism (any reason to be afraid of this term yet?) is a universal automaton which produces other automata like it ... "universality" is probably necessary to organize or *resist* organization by other automata' (cited in Dyson 2012: 223). Information control becomes a common feature transposable between, as Wiener put it, automata 'in the metal or in the flesh' (1948: 42).

If digital automata are children of cybernetics so too are digital networks. By the early twentieth century, as Ford's assembly line mechanized production, the great Bell Telephone Company was developing the electric communication systems of the world market. As David Mindell (2002) shows in his study of the predecessors of cybernetic thought, what Ford would do for automation, Bell did for networks. Automation separates motion from the human bodies. Electronic networking depends on doing the same for communication, creating a signal divorced from human speech and writing, subject to technological modulation and reconfiguration. Telephone and telegraph had made the electrical transmission of voice and print possible. As transmission distances expanded – for example, from coast to coast in the US – maintaining a clear channel became difficult. It required amplification or boosting of the signal, augmenting communication in the same way as simple tools augment physical activity. This enabled more messages to be sent on a single wire, and over greater distances.

Electrical boosting also, however, created new problems. It produced feedback effects of distortion – 'singing in the wires' – that threatened to cancel out the benefits of the process. For a generation of telecommunication engineers minimization of 'noise' became a preoccupation. They learned to 'add power and renew the signal at any point and hence maintain it through complicated manipulation, enabling long strings of filters, modulations and transmission lines' (Mindell 2002: 114). In the process 'voices became signals and could be specified and standardized'; 'Now the telephone company delivered products: signals with a specific frequency range, at a specific amplitude, and with a specified amount of noise ... detached from its physical embodiment' (Mindell 2002: 114). This process was intensified by another corporate concern: creating a medium in which multiple forms of communication – text and speech, but also images from new visual media such as cinema – could be commonly transmitted and combined. This was a priority that reflected telecommunication capital's early ambitions towards the creation of monopolistic conglomerates.

During the Second World War such research was applied to military communication and cryptanalysis. This continued into the Cold War. The Pentagon's Advanced Research Projects Agency's (ARPA) experiments in early digital networks were led by J.R. Licklider, a student of Wiener's. He attended the Macy Conferences and was powerfully influenced by the work of another participant, Shannon. Building on Shannon's concept of information as an entirely quantifiable, and hence machine process-able, sequence of on-off binary signals, the ARPA group began to think of interconnected computers as a new medium of communication, linked by a flow of digital bits and bytes, within which geographically dispersed groups could converse in real time, assisted by various forms of artificial intelligence.

This cybernetics-based network research was not immediately focused on replacing humans by machines. Rather Licklider (1960) envisaged a 'very close coupling' of humans with machines, in a 'symbiotic' partnership. As he put it 'men are noisy, narrow-band devices' with 'many parallel and simultaneously active channels' while computers are 'very fast and very accurate, but constrained to perform only one or a few elementary operations at a time' (Licklider 1968: 1). Networks would maximize the particular strengths of each, marrying speed of machine processing with goal-setting human intelligence. Foreshadowing more recent accounts of inter-species assemblages, Licklider wrote of this human-computer relation as akin to that between the fig tree and the fig wasp, *Blastophaga grossorun*:

> The larva of the insect lives in the ovary of the fig tree, and there it gets its food. The tree and the insect are thus heavily interdependent: the tree cannot reproduce without the insect; the insect cannot eat without the tree; together, they constitute not only a viable but a productive and thriving partnership (1960: 1).

Thus the network side of cybernetics looked forward not so much to self-reproducing robots as to machine-human hybridity – the 'cyborg' (Haraway 1985).

A distinction is therefore often drawn between the distinctly uncanny, human-replacing automata, projects of cyberneticians such as von Neumann, and the apparently friendlier networked, human-augmenting turn of Licklider and his colleagues. The distinction is not, however, clean. Licklider saw the symbiotic moment of computer networking as transitional. In 1960, commenting on a US Air Force estimate that it would require at least 15 years of preliminary man-computer interaction before artificial intelligence was capable of 'problem solving of military significance', he wrote: 'The 15 may be 10 or 500, but those years should be intellectually the most creative and exciting in the history of mankind'; however, he admitted, 'It seems entirely possible that, in due course, electronic or chemical "machines" will outdo the human brain' to the point that it would be necessary to 'concede dominance in the distant future of cerebration to machines alone' (1960: 2).

In both its automating and networking dimensions, cybernetics was a 'knowledge conceived in the hot womb of violence' (Auden 1950: 96), incubated within the US national security state apparatus. It progressed through military projects such as the Whirlwind computer, developed by the MIT Servomechanisms Laboratory for the US Navy as a flight simulator, and prototype for the business computers and minicomputers in the 1960s; the massive Semi-Automatic Ground Environment (SAGE) Air defence system, intended to protect North America from Soviet bombers; and Operation Igloo White, which during the Vietnam War seeded the Ho Chi Minh trail with motion sensors communicating with a central control room to call in air strikes on troop convoys (Edwards 1997). Although the claim that the internet was created specifically to enable US nuclear forces to survive a Russian surprise attack is contested by the scientists who worked on it (Hafner 1998), it undoubtedly arose within a context of military command, control and coordination concerns, whether about the linking of missile bases or university weapons research facilities.

Such research also propelled capital's machinic advance. It was an interlocked 'iron triangle' of military, corporate and academic interests – which met the Pentagon's computing needs (Edwards 1997: 47). Giant electronic and telecommunication corporations – Raytheon, IBM, Sperry – made devices conceived by military-funded academics that then became the basis of a commercial computer industry, which, still supported by military contracts and drawing a new type of scientific worker from university departments funded by military research, branched out to sell computers to other capitalist enterprises.

In its military origins cybernetics was already a weapon for capital against a version of mass worker power. It was the USSR's state socialist mobilization of its own factory labour that had defeated Nazism in the Second World War, building the tank columns that brought the Red Army to Berlin. In the 1950s the USSR was matching or even outpacing the US in industrial growth, to the alarm of American Cold War analysts. Nuclear weapons – such as 'Mike' – and other cybernetic military projects evened the odds (or threatened to overturn the whole board) in this geopolitical conflict. It was not long, however, before cybernetics made it to the home front. From 1945 electronically guided machine tools and production systems pioneered by the US Air Force and other military agencies spread out to civilian aircraft manufacture, petroleum production and metal working (Noble 1984). As Wiener advised Reuther, cybernetic technologies would soon confront labour on the shop floor, for while he declined to put his scientific knowledge to corporate use, others were happy to do so.

Just-in-Time Autoworker

The modern industrial robot was developed in the late 1950s by George DeVol, an engineer who worked for Sperry on servomechanisms during the war, and independently patented a programmable robotic arm that could transfer objects over short distances. In 1960, DeVol, with a partner, Joseph Engelberger, whose electronics firm had supplied military markets, created the company Unimation to produce industrial robots. In 1969 another engineer, Victor Scheinman, working at Stanford University and MIT with fellowships from Unimation, widened robot uses to assembly and welding, then sold the licence to Unimation, who further developed the project with support from General Motors, and eventually marketed the Programmable Universal Machine for Assembly (PUMA), 'the first human-scale, electric robot designed for lightweight assembly' (Marsh 2004: 1).

Adoption was slow. High fixed costs inhibited innovation and 'auto makers preferred to use existing systems for as long as possible' (Dassbach 1986: 54). They were also deterred by the response of workers. GM had rebuilt its plant in Lordstown, Ohio in 1969, making it the most automated automotive plant in the world, building 110 cars per hour with 28 spot welding robots, twice the number of any plant then in existence. Workers resisted the speeded pace of production, the layoffs that preceded it, and the intimidation with which it was enforced. A spate of sabotage and absenteeism culminated in relentless wildcat striking, which persisted until the union, fearing contagious radicalism, colluded with management in suppressing the militancy (Weller 1973; Marsh 2004). Events such as this did not encourage robotization.

The situation did not change until the later 1970s, when the North American auto industry confronted massive competition from Japan. The Vice President of Toyota, Taiichi Ohno, had studied in the United States in the great Fordist factories. At Toyota – originally a textile company that started making trucks during the Second World War, and then entered the car business – Ohno introduced changes to the Detroit mass production system, changes that accelerated as the company faced the 1974 oil-crisis recession. Fordist auto manufacture had achieved immense gains for capital relative to craft production, but had its own limits. Workers were required only to keep the line moving, so quality control was poor. Factories were centralized, so built up huge buffer stocks of parts, tying up capital. The labour process was rigid, so direct line workers were supplemented by indirect labour cleaning up or carrying things. Above all, Fordism generated the mass worker, a formidable force limiting surplus value extraction. Toyotism, also known as lean production, flexible specialization, or simply post-Fordism, broke these limits. Ricardo Antunes (2013: 32–44) summarizes the elements of the new system:

1) *Reduction in the workforce.* Toyotism depended not just on automation, but on what Ohno termed 'autonomation' (1988: 6) – that is, the use of machines sufficiently 'intelligent' to know when to stop their operations. At Toyota, the prototype for such machines was an 'auto-activated

weaving machine' from the company's textile era, but the principle was clearly that of a feedback loop. Ohno called this 'automation with a human touch' – not, however, meaning human-friendly automation, but rather automation that approached the level of human capacities; 'autonomation' aimed not just at 'labour saving' but at 'worker saving' (1988: 6, 113). Toyotism 'allows a worker to simultaneously operate various machines (at Toyota an average of five machines), modifying the man-machine relation on which Taylorism/Fordism was based' (Antunes 2013: 39). In 'classic' Toyotism, as originally introduced in Japan, the trade-off for this reduction of the workforce was guaranteed lifetime employment for those who remained. This would not, however, survive the system's translation to other contexts, such as North America.

2) *Redefining the worker.* Toyota intensified work by demanding workers act not just as 'obedient hands' but as 'active participants' in production (Antunes 2013: 14). The famous *kaizen* system had workers stop the assembly line when it was going too fast for them to keep up, by pulling a cord to alter a set of flashing lights from green to amber to red. The aim, however, was not to permanently slow the line, but, on the contrary, to adjust the production process to get back to maximum pace. Toyotism also introduced cross-functional teams, assigned tasks with no fixed times or workloads, and made worker suggestions for improving efficiency mandatory.

3) *Reduction in inventory.* Rather than building up buffer stocks stored at one central location – the Fordist ideal – Toyota cultivated networks of outsourced suppliers, sending needed parts on call, in a *kanban* or 'just-in-time' (JIT) system that radically reduced the capital tied up in inventory which was a feature of Fordism.

4) *Relating production to circulation.* Ford's motto had famously been that the customer could have any colour car they wanted providing it was black. Toyotism introduced a wide range of automobile models and accessories, so that 'production is varied and heterogeneous, unlike homogenous Fordist production' (Antunes 2013: 38). It also introduced data banks on customers, tracking preferences and orders, converting car consumption into a 'pull-process' guided by demand (Jurgens et al. 1993: 44). This rebounds on production, requiring short-term adjustments to production runs, frequent tool changes, and flexible labour deployments.

Ohno's 'autonomization' was in essence servomechanism automation. Japan's capitalists were more receptive to the workplace application of cybernetics than those of the US, where industrial supremacy bred complacency. In the 1950s and '60s they also absorbed the ideas of management specialists such as Edward Deming, whose 'systems operations' approach was coloured by cybernetic influence. Later they eagerly adopted technologies such as robots, AI and video games, creating the image of 'silicon Samurai'. In Toyotism, however, human reengineering preceded and then paralleled the introduction of cybernetic machines: Ohno declared that 'a revolution in consciousness is indispensable' (1988: 15). This new type of automation required workers who could troubleshoot 'autonomated' machines, answering their need for 'servicing, monitoring and maintenance'; if the Japanese surpassed the US, it was not because they had better robots (they actually bought their automata from the US or manufactured the same models under licence) but because their workforce used them better (Dohse et al. 1985: 116; Jurgens et al. 1993: 69). The first step was re-defining the worker as part of a feedback loop; a sensor component in a goal-oriented process which was adjusted until the biological and machine components of the total system were in balance. The machine is not over and against the worker – because the worker is part of the machine.

Toyota's 'robotics leap' (Jurgens et al. 1993: 67) paired the autoworker with the automatic worker – that is, with the robot. By the 1980s robots were being used extensively in car plants, guiding welding guns and spray guns, and handling parts. Unlike single purpose machines, robots can be reprogrammed to handle different models and variants of car. They 'compete' with manual labour – flexible but expensive – and with dedicated specialized mechanization – cost-effective but rigid. Robots could 'run a model mix ... flexibly adjusted to the market situation' to deal with a 'chaotic succession' of models and techniques required by Toyota's flexible production system (Jurgens et al. 1993: 68–9).

In the context of Toyotism the auto industry became the most intensive user of industrial robots (Jurgens 1993: 67). These still remained far from the 'lights out' scenario of a fully automatic assembly line Wiener had envisaged. Robot 'miscues and breakdowns' were frequent: observers reported that at a GM plant robot problems made car building 'like viewing a film in slow motion, even when the assembly line is moving, which it isn't' (cited in Jurgens et al. 1993: 74). These problems extended to the human part of the equation. In North America, union militants understood the new production technique, with its demand for teamwork and participation, as a challenge to class solidarity that blurred the lines between labour and management, and broke down job descriptions and time demarcations, drawing labour into a self-administered exploitation in the name of company identification. Their ability to fight back was, however, undermined not only by robot replacements but also by cybernetic networks.

From the 1950s US car companies had invested overseas to gain new markets and reduce labour costs. These investments often involved partnership with local companies, some of whom, such as South Korean car makers, in turn became rivals. As competition mounted throughout the 1970s and '80s, this offshoring process accelerated. So too did the foreign investment of Japanese and Korean competitors who built the so-called 'transplant' factories in the US from which Toyota, Honda and Nissan would eventually capture the major share of the North American car market. Car capital developed a 'complex and in some ways surprising geography' (Stanford 2010: 385). It was 'highly global' in that it was dominated by a handful of big makers of cars, trucks and other vehicles, the Original Equipment Makers (OEMS). These planned international operations from centralized headquarters. Factory manufacture was, however, regionalized; transportation costs meant 'most automakers ... continue[d] to produce near their final market' (Stanford 2010: 385). These final markets could however, be far from home base; American auto companies sold in Europe, Japanese enterprises in America, and so on. The picture was further complicated because final assembly is only one part of automobile manufacture. It in turn draws on the networks of independent parts suppliers which Toyotism had separated from central plants and whose operations were sometimes 'far more globalized and outsourced than those of the OEMS' (Sturgeon et al. 2008: 10).

This global production required complex logistical infrastructures which increasingly depended on cybernetic systems. Schiller (1999: 14) has shown that while popular awareness of the internet developed slowly, the most rapid extra-military growth in digital networking was corporate; by the late 1980s company networks accounted for a third of US telecommunication spending. Car companies were at the forefront of this corporate networking, which made it far easier to communicate with assembly plants located far from headquarters, and connect them to suppliers. In 1982 General Motors began to plan a new car, the Saturn, whose production was modelled as a 'stream of resources' (such as raw materials and third-party components) coordinated by satellite-connected computers; though the Saturn was eventually unsuccessful, its factory had built the 'first supply chain management (SCM) system, integrating suppliers, factory and customers' (Scaruffi 2010).

The just-in-time, *kanban* logic of Toyotism was intensified by integrating information on fluctuations in inventories capacities and markets with cybernetic data banks and networks, creating what Japanese auto companies called 'electric kanban'. This increased the scope over which JIT could operate. The importance of delivery speed and defect correction means modern assembly plants often keep suppliers nearby. However, not all parts require close proximity to assembly, and in the automotive sector, as in other industries, foreign direct investment, free trade agreements and cybernetic networks combined to increase global sourcing – especially to areas with low labour costs. From the 1980s on the large automakers of all countries effected a 'gradual investment shift toward locations with lower operating costs' (Sturgeon et al. 2008: 8). In North America, this meant moving production to the non-unionized 'right to work' US South and to Mexico, where automotive labour costs were between 10 and 20 per cent those of the US (Stanford 2010: 392). In Europe, automobile factories and suppliers moved South and East. From Japan, they went to Thailand, the Philippines, other areas of South East Asia and, eventually, India and China.

In the Tornado

The combined effects of automation and globalization were catastrophic for the UAW. The threat of relocation and replacement cowed the once powerful union into a cycle of concession bargaining, and participation in programmes of labour-management cooperation which suppressed struggles against plant closings and mass layoffs in the name of increasing the competitiveness of the Detroit automakers. However even these capitulations were not sufficient to avert collapse. After reaching a peak of 1.53 million members in 1979, the union had shrunk to some 701,000 by 2001 (White 2010).

As North America slid into deindustrialization, cars and their components were certainly being made elsewhere around the globe, in complex new industrial configurations, enabled by new generations of robots and electronic networks linking regional hubs of vehicle body manufacture with contracted-out and offshore supply of parts. In 2005 the world's automobile industry made about 87 million cars, vans, trucks and buses, a reminder that the cybernetic vortex is not weightless, immaterial, or clean; on the contrary, it increases the intensity with which goods made of metal and plastics, powered by fossil fuels, circulate around the planet. Automotive companies still employed about 'eight million people directly in making the vehicles and parts that go into them', accounting for over 5 per cent of the world's total manufacturing employment (OICA 2013).

The workers in the new centres of car production would engage in battles as or more ferocious than those fought by American labour in the 1930s. In India at Toyota's Maruti Suzuki plant on the outskirts of Delhi an 'electronic flow regime' combined high-technology assembly with the 'slum production' of parts by suppliers using out-of-date machinery, attempting through a 'perfectly synchronized supply-chain' to 'reconcile "technical productivity" and "profitability" … tuning the rhythms of welding-robots to those of the dexterous hands of child labour' (GurgaonWorkersNews 2010b). In 2012 a dispute over working conditions exploded into violence and a company official was killed when workers burnt down a section of the plant. Over the next two years there were strikes at Hyundai and Honda plants in India, and in 2014 Toyota autoworkers in Bangalore – a city with a global reputation as a site for outsourced software programming – struck for higher wages (Empire Logistics 2014).

Beverly Silver's (2003: 41–81) detailed tracking of 'world historical patterns' of labour militancy traces a series of waves of automobile worker struggles that moved its epicentre from North America in the 1930s and '40s to Europe in the 1960s and '70s, then to newly industrializing countries such as Brazil, South Africa, South Korea and Mexico, and onward to China in the 2000s. At their high points these waves of autoworker militancy shared 'amazingly similar characteristics'. They 'burst on the scene with suddenness and strength'; relied on 'unconventional forms of protest – most notably the sit down strike' which 'paralyzed the production of huge industrial complexes', exposing the 'vulnerability of the industry's complex technical division of labour to workers direct action'; they involved workforces that were predominantly made up of first- and second-generation international and interregional migrants; strong 'community support' was an important element; they 'rapidly achieved major victories' and often had a 'broad political significance' beyond the industry and sector, such as the crucial role played by Brazilian car workers in the struggles that took their country from military dictatorship to social democracy (Silver 2003: 46).

These successes, however, also elicited managerial counter-strategies. In the short run there would be an institutionalization of collective bargaining and a domestication of the unions. In the longer term work would be 'increasingly automated' in what Silver (2003: 64–6) terms a 'technological fix'. At the same time 'new investments were targeted away from union strongholds'. This was an attempt to find a 'spatial fix' for the problem of labour control – a fix which, we will add, because of the role of cybernetic networks in agile global supply chains, was also in and of itself also another type of 'technological fix'. Ongoing autoworker struggles were thus waged from positions persistently undermined by the threat of global plant relocation, and in the teeth of an automating dynamic that intensified with every victory workers won. The windows of militancy closed more rapidly in each new location as the vendors of industrial robotics and networked outsourcing homed to the beacon of the latest strike wave.

Thus the 'high-point waves' of autoworker strength were not just a series of independent instances', but rather '*linked relationally* by the successive relocation of production away from militant labor forces' (Silver 2003: 46). Silver retained some optimism that post-Fordist, just-in-time lean and mean flexible production techniques might offer opportunities for militant interruption (2003: 69). But she noted that the introduction of 'robots and JIT production methods has pulled the rug out from under all but the lowest wage sites of production (e.g. China, northern Mexico)' (2003: 80). The rapidity of capital's techno-spatial fixes speeds up, so that 'the time required to bring each cycle of militancy under control has decreased over the course of the half century' (2003: 64).

Eventually automobile internationalization 'came full circle' and plants 'began to concentrate in the core regions from which they had fled' (Silver 2003: 66). In the North American Great Lakes region, for example, some plants returned, but this time in small towns, avoiding former bastions of union strength. Moreover, when car manufacture does make such a return it does so technologically metamorphosised. Autoworkers generally continue to be paid better than other manufacturing workers in the same region, partly because of productivity, unionization and the demanding nature of the work, but also because direct labour costs at the assembly level account for less than 10 per cent of the total operating expenses (Stanford 2010: 393). Car capital has so intensified its organic composition as to make the human component almost negligible.

The automobile industry is today the largest sectoral user of industrial robots. These still do not provide the fully automated 'lights out' option that has repeatedly been promised; communication flow – i.e. getting robots to talk to each other – is the main bottleneck. However, the factories that make robots have allegedly solved the problem. At the Mt Fuji factory of Japan's Fanuc Ltd, a major supplier of auto-sector robots, robots have for over a decade been building other robots 'at a rate of about 50 per 24-hour shift and can run unsupervised for as long as 30 days at a time'. When they stop, 'it's because there's no room to store the goods'; trucks haul out the new robots, the lights are cut, and the process begins anew. '"Not only is it lights-out," says a company representative, "we turn off the air conditioning and heat too"' (Null and Caulfield 2003).

What is more, as workers continue to toil alongside robots making cars, the product itself has been cybernetically transformed. The electronics component of cars has risen steadily since the 1970s, now controlling ignitions, fuel economy, emissions, air bags, diagnostics, global positioning systems and on-board entertainment. In the last few years the possibility of self-driving vehicles, operating without human agency, has been widely promoted (Howe 2013). Whatever promises this development might hold for its declared reasons of increasing safety and lessening urban congestion, it looms ominously over the transportation workers who today truck not only auto-parts but a million other commodities across the highways of the planet. In prototyping autonomous vehicles, a leading actor promises to be the world's preeminent information capitalist, namely Google, whose owners embrace the notion of a technological 'singularity' in which machinic consciousness supersedes that of humans (Vance 2010).

Punching Out

After Wiener wrote to Reuther in 1949 the two men did indeed meet and began a sporadic dialogue interrupted by both parties' extreme busyness. Ultimately the encounter was without result. Reuther's reformist trade unionism would never extend to challenge capital's control of computers in the way Wiener suggested. In 1950 Reuther concluded the 'Treaty of Detroit' with the Big Three automakers, a five-year contract signed first by General Motors, then by Ford and Chrysler, tying wages to productivity increases, but relinquishing UAW claims over wider issues such as technological change. On the other side, in 1952 Wiener declined Reuther's invitation to address a national trade union convention, possibly in a bout of the depression that recurrently incapacitated him (Conway and Siegelman 2005: 245–6, 253). Already under FBI surveillance because of his anti-nuclear weapons stance, the scientist's doubts about automation increasingly took the form of religious reflections.

Cybernetics as an organized movement was short-lived. It split between researchers who saw its concepts in purely technological terms and others exploring their psychological and social implications. In the climate of Cold War America Wiener's political positions, including not only his pro-labour sympathies but also opposition to nuclear weapons research, at once isolated him within the movement he founded and made it generally suspect. Cybernetics was also outrun by the technologies it helped develop: identified with research into early mainframes, it would seem anachronistic in the age of personal computers, and be superseded by other currents of thought, including chaos and complexity theory, which developed the notion of feedback but in new 'post-cybernetic' directions (Conway and Siegelman 2005). By the end of the 1950s, even as cybernetic machines raced ahead, cybernetics as an intellectual project seemed over.

Recently, however, it has attracted renewed attention. Katherine Hayles (1999) describes the Macy Conferences as landmarks in the emergence of 'post-human' thought. Johnston nominates cybernetics as the 'historical nexus out of which the informational networks and computational assemblages ... of the post-industrial world first developed' (2008: 25). More critically, the anarchist journal *Tiqqun* (2001) suggests that the 'cybernetic hypothesis' that human and machine behaviours are controlled by programmed and re-programmable feedback loops was intrinsically political because 'it conceives of each individual behavior as something "piloted", in the last analysis, by the need for the survival of a "system" that makes it possible, and which it must contribute to'. We agree; though cybernetics' immediate allusion to 'rulership', 'steering' or 'governance' was to a rather narrow concept of the informational regulation of machinic or biological entities, we can read these terms in a wider way. Cybernetics is about the question of who, or what, will rule in an age of intelligent machines.

And the answer, to date, is capital. Wiener's prediction of a crisis of cybernetic automation 'in some ten to twenty years', would in the short term seem alarmist. The 1950s and '60s were the golden years of Fordist capital, before its crisis in the 1970s. Seen from the present, however, Wiener was prescient. Nowhere was this more apparent than in the city which had symbolized the power of both the US auto industry and its workers. The scale of Detroit's disaster is caught in Paul Clemens' *Punching Out: One Year in a Closing Auto Plant* (2011), whose title refers both to the end of day check-out of assembly-line workers and also, with a sad irony, to one of the most famous accounts of militant auto-factory organizing (Glaberman 1952). Clemens' book is an account of the dismantling of Liberty Motors plant, one of the oldest Detroit factories, which at its peak employed 10,000 workers stamping out car roofs, doors and tailgates; by 2006 there were 350. Then it shut down, and its enormous press lines were taken apart to be shipped to Mexico, where they were then reconstructed to produce the same parts, for the same companies – but for far lower wages.

Clemens writes about the proletarians who disassemble the factory – gangs of roustabouts from Arkansas, making a living taking apart the factory fortresses of the mass worker in the brief moment when deindustrialization itself becomes an industry. They are 'the American working class, mopping up after itself' (2011: 8) in the wake of a stunning cybernetic assault. One tells Clemens, 'I drank thirty-two beers the other night', then remarks 'Hell, I don't even know what e-mail is' (2011: 185). As Clemens watches a piece of large machinery being disassembled, another man, a bystander named Duane, turns to him and remarks: 'You can't measure it. You can't measure the lives; you can't measure the lunches, the allowances, that people were able to give their kids' (2011: 109).

In 2014 Detroit was declared bankrupt. Under what amounted to municipal martial law, the pensions of public sector workers were cancelled and water supplies cut off to predominantly Afro-American neighbourhoods that could not afford to pay their bills. These were communities where urban gardeners were struggling to remedy food deserts created by the flight of supermarkets and grocery stores. Large sections of the city were planned to revert to agricultural production. What had once been the industrial capital of the US was now known to the world as a site of 'ruin-porn', supplying apocalyptic backgrounds for artistic vampire movies. The whole North American auto-belt surrounding it was an area in decline, and the UAW a shadow of its former strength; by 2009, after the Wall Street crash and the mass layoffs required as part of the automaker bailout, it had lost 1.14 million members, or 77 per cent of its membership: many of the remainder were not in the auto industry, but in other industries also in decline (White 2010).

This disintegration mirrored a wider trend: just as autoworkers had led the mass worker on its upward path, so their fall was a benchmark of a collapse in industrial working-class strength. Throughout the whole North American manufacturing sector computerization served as a means to drive down labour costs, whether through automation, from steel sector mini-mills to aerospace CAD/CAM design, or by the digital supply-chain managements systems that outsourced production in electronics and textiles. By 2011 the United States had 'more people dealing cards in casinos than running lathes, and almost three times as many security guards as machinists' (Clemens 2011: 12). With these shifts came the decline in the main organizational form of the mass worker: in 2009 only 12.3 per cent of all US workers were unionized – including just 7.2 per cent in the private sector, compared to 35.7 per cent of private sector workers in 1953 and 22 per cent as late as 1979 (White 2010).

Cybernetics had decomposed the form of labour underpinning working-class advance in North America. The restructuring of the automobile industry was of course not only a matter of technological change. It involved both the engineering of robots and networks and the human reengineering necessary to adapt workers to this new machinic matrix. These changes were set in a larger context of free trade agreements and legislative attacks on labour, political changes that both enabled and were themselves enabled by new technologies. But within this wider dynamic, cybernetics was a major contributor to 'the decline of the mass collective worker' (Murray 1983). To meet the new global proletariat that would replace it we must move on to the other side of North America.

4

Silicon

Birthplace

They 'snap on vinyl surgeon's gloves and don white and blue Dacron: hoods, jump suits, veils, and booties' and, identity and expression extinguished, walk out of the locker room down a corridor towards the work site. Sticky matting cleanses their soles, and nozzles pour 'a continuous fusillade of air at them, removing dust flecks and lint'. Once at their stations in the 'clean room', forced air blows continuously from wall and ceilings, its noise merging with the 'dull whir of the processing machinery' to produce a continuous 'low boom – a crescendo that peaks but never falls off'. Amidst this white noise 'casual conversation is difficult and the distraction often dangerous', so 'like deep sea divers the workers use hand gestures, or like oil riggers they shout above the din'. But mainly 'the crescendo encourages a feeling of isolation, of removal from the world' (Hayes 1989: 63–4). Activity is 'eerily cadenced', like that of 'astronauts slightly free of gravity' in an environment where 'sudden movements raise eyebrows and suggest accidents'. But the gendering of this workplace is no accident. Managers have selected women, generally small, dark-skinned women from Asia, Latin America and the Pacific Rim, for a labour process where the 'time, attention and pampering' given to the final product 'approaches that of a twenty four hour nursery':

> For six to seven days a week on eight to twelve hour shifts round the clock, the women move gracefully from process to process, gently bearing *cassettes* or *boats* of delicate wafers from the photolithography of the *steppers*, to the arsine and chlorine doping of the *ion implanters*, to the acid baths and gas clouds of the wet and dry *etchers*. (Hayes 1989: 71–2).

It was on this labour, amongst the most dangerous and toxic on the planet, the making of semiconductor chips, that the industry which carried cybernetics into homes and hands around the world was founded.

Once the Valley of Hearts Delights, famed for verdant apricot, peach and prune orchards, the Santa Clara Valley in southern California was in the 1970s renamed after a derivative of sand; it became Silicon Valley. In the 1940s computers were built from vacuum tubes like those inside old televisions. In the 1950s they ran on the transistors that powered radios. But it was the discovery of silicon semiconductors in the 1970s that launched the modern computer industry. Silicon is 'a natural conductor of electricity' that 'increases its conductivity exponentially when certain chemicals [are] applied to it' (Pellow and Park 2002: 77). The high-purity grades required for semiconductors are extracted from special sand deposits, such as those produced from quartzite, mined not in Silicon Valley but in very carefully secured and often environmentally devastating quarries in regions such as the Appalachian mountains (Welland 2009). To make the mineral into a cybernetic component, long cylindrical crystals of molten silicon are grown and cut into very fine wafers. The wafers are laced with additives and chemicals to etch in electric circuitry, then broken into tiny 'chips', tested, soldered into boards and assembled into computers, where they relay the binary electric 'on/off' signals that are the basis of digital technology.

The Santa Clara area's transformation from agrarian to cybernetic heartland was shaped by the presence of Stanford University. During the Second World War its research institutes and industrial parks drew in military-industrial corporations such as Lockheed, Fairchild, General Electric, IBM, Westinghouse and Intel. In 1971, Intel released the first commercially available 'microprocessor', a chip containing a computer's entire central processing unit; 30 years later, the company had a market value greater than the Big Three Detroit automakers combined (Pellow and Park 2002: 86). Silicon Valley, ripe with accumulated scientific know-how and rich with defence-related contracts, became the fabled home of information capital's succession of great enterprises – Intel, Oracle, Atari, Apple, Adobe, Google, Facebook; a nexus for software, hardware and digital services; the geographic centre from which PCs, videogames, internet browsers, e-commerce applications, search engines and social media would emerge; and a crucible for cybernetic capital's new mix of billionaire owners, high-technology professionals and low-paid, hazardously employed proletarians. While in the last chapter we examined how cybernetics altered the class composition of a classic industrial-era sector, that of the automobile industry, in this one we will see how in Silicon Valley computer production generated its own distinct information-age composition of labour, a composition that would then become further divided and distributed around the world.

Hacking Class

As computers passed out of the immediate supervision of the military command and control system, they were developed in increasingly distributed and molecular forms. The combination of personal computer and the network would became the basis for internet culture, a culture which, while it grew out of the automation and network experiments of early cyberneticists, is often termed post-cybernetic, because it produced a multiplication of communicational feedback loops flowing not from a single point but intersecting and interacting in complex ways. This networked development took digital technology from the military-industrial complex and disseminated it through the broader capitalist economy which that complex had protected.

Manuel Castells identifies four cultural streams that carried the legacy of cybernetics into Silicon Valley: 'techno-meritocratic', 'hacker', 'virtual communitarian' and 'entrepreneurial' (2002: 37). The 'techno-meritocrats' were the systems managers of military, academic and corporate computing research institutes, highly trained professionals with a code of extreme technological proficiency. The 'hackers' were the junior members of this masculine brotherhood, often graduate students, who in key projects that defined the early history of computing pushed proficiency into unauthorized, playful experimentation. The 'virtual communitarians' were early adopters of networks and computers conducting online explorations in sci-fi, sex, music, games and politics. The 'entrepreneurs', many of whom emerged out of the former three elements, concluded a fateful alliance with finance capital to start the new industry that made Silicon Valley synonymous with money, 'money in staggering amounts' (Castells 2002: 57).

Of these fractions, the hackers pose the major conundrum for class analysis. Working in 'academic circles and ancillary research units ... both in the heights of professorial ranks and in the trenches of graduate student work', this was a grouping outside the Fordist culture of the mass worker and its managerial cadres (Castells 2002: 40). Its ambience was libertarian, scornful of corporate 'suits', often anti-commercial, flouting property and profit to develop computers and networks, but also germinating their commodification. It was Steven Levy's *Hackers: Heroes of the Computer Revolution* (1984) that brought this culture to popular awareness, celebrating a 'hacker ethic' of openness, empowerment and belief that 'information wants to be free'. Other observers were more sceptical. Dennis Hayes criticized the 'vocal minority of computer journalists' who 'identified a highly evolved morality and politics among software and hardware designers', remarking that 'there could be few more misleading notions'. He observed instead a culture fascinated with techniques rather than purposes, infatuated with its own innovations, rendered compliant with corporate and military priorities by the 'seductions of work in a lonely era' (1989: 82).

There are similar divisions of opinion amongst scholars. McKenzie Wark (2004) champions the open experimentalism of the 'hacker class' against the proprietorial logic of information capital; although he acknowledges that much of this subversive potential remains unrealized or co-opted, his analysis assigns to programmers a role in social struggle comparable to that *operaismo* theorists once gave the mass worker. Contra-wise, Christian Fuchs describes the software engineers of Google as a 'labour aristocracy' – 'lieutenants of the capitalist class' – aligned with their employers by virtue of high wages and privileged work conditions (2014a: 229).

These conflicting assessments can be reconciled if we understand hacking culture as an 'intermediate' class strata between capital and labour. Made up of supervisory, skilled or credentialed workers, these strata grow in importance with capital's increasingly complex division of labour, and have always been problematic for Marxism's binary class analysis (Nicolaus 1967). In the 1970s Erik Olin Wright (1978: 80–1) proposed that such workers occupied 'contradictory class locations' with inherently ambiguous, fluctuating identities and political alignments. Sectors in such split locations included mid-level managers and supervisors, small employers and 'semi-autonomous experts' such as university professors or research scientists, who by virtue of special technical knowledge enjoy a degree of control over their labour process even though employed by capital. Early software programmers and engineers were 'semi-autonomous experts' in a technological field whose novelty, speed of development and strategic importance to capital amplified both their independence and the pressures upon it. Seeing hacking in this unromantic way, as a sort of extreme 'middle class' subjectivity with supercharged and freewheeling contradictions, helps explain the different tendencies that appeared within it.

For amongst early hackers some wanted to see the possibilities of cybernetic dissemination actualized within the framework of corporate capitalism while others believed the possibilities exceeded and transgressed those boundaries. This second group was itself internally differentiated between strands which espoused markets but disavowed agglomerations of corporate power and more anarcho-communal threads, stressing the free distribution of goods. All these currents, commonly saturated with a pervasive libertarian individualism, swirled around each other in complex and mutable patterns. Thus in the long arc of hacking culture there is both a great gulf and a certain affinity between figures such as Steve Wozniak and Julian Assange, the one a former phone 'phreaker' who became co-founder of today's mightiest, most secretive and locked-down digital corporation and the other a hunted outlaw with libertarian, pro-market cypherpunk politics (Assange 2012).

Gradually this chaotic set of contradictions sifted into dominant and minoritarian lines. If one hacker section, fascinated and empowered by the technical potential of computers, firmly believed 'information wants to be free', another, implicated in and sharing the ambitions of corporate capital, wanted just as deeply to see it commodified. This split found its exemplary expression in the young Bill Gates' 1976 'Open Letter to Hobbyists', in which he repudiated the free ethic of early computer tinkering in favour of the rights of information property (Levy 1984: 229). From this point two paths diverge. One, broad and upward trending, led to Gates' own corporate empire, and also those of Steve Jobs, Larry Page and Sergei Brin, and Mark Zuckerberg. Another, more twisty and subterranean, was followed by figures such as Richard Stallman (inventor of 'copyleft' protection for Free and Open Source Software), Aaron Swartz (the hacktivist whose breaches of state and commercial systems led to his prosecution and eventual suicide), and Julian Assange (Wikileaks founder).

In Silicon Valley the metamorphosis of hacker culture resolved itself as 'the Californian Ideology' (Barbrook and Cameron 1996), an ostensibly laid-back but actually highly aggressive anti-regulatory free enterprise that narcissistically identified its own lucrative technological success as socially liberatory. As computer-related capital grew, the unauthorized tampering with its systems, intrinsic to the original concept of hacking, was increasingly criminalized. This was a matter both of fact and fiction.

It was 'fact' in so far as there did emerge a subculture of computer experts, technically 'crackers' rather than 'hackers', raiding for credit card numbers, bank access, industrial secrets, and saleable software: Kevin Mittnick was an early, notorious example. This subculture would eventually attain global scale. But the image of the criminal hacker was also 'fiction' to the degree it was invoked to legitimize increasingly restrictive intellectual property regimes, which by outlawing activities such as everyday copying increasingly fettered the new digital apparatus.

Meanwhile programming differentiated into several layers. At the top stood the billionaire hacker entrepreneurs, the select few whose inventions, incubated in universities or stolen from competitors, were successfully financed by venture capital to become the brand names of digital culture. Below were for-hire professional computer savants who found compensation for long hours, high turnover, job insecurity, and a life chronically short of women, in workaholism, high salaries, stock options and dreams of their own start-up. At the bottom were the 'net slaves', from bug-testers to routine coders and on-the-fly freelancers whose silicon hopes resolved into cubicles, commuting and Californian shopping malls (Lessard and Baldwin 2000).

In Silicon Valley, hacker culture was transformed by the 'attempt to introduce capitalist efficiency into the complex process of software engineering' (Hayes 1989: 87). An increasingly hierarchic division of labour distinguished systems analysts, project leaders, programme analysts, chief, associate, assistant, senior and junior programmers. In a classic deskilling process various 'structured programming techniques' (object-oriented programming being the most recent) 'br[oke] up the job of writing software programs into modules, or groups of relatively simple isolated, step by step job tasks'. Leaders assign modules to programmers, who work on them more or less simultaneously, monitored by 'structured walk-throughs' with team members scrutinizing and policing each other's work looking for 'coding irregularities' (Hayes 1989: 91). Capital thus manages software production by Taylorist, Fordist and Toyotist methods.

A striking example of this trajectory is the video game industry, carrier of the most utopian hopes for the digital revolution, and purportedly offering its most 'fun' jobs. In the mid 1970s these claims were embodied in Atari, one of Silicon Valley's first success stories. Game development proceeded to the accompaniment of countercultural company manifestos, lavish parties, a declared 'work smart not hard' ethos, and employee choice as to what projects would be adopted and worked on (Dyer-Witheford and de Peuter 2009: 12–13). Three decades later, the memory of those legendary rebel days was apparently sealed indelibly into the self-image of the gaming business. Atari, however, had vanished into bankruptcy. The new norm of game employment was revealed in the angry blog-postings by programmers' spouses, disclosing their partners' hours of unpaid overtime in the perpetual 'crunch time' of mega-developer Electronic Arts. Surveys of game developers reported a general crisis of labour burn-out, disillusion and a turnover rate sustainable only by the inexhaustible supply of young men eager to hurl themselves under the wheels of the gaming industry's gaudy juggernaut (Dyer-Witheford and de Peuter 2009: 59–67).

Observing this decreasing autonomy and increasing regimentation, Tim Jordan suggests that the 'most important and largest group' of professional programmers are 'those whose ability to define and redefine ... computer and network technologies is not their own, but is decided by the institution that employs them' (2008: 113). These he terms 'the programming proletariat' because they 'have the key forms of control that hackers "own" – the ability to define, modify, make and contest technological determinism – taken away from them and invested in corporate structures' (2008: 113). As Jordan puts it, the 'programming proletariat programs, it does not hack', but their proletarian status is 'masked by various signs of hacking'. The 'campuses' of Silicon Valley corporations invoke academic freedom and offer perks – cool surroundings, nice food, recreational facilities – which 'both cosset and then exploit their programmers as creative workers', disguising 'a lack of freedom in return for a wage' (Jordan 2008: 115). The process by which 'semi-autonomous experts' and other professionals win a limited independence from capital on the basis of special technological knowledge, only to find their autonomy and bargaining power whittled down by the very automating and networking dynamics they helped set in motion is an important part of 're-proletarianization'. The labour of the 'programming proletariat' rested, however, on a far blunter exploitation of other types of workers, to whose role in Silicon Valley we now turn.

Toxic Work

Following Pellow and Park (2002: 85) we can distinguish in the basic industrial processes of computer manufacture 'core jobs' in semiconductor production, performed in 'clean rooms' by the bunny-suited workers we have already met, and the 'peripheral jobs' of preparing printed circuit boards, printers and cables, performed in far less clinical settings – indeed, often in workers' own homes. In addition Silicon Valley featured service workers: janitors cleaning the offices of hacker geniuses, gardeners manicuring the lawns of high-tech campuses, food servers, parking lot attendants, security guards – all labour maintaining the fundamentals of mammalian existence in a world devoted to high-technology machines. Together these industrial and service jobs provided the computer revolution's proletarian manual labour.

In 2000 there were officially about 65,000 electronic assembly workers, 40,000 non-assembly manufacturing workers, and 200,000 service workers in Silicon Valley (RW 2000). These jobs were filled by a workforce shaped in Santa Clara's traditions of female, migrant agricultural labour. In electronics plants the majority of production workers were women from ethnic minorities, while the engineering and management staff were predominantly male and white. Migrants were drawn to production lines and service work in various waves. In the semiconductor industry Latino women were the largest single group in the 1980s, and continued to dominate service jobs, but by the 1990s women from Asia – Vietnam, the Philippines, Malaysia – had become the majority in industrial processing (Pellow and Park 2002: 89). Undocumented migrant workers, not included in official labour estimates but targeted in erratic sweeps by immigration authorities, were variously estimated to compose from 10 to 25 per cent of the workforce (Hayes 1989: 54).

The living conditions of these workers were defined by impoverishment relative to the entrepreneurial and professional superstars of the Valley. At the height of the dot-com boom in 2000 it was calculated that 64 new millionaires were created every day; company heads pulled salaries of over $100 million a year; and top executives took home pay cheques 220 times larger than those of the average worker; meanwhile industrial and service workers toiled for median pay around $11 to $13 a hour (RW 2000). The cost of living in the area was the highest in the US. Housing was the major problem. Rents went up 60 per cent from 1995 to 2000 (RW 2000). For service and industrial workers this meant 'cramming more and more people into tighter living quarters with twenty or more people from multiple families living in a single house, sleeping on rented floors, or in buses and with even the employed resorting to homeless shelters' (RW 2000). In this situation, 'workers sustain[ed] themselves by working extra hours and taking multiple jobs'. Silicon Valley pioneered 'flexible' labour practices that would become hallmarks of cybernetic capital, sacrificing circadian rhythms and social life to the frenetic pace of technological innovation and entrepreneurial start-ups. This had a gendered aspect:

> For women, this really means working three jobs – or 'Three Shifts' as some immigrants call it – one at a sweatshop in the formal economy, a second taking care of the family, and then a third working in the informal economy, taking in laundry or cleaning houses on the weekends (RW 2000).

Temporary work, piece work and home work proliferated. Silicon Valley corporations outsourced not only cafeteria work, garbage removal and janitorial services, but also secretarial and clerical work, subcontracted to temp agencies. These were jobs for which employers assumed 'no responsibility for benefits, pensions or severance pay'; workers were 'hired when needed, dumped when demand slackens, and fired and blacklisted for any hint of opposition' (RW 2000).

Flexible working conditions were particularly pernicious in the 'peripheral jobs' of electronic assembly. The Valley became the home of a new sort of enterprise which would eventually globalize its scope: electronics contract manufacturers. These took on workers as assembly contracts became available; work would in turn be contracted to second or third tier contractors, with pay and conditions deteriorating at each downward rung. This produced the true Silicon Valley sweatshops – assembly of electronic components by workers in their own homes, at piece rates that were only sustainable by mobilizing entire families, including children and the elderly.

The real killer in Silicon Valley, however – the factor that made the computer industry a slow-motion version of the nuclear bomb that destroyed Elugelab – was the toxic waste produced from semiconductors. During the Second World War the microelectronics industry developed new synthetic chemicals from petroleum products and 'capitalized on solvents such as ethylene, benzene, styrene, complex halogenated hydrocarbons ... and various new ketones and resins' (Pellow and Park 2002: 78). These and other substances – 'arsenic, asbestos, chlorine gas, cyanide, freon, glycol ether, hydrochloric acid, isopropyl alcohol, lead, nitric acid, silica, solder, sulphur, toluene, trichloroethylene, ultraviolet ink and xylene' (Fuchs 2014a: 220) – were all applied in semiconductor manufacture. The 'geometries of production' which decreased the size of semiconductor chips 'required more solvents to wash away ever smaller "killer particles" that could jam a circuit, while making the circuits run faster also means using even more toxic chemicals' (Pellow and Park 2002: 107). Accelerated computer production cycles multiplied the chemicals in use, diminished the time to research their health hazards, and minimized corporate interest in doing so.

These toxins were particularly menacing for 'core' workers who encountered the most dangerous substances in semiconductor clean room processes. While their head-to-toe suits were protective, 'they were designed to protect the product from the workers – not the workers from the chemicals'. Those who worked in 'peripheral' jobs often lacked even this degree of protection. US Bureau of Labor statistics showed electronic assembly workers suffering the highest rate of 'systematic poisoning from chemical exposure' of any manufacturing workers, in California and nationwide. Plant closures for worker exposure to nitric acid and arsenic were frequent, and 'it was commonplace for workers to be pulled over on DUI on the way home from work because they were driving erratically after being exposed to high levels of industrial alcohols'. For those who worked out of their homes, assembly processes involving cleaning and soldering chemicals 'so powerful that it could make people bleed from the nose at the end of a day's work', sitting 'next to the family's rice pot with dinner cooking' (RW 2000).

The consequences of exposure were at once terrifying and enigmatic. Workers would suffer headaches, skin rashes, dizziness, respiratory problems, and, a particular threat for a largely female workforce, miscarriages and birth defects. Those who complained about the unsafe working conditions risked being fired and blacklisted. Employers refused to investigate and reclassified complaints to avoid regulations that required reporting accidents. When investigations were conducted the number of chemicals in use and the high turnover of employees made conclusive results difficult. The issue of the relation of birth defects and miscarriages to semiconductor work was the subject of a series of conflicting and contested findings. A recent overview of the controversy concludes that although knowledge of the contribution(s) from specific chemical exposures is still limited, 'most evidence suggests reproductive risks from fabrication jobs, including spontaneous abortion (SAB), congenital malformation, and reduced fertility'. Evidence of cancer risk was equivocal; nonetheless, even though available studies had methodological limitations associated with underestimation, 'excess risks for non-Hodgkin's lymphoma (NHL), leukemia, brain tumor, and breast cancer were observed' (Myoung-Hee et al. 2014: 95).

Pollution was not limited to those who worked in clean rooms or turned their homes into assembly plants. In 1981 the drinking water of homes in Silicon Valley's largest city, San Jose, was discovered to be 'heavily contaminated with the deadly chemical trichloroethane (TCA), a solvent used to remove grease from microchips and printed circuit boards' (Pellow and Park 2002: 73). It soon became apparent that the water sources of other areas had become similarly polluted as chemical run-off infiltrated complex well and irrigation systems dating from the Valley's agricultural era. Toxic effects were not, however, evenly distributed throughout the Valley's various neighbourhoods. Pollution tended to follow, both as cause and effect, patterns of *de facto* residential segregation, heaviest in areas inhabited by service and production workers, lower in those of the hacker-professionals, separating the environmental legacies of the Valley into, on the one hand, palatial billionaire mansions, and on the other, 23 'Super-Fund' abandoned toxic waste sites scheduled for special clean up operations, the most in any county in the US (Baca 2010). The Valley of Hearts Delight became 'the Valley of Toxic Fright' (Pellow and Park 2002).

The new silicon proletariat fought to improve both its working and environmental conditions, but did so under conditions of extreme vulnerability – because of its temporary, dispersed and often undocumented status; discrimination against female, migrant and minority workers; the absence of union traditions in the Valley, and also because of abandonment by most of the US labour movement (Bacon 2011). Nonetheless, organizations emerged to investigate and oppose environmental pollution, involving both workers and wider communities, such as the Santa Clara Center for Occupational Safety and Health (1978) and the Silicon Valley Toxics Coalition (1982). In 1989 a Justice for Janitors campaign by the Service Employees International Union won an important battle by systematically embarrassing Apple about the wages and conditions of its subcontracted cleaning staff. Other efforts did not end so well. In 1992 workers at the Versatronix plant for PC computer boards took the unprecedented step of voting to unionize an assembly operation in the Valley. The owners greeted the victory by immediately closing down operations and moving overseas – a response that foreshadowed the precarious future of Silicon Valley's industrial workforce.

A Tale of Three Cities

Silicon Valley was from its origin globalized; it grew from migrant labour. Then, however, the Valley itself migrated, extending its class dynamics on a world scale. Silicon Alleys (New York), Glens (Glasgow, Scotland), Plateaux (Bangalore, India), Gulfs (Mindanao, Philippines) and Savannahs (Nairobi, Kenya) sprung up as regions and nations attempted to copy the Californian computer industry success. In reality, however, the Valley did not so much replicate as explode: different shards of its division of labour were broken off, externalized, and offshored, creating new, specialized international centres whose class consequences we will illustrate with snapshots of three sites: Mexico's Ciudad Juárez, India's Hyderabad and Taiwan's Hsinchu.

Ciudad Juárez stands on the US-Mexico border, across the Rio Grande River from El Paso, Texas. It is the largest city of Mexico's *maquiladoras*, in the factory frontier zone that from the 1970s attracted US industries to take advantage of low Mexican wage rates. The North American Free Trade Agreement (NAFTA) of 1994 increased this draw. It also undermined Mexican farmers' ability to compete with US agribusiness. The rural unemployed flooded into Juárez's factories – many of them 'twinplants' managed from El Paso – including automotive, light industry and computer assembly plants. US computer makers had been outsourcing assembly work since the mid 1960s when IBM shifted its labour-intensive production to Japan. In the 1980s an industry downturn accelerated the process. Atari, pioneer of personal computers and video games, and Apple, which initially produced its own machines, sent assembly work to Asia. Electronics assembly for the US computer industry grew rapidly in Taiwan, South Korea, Singapore and Hong Kong, and then in the export processing zones of Malaysia, Thailand, Indonesia and India. Outside Asia, Mexico's *maquilas* were a main destination for such outsourcing. Hewlett-Packard, Dell, Cisco and other US computer companies set up in Juárez.

Like many *maquila* operations, Juárez's featured low wages, environmental pollution, lack of social services, an absence of labour protections, and substandard housing, which stretched out into the deserts to the south and east of the city. Young women 18 to 25 years old composed the main labour force in the 1990s, though in electronics the age was higher. Electronics factories were considered desirable workplaces because they seemed clean and modern (Fernández Kelly 1983: 106). Nonetheless even today Mexican electronic manufacturing plants are generally 'Taylorist assembly line organizations' with 'hierarchic control and an authoritarian and paternalistic style of management'; employees must behave deferentially, and are 'treated arbitrarily and yelled at by their supervisors and managers'; trade unions, if they exist, compact with employers (Lüthje et al. 2013: 167). Hiring is increasingly handled by temp agency short-term contracts; problems with pay and deductions are frequent (Paterson 2010). Women are subjected to intimidatory, sexualized discipline, overseen by male supervisors, questioned about sexual habits, menstruation and pregnancy, and sternly choreographed in the routine movement of assembly work (Wright 2007).

Melissa Wright argues that *maquila* capital sees its female workforce as 'disposable women' (2006). This phrase acquired ghastly connotations in Juárez. As the population exploded with the influx of *maquila* workers in the early 1990s, it saw a wave of several hundred murders, most unsolved. Many victims were women working in *maquila* factories. The killings subsided somewhat, then surged again in the late 2000s as Northern Mexico was submerged in a tide of drug trade related violence. The Juárez murders, which often involved the torture and rape of female victims, have been called a 'femicide' (Wright 2007; Gaspar de Alba and Guzmán 2010; Rodríguez 2013). This is controversial; the victims also include many men (Hooks 2014). Whether Juárez is actually the most violent city on earth, as is sometimes claimed, or just one with murder rates comparable to other zones of slums and poverty, is also debated. What is widely agreed is that the killings, whose immediate causes include domestic violence, sexual predation, crime and the drug trade, were fostered by the social conditions of *maquila* industry: social dislocation, poverty, and disrespect and brutalization of workers.

Juárez's reputation as 'Murder City' did not prevent further outsourced computer work. In the 2000s Asian competition threatened its electronics factories and several closed. Then, in 2009, Foxconn, the Taiwanese electronics contractor whose China operations would later become infamous, opened a plant producing desktops and laptops for Dell. Its 'landscaped grounds ... surrounded by walls and razor wire', were like 'a prison with a campus'; wages were around the average for *maquiladora* industry, $80 a week; managers stayed in adjacent dormitories, workers came in from surrounding areas on white school buses (Rice 2011). One night the bus didn't show up, allegedly stopped by one of the city's many military checkpoints; employees were forced to work until 4 a.m. When the bus was then discovered safely parked in a corner of the grounds, workers rioted and burnt down part of the plant.

The desolation and violence of Juárez have made it notorious. It appears in the work of the Mexican novelist Roberto Bolaño as the city of 'Santa Teresa', a place which 'would have swallowed Heidegger in a single gulp, if Heidegger had had the bad luck to be born on the Mexican-U.S. border' (Bolaño 2004: 114). But the logic that creates this scene is not exceptional. In an all too literal way, Juárez can be taken as representative of the conditions of 'bloody Taylorism' – the transfer of production to zones with labour repression and high rates of exploitation in terms of wages, length and intensity of the working day (Lipietz 1987: 74) – that characterize the global outsourcing of computer assembly work.

Our next stop is Hyderabad, in central India, sometimes known as Cyberabad (Cyber City). It is an old town, with a thriving gold and pearl trade, but also numerous slums and child labour industries. On hills a few kilometres outside is HITEC (Hyderabad Information Technology Engineering Consultancy) City. As the road winds out of the city centre, crowded narrow streets give way to increasingly Californian vistas: wide highways, landscaped verges and gleaming buildings, fenced and guarded. Central to HITEC's 150 acres is the Cyber-Tower, a ten-story, four-quadrant building with a large fountain in the middle. Its construction in 1998 began the development of a zone that now includes a Cyber-Gateway, exhibition and convention sites, and several IT parks: Info City, Futura, Mind Space, Cyber Pearl. These are home to the offices and workspaces of global conglomerates such as Microsoft, Google, IBM, Yahoo!, Dell, Facebook, and major Indian firms, such as Infosys, Tata and Wipro.

If Ciudad Juárez represents the outsourcing of computer assembly work, Hyderabad exemplifies a similar logic applied to software development. India has been the most important partner to US cyber-capital in this process because of its widespread use of English, an education system relatively strong in mathematics, science and technology, pre-existing business connections, and, of course, massively lower wage rates. The relation began in the 1970s with cyber-labour moving *to* the US. Burroughs Corporation, which had dealings with India's nascent computer industry, recognized the cost advantage of hiring Indian personnel to install software for US customers (Aspray et al. 2006: 109). This was the genesis of the 'body shopping' (Biao 2007) system by which Indian consultancy companies arranged visas for IT workers to find temporary employment in the US doing routine programming, garnishing wages to pay for the placement.

'Body shopping' soon overlapped with a reverse 'virtual migration' (Aneesh 2006). In 1984 Texas Instruments leased a data line from Bangalore, India, to the United States. Indian programmers were contracted to work on software projects at a distance, taking advantage not only of wage differentials but also of time zones to enable a 24-hour work cycle. This practice was boosted by large-scale conversion projects such as business switches from mainframes to PCs, and, later, the Y2K scare which saw Indian programmers labouring to ensure American computers recognized the start of a new millennium. American manufacturing, airline and financial corporations sent development and operation of back-office digital systems to India. From the 1990s the process was promoted in India's new, neoliberal economic policies, which included tax and trade incentives for special software development zones. IT services became the country's largest export, the centrepiece for a market-oriented 'shining India'.

The cost differential between US and Indian software work has varied widely, but in the early 2000s was often reckoned at between 1:6 and 1:10. Wages for an entry level software engineer in the US might be around $45,000, and in India $4,500 (Ilavarasan 2007; Thibodeau 2012; Fuchs 2014a). The Indian rate, amazingly low by American standards, is very good in a country where GDP per capita during the 2000s was less than $1,500 (in the US, by comparison, it was it around $50,000) (World Bank 2014a). However, with the 'middle class' salaries for India's programmers also came the social and psychological problems of Silicon Valley's cybernetic workers, exacerbated both by the vagaries of outsourced work and the contrast between high-tech corporate culture and traditional Indian lifestyles. Complaints of extreme demands for flexibility, very long hours, high stress, intermittent employment interrupted by long periods 'benched', collapsing social life, and an absence of women in the workplace were common; there were also increasing concerns that, as wages rose, automation would replace outsourcing as a US software strategy.

The expansion of India's IT industry is a microcosm of capital's aspirations to build a global 'middle class' to counterbalance the proletarianizing, low-wage effects of cybernetic production. It certainly presents a more benign face than the grim visage of bloody Taylorization. The IT-based development strategy of 'shining India', focused on a sector that employs at most 2 per cent of the country's population, has however been criticized for creating islands of high-technology disassociated from a local context of continuing poverty (D'Costa 2003; Saraswati 2012). The surroundings of Hyderabad remain extremely bleak, despite HITEC City; literacy rates are low; millions lose crops because of insufficient power or irrigation; slave-like conditions of bonded-labour are not uncommon (Hawksley 2014). Even tourist guides observe that 'While the cyber literate shelter in their cyber tower travelling the virtual highway, the homeless know the harsh realities of the real highways of Hyderabad' (Singh et al. 2003: 892).

And indeed such surrounding poverty is an intrinsic factor in the success of India's software industry in capturing global markets for cheap computer programming. It is not simply that this general immiseration sets the baseline against which so-called middle-class programming wages are set. No less than Silicon Valley itself, IT parks such as HITEC City depend directly on a low-wage 'facilities management' staff – security guards, janitors, drivers, fast food workers – now reproduced under Indian wage conditions by first generation migrants from the countryside. As Indranil Chakraborty (2014) discovered in interviews and surveys with over a hundred of these workers in Hyderabad, Bangalore, Puna, Delhi and Calcutta, they generally earn less than $30 per month, working 12–13 hours a day, six and sometimes seven days a week, without benefits or job security, living in rows of shacks beside open drains stacked behind the imposing cyber-towers. Thus the triadic pattern of lucrative high-tech capital, professional informational work and grinding proletarian labour is replicated globally.

Our third stop is Hsinchu Science Park on the island of Taiwan. It takes us back to the semiconductor clean room with which we began this chapter – but with a significant difference: this time there are hardly any workers inside it. In the 1960s and '70s US chip manufacture followed the same low-labour-cost logic that took assembly work to Asia. However, in this case, having found cheap, female assembly labour in developing world locations, semiconductor companies also discovered low-cost male engineers and managers. At the same time the industry underwent a deep restructuring driven by escalating costs. Moore's Law, which we encountered in Chapter 1, states that the number of circuits on a chip doubles every 18 months at a constant price. This has proven correct, but with a catch – sometimes referred to as 'Moore's Second Law'. Regular reduction in the cost of chips has been achieved only by increasing the costs of making them. Chip fabricating factories – 'fabs' – have become ever larger and more automated: in 1966 a new fab cost $14 million; by

1995, $1.5 billion; today, the price of a leading-edge fab exceeds $6 billion (Economist 2009a).

Originally, all chipmakers were vertically integrated, meaning they designed their chips, built the tools to make them and ran the fabs and associated services. As costs went up and manufacture became increasingly complex, parts of the process spun out to specialized firms. Some 'fabless' companies now only design chips. Others only fabricate designs from other companies. These 'foundries', the 'smelters of the information age', are now centred in Taiwan. An island of 23 million people, in the 1960s Taiwan became a site for US electronics outsourcing. An aggressive state-led development process enabled the growth of a domestic electronics industry, including chip manufacturers. The foundry business was created in the 1980s by the Taiwan Semiconductor Manufacturing Company (TSMC), today the world's biggest chip maker; Taiwanese foundries now make more than half of the world's chips (Economist 2009a). Foundries have to produce huge numbers of chips to offset their costs: they depend on economies of scale. Taiwan's three Science Parks, of which Hsinchu, opened in 1980, is the oldest, were the first home for giant 'Gigafabs' operated by TSMC. These cost between $8 billion and $10 billion, 'which would buy you four nuclear power stations'; the largest can produce 3 billion chips a year, and has a clean room area of 104,000 square meters, the size of fourteen soccer fields (Economist 2009a; TSMC 2010).

It is not only the size of these monster factories that is striking, but the absence of people within. Workers have increasingly become the enemy of chips, for 'of the many potential sources of contamination in cleanrooms … none is more persistent, pervasive, or pernicious than the human beings who occupy them' (Eudy 2003). Clean room operators generate millions of particles with every movement; each particle is a source of potential accident or contamination that can cripple millions of dollars of fixed capital. Furthermore, the issue of medical claims by fabricator workers, with the risks to capital of litigation costs and awards, persists: recently, young South Korean workers in Samsung's semiconductor plants reported high incidences of leukaemia, lymphoma, brain cancer, and other serious diseases (Grossman 2011; Han et al. 2013). The Hsinchu Science Park itself has ignited conflicts with city residents over toxic releases and water pollution (Chang et al. 2006; Chang 2006). Finally, and perhaps most important, chip manufacturing now proceeds at a microscopic scale for which human perception is inadequate: only robots will do.

Despite repeated claims and promises, chip manufacturers have not yet attained a fully automated fab; a labour force of maintenance technicians and engineers must be maintained on location for immediate response to breakdowns. Some technicians physically exiled from the clean room are still 'driving or operating the tools from client devices (such as a laptop computer) from outside' (Rulison 2011). However, the impressions of the rare visitors allowed into these facilities are unequivocal:

> What struck me was the total automation of a GigaFab. Machines outnumbered man exponentially with 99 per cent automation. Shuttles zoomed around on tracks above delivering thousands of 40nm wafers to the 300+ steps in the semiconductor manufacturing process. The few people I did see were at monitoring stations. Even more impressive than the billions of dollars of hardware in a GigaFab, is the millions of lines of software developed to run it: Automated Material Handling Systems (AMHS) for transporting, storing, and managing semiconductor wafer carriers and reticules plus Manufacturing Execution Systems (MES) software to manage overall production efficiency. (Nenni 2010)

TSMC promises more: in a recent presentation in Hsinchu, company officials showcased a 'Super Manufacture Platform' (SMP) that would 'enable a people-less GigaFAB operation' where 'the defect-free rate can reach to 99.8 percent' (Wang 2014). GigaFabs mark the point at which capital's increase in its organic – that is, machinic – composition asymptotically approaches the elimination of the human.

Back at the Ranch...

Silicon Valley's manufacturing base of chip production and assembly, which in the 1980s made it 'as important a manufacturing center as Detroit or Pittsburgh', has today been globally dispersed: what remains are suburban software parks built on top of the contaminated aquifers (Madrigal 2013). But while Detroit went bankrupt, Silicon Valley, the world's largest centre for venture-capital-backed high-tech industry, and headquarters of hundreds of software and internet companies, boomed. The growth of social media, most of which occurred after 2008, means that it is today adding jobs faster than it has for a decade; in 2013 Twitter's stock offering made millionaires of 1,600 of the company's employees (Florida 2013).

The Valley also, however, persists as a deepening cauldron of inequality. As George Packer records in a stinging indictment of the digerati's pretensions to progressive politics:

> There are fifty or so billionaires and tens of thousands of millionaires in Silicon Valley ... There are also record numbers of poor people, and the past two years have seen a twenty-per-cent rise in homelessness ... After decades in which the country has become less and less equal, Silicon Valley is one of the most unequal places in America. (Packer 2013).

The Sacred Heart Community Center in San Jose provides free food for about 70,000 people a year – families, working couples, disabled people and elderly. It is within a few miles of the high-tech campuses of Google, Facebook, Apple and other companies, 'designed to be fully functioning communities, not just places for working ... inward-looking places [that] keep tech workers from having even accidental contact with the surrounding community' (Packer 2013). Facebook's buildings, where 'employees can eat sushi or burritos, lift weights, get a haircut, have their clothes dry-cleaned, and see a dentist, all without leaving work', surrounds a 'simulated town square whose concrete surface is decorated with the word "HACK", in letters so large that they can be seen from the air' (Packer 2013).

Food stamp participation hit a 10-year high in 2014; the average income for Hispanics, one in four of Silicon Valley residents, dropped over the last five years to a new low of about $19,000 a year (Mendoza 2013). Private-school attendance has surged as public schools in poor communities fall into disrepair and lack basic supplies (Packer 2013). Housing costs yet again doubled from 2009 to 2014, while wages for low- and middle-skilled workers are stagnant, so that 'nurses, preschool teachers, security guards and landscapers commute for hours from less-expensive inland suburbs' (AP 2014). In 2014 security guards rallied outside Apple's shareholder meeting demanding better wages. Their banner read 'What's the matter with Silicon Valley? Prosperity for some, poverty for many' (AP 2014).

Over the past decade software production expanded north from the Valley to the edges of San Francisco and the Bay area. Among the US's fifty largest cities, San Francisco experienced the highest increase in income inequality between 2007 and 2012 (AP 2014). The influx of high-technology professionals from companies such as Twitter, Yelp, Spotify and Google has transformed the area, sharply raising housing prices, income disparity and urban tensions. The fleets of Google buses that transport workers to the company's headquarters in Mountain View and back – 'some of the city's hottest restaurants are popping up in the neighborhoods with shuttle stops' (Packer 2013) – have become a flashpoint:

> Sometimes the Google Bus just seems like one face of Janus-headed capitalism; it contains the people too valuable even to use public transport or drive themselves. In the same spaces wander homeless people undeserving of private space, or the minimum comfort and security; right by the Google bus stop on Cesar Chavez Street immigrant men from Latin America stand waiting for employers in the building trade to scoop them up, or to be arrested and deported by the government. (Solnit 2013: 35)

The buses became a target of protests against gentrification, displacement and congestion (Goode and Miller 2013). Signs taped to the buses read: 'Gentrification & Eviction Technologies: Integrated Displacement and Cultural Erasure' and 'F--- Off Google' (AP 2014). Even as engineers and designers were taking legal action against Apple, Google, Intel and Adobe for collusive agreements holding down salaries, 'tech employees who united against their bosses in court [found] themselves denounced by protestors blocking the Google bus' (Pollak 2014). The demonstrations also became an occasion for a wider critique of the computer industry: one group, The Counterforce, distributed leaflets accusing Google of 'building an unconscionable world of surveillance, control and automation' (Streitfield and Wollan 2014). In reply, venture capitalist Tom Perkins, in an open letter to the *Wall Street Journal*, likened what he called 'the war on the one percent, namely the "rich"' with fascist Nazi Germany: 'Kristallnacht was unthinkable in 1930; is its descendent "progressive" radicalism unthinkable now?' He backed down a few days later, calling his choice of words 'terrible' (AP 2014).

Shamed or intimidated by such episodes, some of the Valley's largest companies stepped up (or started) donations to local anti-poverty groups. The proprietors and professionals also continued unabashed with their endemic rhetoric of 'world changing' digital innovation and serious discussions as to whether Silicon Valley could 'save the world' through philanthropic development projects (Kenny and Sandefur 2013). They had indeed changed the world, but largely in the direction of pioneering a production model that intensified the gulf between those at the top and those at the bottom of capital's hierarchy. The new class composition forged by the computer industry as it applied its own networking and automating inventions to the making of cybernetic devices intensified both the global division of labour and the technological liquidation of labour, with both these apparently contradictory tendencies deployed to the advantage of capital. In the next chapter we will see how this pattern would be repeated on a yet wider scale as Silicon Valley's inventions were adopted around the globe.

5

Circulation

Chimerica

In the evening millions of migrant workers return from a brief holiday in their rural villages celebrating the lunar New Year. After hours of travel they press through thronged railway stations, back to their dormitories. In the morning they will put on uniforms and pour out into the streets of factory complexes as big as cities, hurrying to start their shifts; the assembly lines are waiting, and on the pallets are the parts of myriad cybernetic machines.

Across the world a generation wakes and reaches for laptops, tablets and smartphones, to find friends, share news, learn of parties, meetings, artists, lovers, school. As they do so, every click is tracked, graphed and banked; recommendations offered; trends announced; advertising recalibrated; the flows of information tweaked; the revenue stream maximized; reality adjusted.

Overnight the software agents seethe in the dark pools of electronic environments visible only on computer screens in glittering towers of finance; they compete, evolve and reproduce at millisecond speeds, predate and parasitize upon each other, learn from every attack and evasion. Dependent on their desperate struggle, the value of factories, commodities and people rise and fall; suddenly, a million homes are worthless.

In the previous chapter we looked at the class composition of the computer industry; we now turn to examine a much wider set of cybernetic de- and re-compositions of class, focusing on the role the internet played in reconfiguring the relation of American and Chinese proletarians, a turbulent reorganization that set the scene for the great crash of 2008. This analysis will focus on the circulatory flows of the cybernetic vortex. In the vortex, production, where surplus value is siphoned into commodity form, is the ground zero of class composition and decomposition. But production connects in manifold ways to circulation, where commodities – including the commodity-creating commodity, labour power – are bought and sold, and to financialization, where processes of credit, debt and speculation accelerate circulation, or bring it to a crashing halt.

Circulation is a process distinct from production, one which increases value not by extraction but acceleration; it does not siphon value from labour power into commodities, but speeds commodities through the process of exchange, increasing capital's turnover, the rate at which it changes from commodity into money and then back into the labour process that creates yet more commodities. Financialization hyper-accelerates this circulation, attempting to overleap both production and exchange, and, by means of interest on debt and speculative gambles, directly morph from money to yet more money. These circulatory processes both rebound on and are shaped by the composition of classes.

Autonomist analysis by Brian Marks (2012) has examined the circulatory connections and changes in the working classes of China and the United States, whose perverse linkage at the turn of the millennium formed the main axis of capitalist globalization. Building on this analysis, we examine the making of 'Chimerica' (Ferguson 2008: 283) in three cybernetic dimensions, all involving the circulation of commodities. First, we look at the induction of China's rural migrant workers, bearers of labour power, into assembly-line factories at the end of electronic supply chains, where they produce cheap digital devices. Second, we examine how these devices, in the US and then globally, provided the basis for the rising popular use of an internet that was increasingly devoted to the circulation of commodities speeded by the free labour of its users. Third, we see how networks, automation and algorithms enabled the rise of a financial sector which, pumped with the profits from low-wage labour in China and free labour online, generated credit, debt and speculation that first accelerated commodity circulation, and then brought it to a crashing halt in the sub-prime mortgage crisis that sent the world economy to the brink of collapse. This is a story of chains, nets and bubbles.

Chains

Marx and Engels (1964) called 'workers of the world' to a revolution in which they had 'nothing to lose but your chains'; today, those chains are 'supply chains', a term not of radical exhortation, but management art. With its many close synonyms and sophisticated elaborations – 'value chain' (Porter 1985), 'commodity chain' (Gereffi and Korzeniewicz 1994), 'production network' (Henderson et al. 2002; Levy 2008) – 'supply chain' names the process by which a capitalist enterprise organizes the commodification process by dispersing each element to geographic locations that optimize labour costs, access to raw materials, or proximity to markets, and then links the chain in a continuous, integrated sequence.

In its ur-form the supply chain headquarters research, design and marketing in the high-wage areas of the global economy, subcontracts manufacturing, assembly and back-end office functions to new industrialized territories where they can be rapidly scaled up or down with market fluctuations, and sends mining, waste disposal and other indiscreet activities to abyssal sacrifice areas where they vanish from sight. In the 1980s and '90s, as capital decomposed the industrial mass worker, breaking through its former partitions of the globe into first, second and third worlds and sending itself snaking across the planet, the supply chain became key to the technical composition of a global proletariat.

Supply chains are forged from cybernetics. As Richard Baldwin observes in a lucid management-side exposition, 'Globalisation made a giant leap when steam power slashed shipping costs. It made another when ICT decimated coordination costs' (2011: 4). In the industrial era production clustered in factories with various sections or 'bays' because coordinating the manufacturing process demanded 'continuous ... flows among the bays of things, people, training, investment, and information all in constant flux'. However, from the mid 1980s as telecommunications became cheap, reliable and widespread, alongside 'vast strides in computing power, transmission capacities, and software', the 'co-ordination glue' began to loosen. It 'became increasingly economical to geographically separate manufacturing stages – to unbundle the factories'. The most radical change, Baldwin notes, was the way ICTs 'made it easy for rich-nation firms to combine high technology they developed at home with low-wage workers abroad' (2011: 6).

Email and exchangeable software packages made it easier for corporations to manage work across great distances. The relations of suppliers to a chain's 'lead firm' were increasingly dictated by 'modular production processes' and 'routinized interfaces with suppliers and customers' (Levy 2008: 7–8). From the mid 1990s such practices spurred Electronic Data Interchange (EDI) formats, which set standards for exchanging data via any electronic means to 'enhance communications between supply chain partners' (Bonacich and Wilson 2009: 5). Supply chains, however, connected more than people; they created an 'internet of things' (Gershenfeld et al. 2004). The crucial innovation was the Universal Product Code – or bar code – developed by IBM in the early 1970s. This was only the first stage in a process in which, in an uncanny realization of Marx's darkly comic fantasies of commodities discussing their source of value with each other, sensor-instrumented goods 'speak' electronically to each other and their owners about their location, destination and price. This was integral to a 'logistics revolution' in which communication and transportation became linked in detailed cybernetic tracking, inventory control and labour monitoring systems (Bonacich and Wilson 2009; Bernes 2013; Cowen 2014).

As supply chains grow in length and complexity, intersecting with one another to form intricate supply-and-production networks, managing their cybernetics itself becomes a whole sub-sector of capital. Entire Enterprise Resource Planning systems are sold by vendors such as Microsoft, Oracle, Epicor and SAP, offering automated alerts as markets move, and simulated scenarios to assess the impact of replacing suppliers, switching transportation modes, establishing new routes, increasing product prices and sudden labour troubles. The objective was to forge a supply chain both 'lean' and 'agile', reaching down to cheap labour and resources, moving commodities with minimum costs and maximum speeds through every stage of commodification from production to final sale, with the capacity to identify actual or potential problems and route around them.

Large corporations develop their own systems. Wal-Mart is the classic example of a colossal retail-led supply chain that links the logistics revolution with just-in-time-production. By the mid 2000s its data-centres were tracking over 680 million distinct products per week; barcode scanners and point of sale computer systems identified more than 20 million customer transactions per day and stored this information. Satellite telecommunications linked directly from stores to the central computer system and from that system to the computers of suppliers to allow automatic reordering. The company's early adoption of Universal Product Codes led to a 'higher stage' requirement for Radio Frequency Identification (RFID) tags in all products to enable tracking of commodities, workers and consumers within its global supply chain (Haiven and Stoneman 2009).

The consequences of supply chains for class composition were immense. We have already seen their role in the shattering of the auto-sector's mass workers. During the 1980s and '90s the drain from old industrial centres to new export zones intensified; by the beginning of the twenty-first century not only car production, but shipyards, textile factories, electronics plants and chemical processing had all been moved (Roth 2010). Creating supply chains and running them profitably required radical reorganization of transportation and communication sectors, placing the labour of longshoremen, truckers, sailors, pilots, couriers, warehouse and distribution workers under immense pressure from capital, making these areas flashpoints of class conflict; we will look more at this in Chapter 9.

The biggest changes were, however, at the end of the supply chain, where deindustrialization of the global North met, as both cause and effect, the rural depopulation of the global South. Here the subsistence farming that had for millennia supported the largest part of the planet's population was slowly collapsing under the pressures of the world market, creating a new phase of the primitive accumulation whose release of the landless labour had provided capital's early proletariat. In Asia, Africa and Latin America migrants streamed into vast new metropolii (Davis 2007), to eke out a living in 'informal' economies, attempt further journeys towards service labour in the global North, or enter the factories of *maquilas* and special export zones in Mexico, the Philippines, Malaysia, Thailand, Cambodia and, above all, China.

The Chinese Communist Party (CCP) had in 1978 made a sharp turn from Maoist revolutionary communism to embrace the world market. The country opened to foreign investment; free enterprise was enforced by party bureaucracy; authoritarian capitalism was accompanied by epic corruption as political elites and transnational corporations fawned over one another. The process also triggered the largest migration in the history of the world. Over 25 years some 150–200 million Chinese moved from the countryside to urban areas, pushed by the dismantling of communal village life, drawn by the promise of wages and city excitement. Not all went into factories. Most found 'irregular employment' in 'construction, cleaning, and maintenance of premises, retail trade, street vending, repair services or domestic services', paralleling the 'informal' employment proliferating elsewhere around planet (Hart-Landsberg 2013: 49).

Nonetheless by the 1990s internal migrants made up 70 per cent of the labour in the manufacturing industries of the new 'workshop of the world' (Hart-Landsberg 2013: 47–9). Between 1990 and 2008, China's share of total world exports grew five-fold. In 2003, it became the second largest exporter to the United States, trailing only Canada, which it would then pass in 2007. Clothing, shoes, toys, furniture, appliances, light engineering goods and electronics flowed to the US from China's factories. Many of these stood at the foot of global supply chains of transnational corporations, which after 2000 accounted for more than half of China's exports, drawn by a massive wage differential: in China, manufacturing wages in 2002 were about 2 per cent of those in the US, rising to about 4 per cent in 2008 (Hart-Landsberg 2013: 43–5; US Dept. of Labor 2011).

China's factories not only connected to digital supply chains but made the links on those chains. China became the planet's top producer of computers. Transnational corporations (TNCs) produced about 85 per cent of China's high-technology exports. The leaders were Taiwanese manufacturers who shifted production of laptops and motherboards and monitors to the mainland; the largest would eventually be Hon Hai Precision Industry Co, which in 2000 set up a China subsidiary, Foxconn International Holdings Ltd. The computers, video game consoles and, later, smartphones produced in these factories were largely destined for the North American market, and often subcontracted by North American companies, creating a 'triangular relationship' between capital in the United States, China and Taiwan (Lynn 2005: 63). Electronics and electrical equipment industries were one of the largest magnets for rural migrant workers; by 2006 migrant workers made up half this sector's workforce, most employed in Shenzhen at the heart of China's south coastal industrial area around the Pearl River (Hong 2010: 61).

In *Made in China*, the labour ethnographer Pun Ngai (2005) draws on her own time working in an electronics plant in Shenzhen to describe the experience of the *dagongmei*, the young women who migrated from countryside to factory. The *dagongmei* and their male counterparts, the *dagongzei*, did not correspond to the Chinese state's concept of the working class (*gonggrenjieji*), defined in the Maoist era as comprising workers in state-owned heavy industry. *Dagong* meant 'working for the boss', and also 'disposable' – a new term to encompass what Ngai calls the 'postsocialist' appropriation of labour by capital (2005: 12). Rural, young, itinerant, usually working in factories for a four to five year period in their 'pre-marital life cycle' (Ngai 2005: 6), *dagongmei* were an object of contempt from urban residents, and of extreme exploitation by their employers.

Ngai details the process of 'subjectification' by which firms strove to shape the *dagongmei* into a plaint workforce, through 'techniques of labor appropriation' that include authoritarian supervision, repetitive operations, and psychological and material devaluation of their rural and female identities. Under China's state administered residential system, migrants pay fees to register as temporary urban residents; they, and their children, even if these are born in an urban area, do not have access to public services such as education, health and housing (Hart-Landsberg 2013: 51–5). This system forces workers into dormitory residences and enables 'both foreign and local enterprises to maximize working time and extract labour power without worrying about the reproduction of labour in the long run' (Ngai 2005: 5). The conditions described by Ngai correspond to those documented by others throughout Shenzhen factories: working six days a week for up to 11 hours a day; wages of 80–90 cents an hour; no functional trade union protection; subject to late- or non-payment of wages; a high rate of accidents, including factory fires in which scores or hundreds of workers perish.

But Ngai also describes how in the face of a 'triple oppression of global capitalism, state socialism, and familial patriarchy' (2005: 4) the *dagongmei* developed 'life tactics from below', reworking communal village traditions to create collectivities of mutual support, now re-made outside the traditional strictures of patriarchal authority and localism. Female identity, which made *dagongmei* objects of discrimination, became the basis for a 'minor genre of resistance', as workers responded to assembly-line speed-ups with fainting, menstrual pains, other illnesses and psychological crises (Ngai 2005: 2). Ngai wrote at a time when many academics believed the difficulties facing migrant workers in China would prevent their political organization. In 2004, however, what she called a 'symphony of migrant worker transgression' (Ngai 2005: 6) suddenly swelled in volume as an unprecedented series of strikes and walkouts hit factories in the Pearl River Delta. China began to emerge as a new 'epicentre of global labour unrest' (Silver and Zhang 2009). In the meantime, however, the digital devices made by the *dagongmei* had travelled back up the supply chain, and were transforming North America.

Nets

By the 1990s manufacturing jobs in North America were being both automated and offshored, and real wages were stagnating, but US consumption continued to account for some 70 per cent of GDP (Lapavitsas 2013: 274). If China was the new workshop of the world, the US was its shopping mall, consistently ranked at the top of global per capita household expenditures, vying only with contenders such as the

United Arab Emirates (World Bank 2014b). As these measures exclude house purchases, which as we will see were a major item, they massively underestimate American spending. Much of this came from the luxury purchases of capitalists and new intermediate strata such as Silicon Valley software engineers. But North America's proletarians were also buying. This was made possible by a growth in two- or three-income households, as women entering paid work made up for declining wages; by debt; and by cheap imported goods – largely from China.

North American workers were not only consuming, but increasingly working in the sphere of circulation, selling to other consumers, as de-industrialization shifted employment towards service jobs. By 2000 retail, including advertising and promotional activities, employed as high a percentage of the workforce as manufacturing. Wal-Mart replaced General Motors as the largest employer in the US (US Dept. of Labor 2013). Its combination of low-wage workers, even lower waged suppliers, rock bottom prices and big corporate profits encapsulated the dynamics of the US economy. Other rising areas of consumption-related work included fields such as tourism, hospitality, and the cultural industries, whose films, TV shows, radio programmes, websites and digital offerings serve as both objects in and vehicles of the ongoing circulation of commodities.

It was in this context that the greatest technological discovery of the late twentieth century became a gigantic sales engine. If the digital revolution's dirty secret is the supply chain, its happy-face would seem to be the vast expansion of communication created by the internet. Yet at the turn of the millennium, this network of networks was increasingly becoming defined as a path for the circulation of commodities out of production, towards consumption, streaming advertising, capturing sales and tracking consumers. Such a destiny was not apparent at its origin. From the moment hacker labour took networks on a line of flight out the Pentagon, different models for their organization contended in sub-cycles of struggle moving at net speed.

In the early phases of the internet, the policies of the National Science Foundation, the US government agency that officially managed it, excluded commerce from its use for 'research and education'. In practice this meant that, though superimposed on commercially sold computers, and commercially owned telecommunications, and developing alongside private networks, the internet existed as a 'temporary autonomous zone' (Bey 1991), a counter-cultural playground for early intermediate-strata adopters. This moment, short-lived as it was, left deep archaeological traces – open network architectures, dissident political shards and stranded cyber-cultural colonies – rotating through the cybernetic vortex, even as it rose away from them towards intensifying levels of capitalist subsumption.

From the 1990s on, however, the initially tiny internet population first steadily increased and then suddenly started growing dramatically: in 1997, 18 per cent of the US population had internet use at home, but by 2000 this had risen to 41 per cent, and by 2011 to 72 per cent (US Census Bureau 2003–2011). Much of this can be attributed to the decreasing costs of digital devices, a result in part of low-wage production in China. Between 1999 and 2003 the US consumer price index for computers and peripherals fell sharply, and continued falling subsequently, though more slowly. As the number of online users grew, US capital became increasingly aware of the internet as a potential arena for commodification.

In the 1990s changes in US state policy steadily created a privatized, deregulated, business-friendly 'information superhighway'. 'Dot-com' addresses were created; allocation of domain names outsourced to a fee-charging, CIA-linked company; ownership of the Net's telecommunications backbone, to which other networks connected, sold to a corporation. These high-level changes sent commercial ventures cascading down through the entire system. 'Netizens' used to the non-profit ethic responded with libertarian outrage. Complaints burned out e-advertisers fax machines and brought down their servers. One senior systems administrator attempted to divide the official – that is, commercial – Net from some remainder of the initially commerce-free system, until the FBI visited him: capitalization rolled on.

The signal that the internet had become a new frontier of corporate expansion was the 'browser wars' of the mid 1990s between Microsoft and upstart Netscape for control of technology giving easy access to the World Wide Web, a contest won by the monopoly. The subsequent digital gold rush involved many actors: the computer sector, producing the software and hardware; telephone and cable carrier conglomerates laying wired and wireless connections; retail and business-to-business (B2B) sectors, trying to transcend bricks-and-mortar; media companies racing each other to find digital channels for entertainment and news; the pornography business, persistently at the leading-edge; early search engines, mired in ranking scams and portals; eBay's online auctions; and the growing world of e-advertising, vital to many of these experiments, soon spawning its own specialized agencies. In 1991 there were only some 181,361 '.com' hosts, 12 per cent of the total; by 2000 there were 32,696,253 commercial sites – 35 per cent of the total (Dyer-Witheford 2002: 135).

NASDAQ, the high-tech stock market index, increased its value eightfold between 1996 and 2000. Of the myriad of dot-com start-ups, most were ill-conceived, and many were cynical get rich-quick schemes, touting vapourware to make money from stock sales or acquisition by larger corporations. Venture capital had raised high-risk money for such investment. Shares priced on expectation not performance. Some investors bought stocks they knew were overvalued on the 'greater fool' theory of selling to someone yet more gullible than themselves. Online day-traders and credible financial advisors alike pumped and dumped worthless stock. Rising stock prices supported profit-less development in a virtuous circle, but when dot-coms failed to meet financial targets, the cycle went into vicious reverse.

Friday, 14 April 2000 saw what was at the time Wall Street's largest one-day fall in history. As venture capital hesitated, then fled, thousands of dot-coms with meteoric burn-rates of daily expenditure flamed into oblivion. This set off a telecommunication meltdown, as companies that had invested in thousands of miles of fibre cable and internet equipment found themselves holding vast overcapacity. A third act, a criminal conspiracy, followed, as giant corporations such as Enron, WorldCom and Global Crossing covered up losses, hoping to ride out the crisis or allow executives to sell stocks while they were still high. The discovery of multi-million-dollar fraud, implicating major accounting companies and leading investment banks, completed the rout of investor confidence. Between 11 March 2000 and 9 October 2002, NASDAQ lost nearly 80 per cent of its value: Net capital had imploded.

Beyond venality, the basic flaw in dot-com dreams was that digital consumers didn't consume enough. Internet use continued to grow, giving rise to expectations of unlimited online markets, but as *The Economist* (2001) observed, 'The real problem … appears to be that internet users have come to expect online services to be free.' The legacy of the Net's early un-commodified origins had left a great residue of non-commercial sites and gift-economy practices, reproducing and circulating digital content without regard to intellectual property laws. Even as internet commercialization was getting underway, a parallel process of vernacular, not-for-profit networking, rooted in the 'information wants to be free' lineage of hacker culture, continued to point in a very different direction.

By the late 1990s these practices were hitting a mass scale. This was largely thanks to the invention by tinkering college students of peer-to-peer (P2P) networks, first Napster and, later, Gnutella, Kazaa and Bit Torrent – networks which, dispensing with a central server, were almost impossible to repress, and hence ideal for unauthorized copying. Internet populations didn't just copy for free: they also created *gratis*, from individuals throwing up web pages to the volunteer digital encyclopaedia Wikipedia which appeared in 1999. The most striking example of such creativity was the Free and Open Source Software (FOSS) movement, whose 'copyleft' practices seemed a practical counter-logic to that of Microsoft and other corporate software producers. As Richard Barbrook observed, in the course of North America's everyday online activities, 'cyber-communists' seemed to be pragmatically 'engaged in the slow process of superseding capitalism in cyberspace' (2000: 5).

Regardless of the dot-com bust, going into the new century the number of internet users continued on a steep increase. And it was not long before the process of 'superseding capitalism in cyberspace' started to run the other way again, as digital capital resurrected itself and make a new effort to subsume the networks. Although 21 million dot-com domain names had been created between 1985 and 2000, 57 million were registered between 2000 and 2010, bringing the number of global dot-com domain names to close to 80 million (Atkinson and Stewart 2013). The new commercial offensive took the form of 'Web 2.0', with Google and Facebook as its flagships. In a classic strategy of recuperation, these companies made the very voluntary and unpaid practices that had frustrated Web 1.0 capital into a new form of cybernetic accumulation.

Web 2.0 capital was characterized by platforms mobilizing unpaid 'user-generated content', whether as the passively provided raw material processed by search-engine crawlers or as active contributions to various forms of social media. Many of these platforms themselves used open source software for commercial purposes: Facebook's adoption of the free Hadoop data-processing program to calculate the social graphs with which it maps the connections between its users is typical. Networked advertising is usually a primary revenue source, supplemented by various forms of virtual and physical commodity sale. It is, however, the participants who generate the content that attracts advertisers, relieving platform owners of the costs of employing cultural workers – comics, critics, analysts, videographers, animators – for this purpose. A major feature is the accumulation of data about users, data either directly deployed by social media capital or sold on to third-party capitalists to precisely and predictively target advertising.

The 'free labour' sucked into such social media activity was first identified by Tiziana Terranova (2000) in relation to early chat rooms, virtual games and fan sites. Subsequently, the manner in which online capital came to normalize a business model that employed a small number of permanent staff to draw on the voluntary or unknowing contributions of millions of users was analyzed in regard to MySpace (Coté and Pybus 2007), YouTube (Andrejevic 2009), Google (Fuchs 2012), Facebook (Böhm et al. 2012), Flickr (Brown 2013), alongside more overarching accounts of social media accumulation (Terranova 2010; Fuchs 2014b). Such analyses inspired the Wages for Facebook manifesto that appeared in 2014: 'They say its friendship; we say its unwaged work. With every like, chat, tag or poke our subjectivity turns them a profit. They call it sharing. We call it stealing' (Ptak 2013). The echo of the autonomist feminist 'wages for housework' campaign against the unpaid contribution of domestic work to value creation is intentional and apropos. Free online labour for Web 2.0 capital is one of the manifold forms of shadow work through which capital supplements surplus value extracted through the wage, a process labour historians such as van der Linden and Roth (2014) see as always having been constitutive of capitalist proletarianization and that now takes fresh form at a new level of technological subsumption.

In terms of class composition, the free labour model of Web 2.0 capital had at least six consequences: i) a limited expansion in the number of techno-scientific workers employed in Web 2.0 businesses; ii) a mobilization of 'prosumer' content provision amounting to collective digital extension of the unpaid working day; iii) a subversion of 'old media' professionals by the competition of free labour (as in journalism, where the rise of so-called citizen journalism, based in blogs and Web 2.0 related practice, has contributed to a 're-proletarianizing' collapse of stable employment opportunities); iv) an encouragement of precarious micro-business ventures, spurred on by niche advertising opportunities on Facebook or through Google's Ad Sense; v) a further intensification of the circulation of commodities through the saturation of social interaction with commercial messaging, including especially vi) promotional, auto-commodifying rep-utation-management by current and potential professional and cultural workers, for whom an active social media presence (e.g. LinkedIn) became a necessity in the search for work, even as their voluntary contributions might actually decrease their chances of a job by enabling social media to run on unpaid content.

The idea that networked free labour is exploited is anathema to boosters of social media. It has also attracted criticism from thoughtful observers. David Hesmondhalgh (2010) has criticized any equation between Facebook posting and sweatshop work. He is correct to reject a direct equivalence between the experience of, say, the *dagongmei* and Facebook users. But vampire bites come in many ways. Facebook posting is a form of exploitation, which, without explicit violence, is nonetheless parasitic. It does not replace the 'normal' structures of daily class exploitation at work and home, but is added to and superimposed upon them, to constitute a regime in which the user is habituated, on pain of exclusion from social worlds, to surrendering the elements of their personality – identity, creativity, sociality – to enhance the circulation of capital. This submission is not the same as the brutal bodily discipline inflicted on the *dagongmei*, but it is a form of subjectification that is both infiltrative and extroversive in the abject submission to the commodity form it elicits.

There is a clear connection between the young Chinese woman who spends her 'pre-marital life cycle' on the assembly line of fire-trap factories, and the young American woman who discovers Facebook 'knows' she is engaged, even though this was never announced (Watson 2012). This relation is in one way, as 'Third World' Marxists have repeatedly and correctly pointed out, that of conflicting global class interests (Cope 2012): the relative affluence of the North American Facebook user is based on the cheap commodities, including computers, produced in China's factories, so that s/he benefits from the exploitation of the *dagongmei*. Yet the relation is also, simultaneously, one of complementary exploitations, in which the computer made by the *dagongmei* becomes the means for the Facebook user's surrender of free labour and subjective subordination to the commodity form. Each exploitation drives the other; the toil of the *dagongmei* creates the material basis of the social media platforms that generate 'voluntary' labour for digital capital which in turn propels further low-wage physical exploitation of electronics workers. The result of both was an increase in the power and wealth of major information corporations and in the overall buoyancy of capital, whose mid-decade stock market boom these companies contributed to – and whose sudden disruption would send reverberations from the Potomac to Pearl River.

Bubbles

Financialization involves 'the escalating importance in advanced capital of banks, stock markets, loan agencies, shadow banks and other agencies that make their profits primarily from trading money and various monetary instruments' (Lapavitsas 2013: 214). In autonomist analysis financialization is seen as a means by which capital escapes or attacks proletarian power (Bonefeld and Holloway 1995). During the era of Fordism, the expansion of credit served to defer confrontation with a powerful working class over wages. As automation and offshoring destroyed the power of the mass worker, however, other dynamics came into play. Wage rates were held in check in the capitalist centre. But this very success brought other problems. A high-tech low-wage global economy did not generate either wide enough purchasing power or high enough profits to provide adequate investment opportunities. Capital increasingly played games with itself involving exotic speculative devices such as derivatives, or turned to extracting revenues yet more deeply from decomposed proletarian strata through financial instruments such as sub-prime mortgages. In the United States, where financialization was particularly extreme, the share of financial profits versus overall profits rose from under 10 per cent in 1945 to about 40 per cent in the early 2000s, an increase that was particularly sharp after the 1970s (Lapavitsas 2013: 214).

Carlotta Perez (2009) has shown how, from the expansion of roads and canals to the invention of railways, telegraph and radio, successive waves of technological innovation in the means of communication have ignited frenzied speculative financial activity, followed by spectacular crashes. Finance capital both gambles on investment in new technologies and adopts them to enlarge the scope, speed and complexity of its operations. These two processes were on display in the escalation of finance in the US in the cybernetic era. As we have seen, the commercial exploitation of the internet depended on investment by techno-scientifically oriented venture capital which underlay the dot-com boom and bust of 2001. The repercussions from this disaster shaped the remainder of the decade. The larger speculative bubble that burst in 2008 arose from the easy-money, low-interest-rate policies by which the US Federal Reserve sought to escape the earlier crisis. Thus, although the crashes of 2001 and 2008 apparently had different points of origin, one in cyberspace, the other in housing, they should be seen as two moments of a single episode.

Finance capital not only funded Silicon Valley but also adopted its cybernetic instruments. After the internet escaped from the Pentagon, banks were amongst the commercial early adopters (Schiller 1999). From the start of the 2000s finance and insurance has been the US business sector with the second highest annual expenditures on computer and telecommunication equipment, after the information sector itself, and above third place manufacturing (Schiller 2012). Stock exchanges were part of this digital transformation (Zaloom 2006). From the mid 1980s, open outcry pits where traders met physically on floors and bid for orders with shouts and signs were increasingly replaced by computerized matching and display systems, usually still within the dealing rooms of stock exchanges.

The first complete electronic trading floor conversion was NASDAQ, the centre of the dot-com bust. The cybernetic metamorphosis of finance only really got under way, however, in the 1990s, accelerated not just by the diminishing cost of computers, but also by the excess bandwidth left by the telecommunications meltdown that followed the dot-com crash; such 'dark fibre' enabled the 'dark pools' of secret finance and shadow banking. By the mid 1990s, the internet was connecting investors directly to trading activities, and also linking exchanges internationally. This was followed in the 2000s by the creation of financial information protocols as 'a global language for the automated trading of financial instruments' (Wójcik 2011: 131). These networks – the 'money grid' – were second only to the Pentagon's, and indeed borrowed largely from military research (Patterson 2010: 118).

The main impetus to automation came from derivative markets. As David McNally (2011) has pointed out, the growth of high-risk derivatives was closely associated with supply-chain-driven globalization. Various forms of futures were initially developed to hedge against the uncertainties of foreign investments – in particular currency fluctuations. They then became transformed into offensive, high-risk instruments, involving an increasing range of speculative objects, and an ever-extending sequence of traders selling chancy gambles on to one another. The estimation of risk, which has of course always been a part of banking and speculative activity, was increasingly computerized, made dependent on the elaborate mathematical modelling of the best and brightest of graduates in mathematics, physics and computing science – 'the quants' (Patterson 2010) – and the algorithmic trading programs they produced, programs whose accuracy was of course constrained by the adequacy of the data sets on which they were based, which, as it transpired, were dangerously thin.

Algorithmic trading in turn placed enormous pressure on the speed of networked connections because of the rapidity with which risk-based transactions must be identified and executed. They depend on taking advantage of arbitrage possibilities that exist for fractions of a second. Paradoxically, such speed required stock exchanges to build aircraft-carrier-sized computing facilities next to their main sites, because the time lags of satellite uplinks were too long. In the mid 1980s it was considered a fantastic achievement for financial computer systems to generate ten orders a second; by 2010 they could execute tens of thousands a second (Wójcik 2011: 131).

Where this cybernetic apparatus touched directly on the mundane reality of class composition was in the growth of household debt. As Costas Lapavitsas observes: 'The most striking aspect of financialization is the penetration of financial transactions into the circuits of personal revenue ... Households have been driven into the arms of formal financial systems with respect to both liabilities and assets' (2013: 238). This has been especially marked because, with reductions in public provisions for health, education and housing, 'the financial sector has mediated the private provision of goods and services in households'. Intrinsic to this process is an increase in 'financial expropriation' – that is 'the transfer of personal income directly to the profits of the financial institutions that have played this mediating role' (Lapavitsas 2013: 240).

The US household debt-to-income ratio went from 60 per cent in 1984 to 120 per cent by 2005. The personal savings rate fell after 1980 from a long-term average of 4 per cent to zero in 2005. By far the largest component in debt was mortgages for housing purchases made attractive by the low interest rates with which the Federal Reserve Bank buoyed up the economy after the 2001 crash:

American workers, fleeing south and west from the downsized rust belt towards the new centers of high-tech industry, finance, and construction, sought to compensate for their falling incomes at work by participating in the housing bubble, wresting from their rising equity a part of the surplus wrung from them on the job. (Marks 2012: 473)

In the mid 2000s close to 10 per cent of American disposable income came from extracted equity (mostly refinanced mortgages), boosting consumption despite falling wages (Marks 2012: 473).

The extreme, and, for proletarians, ultimately disastrous manifestation of this dynamic was in sub-prime mortgages. Such mortgages can be seen as a perverse response to demands by segments of the US working class for the house ownership that was a traditional part of the American Dream. Ethnic minorities had for decades protested the 'red-lining' that excluded them from mortgages. Sub-prime was the answer to this, but in a form that was calculated to benefit finance capital, with mortgages offered at initial low rates that would then balloon to un-payable levels, with 'far higher costs and penalties for noncompliance than "normal" loans': 'racial exclusion' was partly replaced by 'extortionary racial inclusion' (Dymski 2009: 162).

This expansion of financial markets was facilitated by cybernetics. Banks and mortgage agencies used enlarged information-processing capacities that should, in principle, have produced accurate estimates of what households could afford, but in practice were used to trawl for sub-prime applicants with online applications and automated underwriting. In sub-prime mortgages, debt and speculation met. Mortgage companies offered loans they knew would not be repaid because they did not intend to be holding them when they fell due. They 'securitized' such debts, bundling them up and selling them on to other investors as a supposed source of revenue on an international market where the speed and scope of cybernetic transactions made the distribution of these ticking, toxic financial time bombs all but untraceable.

After the bombs went off and the bubble burst, the sub-prime mortgages would reveal very complex 'cartographies of race and class' (Wyly et al. 2009). Almost everywhere however, African and Hispanic Americans were more likely than whites to be offered sub-prime, rather than normal, mortgages. Some autonomists have suggested the sub-prime mortgage boom can be seen as an exercise of proletarian power from below, a use of cheap credit by the most disadvantaged sections of the American working class to claim housing and other goods from which they had been historically excluded, with a rebellious disregard for apparent 'irresponsibility' (Midnight Notes 2009). There may be a grain of truth in this. But such rebellious aspirations were calculatingly fostered and ruthlessly exploited by capital.

Rather than rebellion-by-debt, what sub-prime mortgages demonstrate is finance capital's opportunistic exploitation of the extreme political decomposition of the US proletariat after the collapse of the mass worker. This decomposition was taken as an occasion to develop new forms of financial expropriation that targeted the most vulnerable members of the class. And such financial expropriation was, once again, connected back to the workplace exploitation of Chinese workers. For fuelling the North American housing boom was a financial flow between US banks and housing agencies and East Asian manufacturing in which profits from Asian exporters were recycled into the US mortgage market. It is now generally accepted that investment from China and Taiwan significantly pumped up the housing bubble (Duncan 2012). There is thus a trans-Pacific circuit which connects the exploitation of the *dagongmei* in Shenzhen with the eventual evictions of the sub-prime mortgage-holding proletarians in Detroit, Cleveland or Stockton.

Counter-Rotations, Power-Ups

From the early 1990s to 2008, capital's cybernetic intensification in its circulatory and financial processes began to interact at multiple global levels. Sophisticated and speedy supply chains enabled by digital communication enabled the shifting to low-wage zones of industrial production, including the manufacture of computers. In the factories of South China, the migration of rural populations created a vulnerable, unorganized and highly exploitable workforce serving the world market. The cheap digital devices produced by these workers laid the basis for the expansion of internet use by North Americans, with personal computer and network connections transformed from hacker experiments to consumer commodities. This internet expansion in turn spurred the venture-capital financed dot-com boom that reached its climax in 2000.

This period was not without counter-forces. The Zapatista's 1994 internet communiqués announcing the revolt of Mayan peasants against the consequences of US-Mexican free trade can be taken as a starting date for an 'alter-globalist' movement asserting that 'another world is possible'. This movement combined an unstable mix of, from the planetary North, trade unions and middle-class groups defending fast-fading Fordism with, from the South, workers and communities fighting structural adjustment programmes and special export zones. To these were added dissident hackers, students and young people raised in an increasingly networked context, with a strong sense of its pirate, alternative and common potentials.

The digital organization of anti-summit protests by this 'cyber-left' (Wolfson 2014) was at once antagonistic and akin to the optimism of the dot-com boom. Its experiments in a cybernetic version of the circulation of struggles theorized by *operaismo* (see Chapter 2) created the moment of Hardt and Negri's *Empire* (2000) and of this author's *Cyber-Marx* (1999). For several years, alter-globalism travelled a path of intensifying confrontations with the state through violent demonstrations in Seattle, Gothenburg and Genoa. It is impossible to say whether interruption by the 9/11 World Trade Centre attacks and the war on terror halted the movement's radicalization or saved it from falling apart under its own internal contradictions. What is certain is that its end was effectively marked by the failure of worldwide mass protests against the invasion of Iraq in 2003, even though anti-summit mobilizations continued at Gleneagles in 2005 and Rostock in 2007.

Alter-globalism had little connection to China. At a leadership level its World Social Forums linked activists in North and Latin America, Europe, India and some Asian countries, such as the Philippines. But what would turn out to be the most important axis of capital's globalism was largely outside its orbit. The one important exception was the 'anti-sweatshop' activism that flowed in and out of alter-globalism. This was a largely student-based politico-ethical attempt to 'run the supply chain backwards', making visible the connections between exploitation in the global South and consumption in the global North. It campaigned to pressure subcontracting transnational corporations to improve working and environmental conditions. Especially strong around the garment industry (Ross 1997), anti-sweatshop activism eventually also extended to computer manufacture, largely through the connection of international 'clean electronics' campaigns that had originated in Silicon Valley's poisoned communities (Smith et al. 2006) with exiled Chinese labour activists and exiled Tiananmen Square dissidents.

Such campaigns against Foxconn, Samsung and other electronics corporations have provided an important relay of information from China to North America. They are, however, generally constrained by their focus on corporate social responsibility and codes of conduct. This is not just because the complexity and agility of supply chains gives plenty of opportunity for such codes to remain unenforced even when adopted. It is also because, as Dorothy Kidd (2012b) observes 'monitoring and "codes of conduct" ... take the pressure off local authorities to establish and enforce labour regulations; and, in effect, contribute to privatizing labour law and increasing corporate power'. Ultimately a strategy of supply-chain reform represses the knowledge that in a globalized capitalist economy where workers must competitively bid against each other for jobs, proletarians are required to sell themselves cheap to get a wage. It thus avoids the issue of whether capitalist supply chains should exist at all (Friends of Gongchao 2013b).

Behind anti-sweatshop activism there also lay an assumption that China's impoverished worker-victims had to be saved by affluent North American consumer-activists. As it turned out, the Wall Street crash would see many of these activists themselves plunged into deep, debt-and-unemployment-driven proletarianization. Alter-globalism knew almost as little about finance capital as it did about China. Yet in the same period as it was summit-busting, the money-grid was expanding and speeding astronomically. The dot-com crash generated the low-interest-rate policy which fed the housing bubble, providing a huge if temporary 'power-up' for US capital. A resurrected commercial internet, which took the tactics of alter-globalism's digital circulation of struggles and made them into the basis of a commodity circulating Web 2.0, using participatory 'activism' as free labour, was part of this stock market revival (Marazzi 2010).

In this context US workers with stagnant wages sustained living standards partly via cheap consumer goods (including computers) from China, but also by growing debt, especially mortgages. This debt bubble was swollen by investment funds flowing into the dollar from China-based capital profiting from the influx of super-exploitable migrant labour into export factories. Marks explains the symbiosis of class decompositions on opposite sides of the Pacific:

> The more people unable to survive in rural China, the more, and cheaper, the migrant labor pouring into the cities; the faster people ran up credit card debt, the higher went American (and Chinese) economic growth. The two trends had a striking complementarity: Americans dealt with non-reproduction by excessive spending and debt; Chinese, shorn of the social safety net of the old Communist state, squirrel away money to pay for hospital visits, housing or retirement – i.e. cover their precarity by excessive saving. (Marks 2012: 476)

The cheap electronics produced by the sweat of the *dagongmei* provide both the links in the supply chains that bound China's workers to the assembly lines, and the cybernetic financial manacles snapped onto the wrist of black and Hispanic proletarians by sub-prime mortgages. It was the very success of capital in extinguishing the circulation of struggles and accelerating the circulation of commodities that would lead to collapse when mortgage markets began to fail in 2007. Before turning to that meltdown, however, we should look at the motions of the cybernetic vortex, not around its central Chimerican axis, but in its peripheral zones.

6

Mobile

Cell Phone, Cell Form

In Morazán province, El Salvador, mobile phone companies rule the horizon; as Rafael Alarcón, who researched the spread of mobiles through this small Latin American country, writes: 'antennas erected by Claro, Tigo, Movistar, and Digicell fill the landscape, their electric needles pointing skyward. Every town in northern Morazán welcomes visitors with huge signs donated by cell phone companies' (Alarcón 2014: 5). Twenty years ago this skyline was a frontline circled by helicopter gunships in a war between leftist guerrillas of the Farabundo Martí National Liberation Front (FMNLF) and the US-backed government. In 1992 the insurgents laid down their arms. Today, they and their children labour in low-wage work in the coffee plantations, *maquila* factories, call centres and tourist industry, or await remittances from relatives in the US.

As a Salvadorian saying has it, 'En El Salvador hasta los perros andan celular' ('In El Salvador even dogs have cell phones') (Alarcón 2014: 11). Some 30 to 40 per cent of the population live below the official poverty line, but there are 123 cell phone subscriptions per 100 inhabitants. When Alarcón saw the vans of a cell phone company's sales force arrive in the small town of Perquín:

> The air was suddenly filled with a loud voice booming from a megaphone on top of a small blue truck ... completely covered with Tigo publicity. As the recording invited people to purchase a Tigo cell phone, a couple of speakers played dance music at a high volume ... about a dozen young people exited the rear of the vehicle. Wearing blue pants and Tigo T-shirts [they] traversed every street in Perquín and the adjacent hamlets of Casa Blanca and El Carrizal, knocking at every door and offering cheap Tigo cell phones with the lowest rate per minute and the largest number of *mensajitos* (cell phone short message service

(SMS)) per dollar spent ... the people in Perquín were accustomed to this spectacle, because different companies had been doing the same thing once or twice a week for several months (Alarcón 2014: 6).

In his study of mobile adoption in the aftermath of revolutionary war, Alarcón shows how *saldo* – cell phone credit – has become a Salvadorian preoccupation; a practical necessity for the coordination of work and handling of emergencies, a channel for remittances, a nexus both of *consumismo* (consumerism) and crime, and a symbol of life in the world market:

> Just like cell phone saldo, capitalism in Morazán is fleeting, ubiquitous, and unstable ... As a metaphor for the precariousness of life in these communities, the ghostly appearance and disappearance of saldo in everyday life is the backside of the instability of wage labor and the increasing difficulties of making ends meet day to day. (Alarcón 2014: 17)

Building on Alarcón's work, we suggest that when the cybernetic vortex touches down, it is heard as the ring tone of a mobile phone. Marx (1977: 90) described the commodity as the 'cell form' of capitalism. Today a bad pun and an inversion give us the *cell phone* as the genotypic commodity of the world market, ready-to-hand techno-science for a system that requires people in perpetual motion, in touch, up to speed, 'always on' (Chen 2011), constantly involved in the technological 'annihilation of space through time' even while continuing to move through space, the practical realization of the 'universal intercourse' that accompanies the global circulation of commodities – including that most migrant of commodities, human labour power (Marx 1973: 539; 1970: 56). Whereas the last chapter examined the cybernetically mediated relation of US and Chinese working classes that became a main axis of the world market, this one looks at the special significance of the mobile phone to capitalism in some of the most impoverished and marginalized regions of the new global economy, and also to proletarian attempts to cope with or escape this immiseration.

The International Telecommunication Union (ITU 2013) estimates there were 4.6 billion mobile cellular subscriptions in 2009, 5.4 billion in 2010, 6.0 billion in 2011 and in 2012, 6.8 billion – a number equivalent to 96 per cent of the world population. However, as those numbers include multiple handset ownership (for the rich) and multiple SIM cards in single handsets (for the poor), estimates of actual users hover round

4 billion. Expansion has been especially fast in the poorest parts of the world. These often have no landline infrastructure, so mobiles – cheap, usable by the illiterate, not needing constant electricity, cost controllable by pre-paid cards and shared use – often provide the first telecommunication experience for their populations (Burell 2010).

Between 2005 and 2011, subscriptions per 100 people in what the World Bank (2013a: 9–10) lists as 'low income' countries rose from 4.7 to 41.7; in India, from 7.9 to 72; in the Middle East and North Africa from 22 to 90 and in Sub-Saharan Africa from 12 to 53 (World Bank 2013a: 104, 8). In 2008, three-quarters of all mobiles were in developing countries: most are cheap cell phones, but digital smartphones (the mobiles that actually qualify as truly digital, rather than analog devices) are also spreading fast (ITU 2012). It is therefore not surprising that visions of 'mobile-led economic development' (Bhavnani et al. 2008; Economist 2009b; Aker and Mbiti 2010) have become important to cybernetic capital, with the cell phone seen as a – if not *the* – means for the poor to better themselves within the context of a global markets, providing employment, entrepreneurial and financial opportunity, and permitting entire societies to leapfrog from peasant life into the information age.

Here, however, we explore a different proposition: that while there *is* an emancipating aspect to the planetary spread of the mobile phone and the 'universal intercourse' it activates, this potential is superimposed on and subverted by the class divisions that are the basis of commodity production (including the production of mobiles themselves). We develop this argument in three stages. First, we look at the production cycle of cell phones, in which various forms of insecure and often highly exploitative and hazardous work are prevalent. Second, we examine how the use of mobiles to cope with everyday conditions in low-wage global zones is also a mode in which those conditions are reproduced. We conclude by, third, suggesting that mobile phones are paradigmatic technologies for a new global level of capitalist subsumption that simultaneously includes and ejects vast surplus populations, exploiting a constant condition of transient and intermittent employment.

Moments of Exploitation

Inspired by Ursula Huws' (2003) concept of a 'cybertariat', Enda Brophy and Greig de Peuter (2014) have identified the 'moments' in a 'circuit of exploitation' travelled by the mobile phone as it proceeds from cradle to grave. We will broadly follow this model, tweaking it slightly and changing examples, to explore the five phases of mobile phone production currently most commonly situated in the developing world – *extraction, assembly, sale, service* and *disassembly* – reserving the moment of *design* for a longer discussion of the 'app economy' in Chapter 9.

Extraction

In the Amazon jungle at the frontier intersection of Columbia, Venezuela and Brazil, in an outlaw area controlled by paramilitaries, guerrillas and drug traders, indigenous miners pick-and-shovel heavy black ore nuggets out of mines scattered throughout the jungle. They carry the rocks out by foot to collection zones, from whence the nuggets will be clandestinely transported and eventually sold over the internet. The ore goes into smelters in Asia and thence into the transnational value chains of electronics manufacture (Gómez 2012). This is just the most recent phase in the history of electronics' most notorious blood mineral, coltan.

Coltan – columbite-tantalite – is the source of the tantalum used in the capacitors of mobiles, game consoles and many other digital devices. It came to public attention in the global North in 2000 when supply shortages delayed the Christmas debut of Sony's new PlayStation 2 on store shelves. Press investigation of this consumption blockage disclosed that the world's largest deposits of coltan were the Democratic Republic of Congo (DRC), one of the poorest countries on earth (second-to-last on the United Nations' Human Development Index) and central battleground of what has become known as 'Africa's World War' (Prunier 2011), a protracted conflict involving the DRC, Rwanda, Uganda and semi-autonomous warlords and militias in a struggle largely focused on control of resources such as cobalt, gold, diamonds, copper, timber – and coltan.

Because large mining corporations abandoned DRC's conflict-ridden post-colonial conditions, Congo coltan mining, like that in Columbia, is informal, conducted in

> primarily small-scale, artisanal, and fleeting mines, dispersed across remote forests, where diggers – typically migrant, young, and male – use rudimentary tools to variously strip land, burrow underground, crush ore, or haul coltan – jobs whose growth has coincided with deteriorating agricultural skill. (Brophy and de Peuter 2014)

Migrant miner camps are controlled by contending factions in Eastern Congo's chronic war, overseen by juvenile soldiers paid from coltan revenues (Dyer-Witheford and de Peuter 2009: 223). A miner could hypothetically make anywhere from $10 to $50 a week, well above Congo's national average of $10 week. However, various forms of coerced labour are common in the mines, including outright slavery (Fuchs 2014a: 178–9), and child labour endemic; at one time perhaps a third of Congolese children left school to go to the mines.

Though game consoles broke the coltan story, since 2000 cell phones have been the 'main attractor' for the mineral (Brophy and de Peuter 2014). Under pressure from 'clean electronics' campaigns, major digital companies first denied the use of DRC coltan, and then promised monitoring to prevent it. In 2010 the largely cosmetic Wall Street reforms of the Dodd Frank Act required disclosure (but not cessation) of the use of coltan and other 'blood minerals' from DRC. However, there are serious doubts about the efficacy of these measures, given the powerful price incentives for corporate blind-eyes, the complexity and opacity of electronics supply chains, and their agility in routing round disruptions – demonstrated by the recent news of black market coltan production in Latin America.

Coltan is the most infamous cell phone mineral, but mobiles and other cybernetic devices also contain gold (whose high-technology use accounts for 12 per cent of global production), copper, aluminium, silver, palladium, and various rare earths, as well as lithium, graphite and platinum in batteries (Sharpe 2013). Consequently there is a general involvement of mining in cybernetic production. Given the range of minerals and various production locations, conditions of work vary enormously. It is however fair to say that mining is an industry known for the danger of its working conditions, industrial conflict, and community and ecological disruption, especially in low-wage, unregulated zones. Fuchs (2014a: 173) points out that South Africa's infamous Marikana mine, where in 2012 34 striking miners were killed by security forces, produced platinum, a mineral of which more than a third of the world's output is used in computer hard-drives. In Bolivia, mines producing the lithium used in batteries for mobiles and computers have seen recurrent disputes over both lithium miners' wages and conditions and indigenous people's rights to control of resources (Achtenberg 2010). China's mines for rare earths vital to smartphones are highly toxic (Kaiman 2014). Mobile's mineral components emerge out of such contexts.

Assembly

We have already looked at electronic manufacturing's 'bloody Taylorism' and 'peripheral Fordism' in Ciudad Juárez and Shenzhen (Lipietz 1987); Brophy and de Peuter (2014) discuss similar conditions in India's Special Export Zone's. Here we add to the roster the Batam-Bintan-Karimun free trade zone (BBK FTZ) in Indonesia, drawing heavily on a report by the Asian Monitor Centre (Wulandari 2011), one of the most important organizations monitoring electronic industry supply chains.

In 2007, Singapore, a star economy of Asian capitalism, signed an agreement with Indonesia making an adjacent cluster of islands, centred on Batam, a free trade zone. The aim was to create an assembly work 'backyard' for Singapore's burgeoning electronics industry, which was upgrading from contract manufacture to higher-end activities such as design and services, 'relocating low end manufacturing to other countries'. BBK soon housed '21 industrial parks, surrounded by corridors and ports, with over a thousand foreign companies, including major brands and their subcontractors'. Amongst these were factories manufacturing disks, drives and parts for electronic devices, and assembling mobile phones, including a plant of the contract assembly giant Flextronics, one of Foxconn's global competitors. Enterprises were attracted by 'free land, water and other natural resources' and by a supply of cheap labour. Wages were low, even by Indonesian standards, though Batam was expensive because of its proximity to Singapore. Most workers routinely did '100–200 hours' overtime a month to make ends meet. Nevertheless, as 'some 70% of the Indonesian population lacks regular work', the zone attracted workers, many recruited through agencies taking a cut of wages as fees (Wulandari 2011: 27–31).

Over a decade, BBK's population doubled from half a million to over a million. This included not only factory workers, but also casual construction and port labour, and an informal 'underground service industry' of food vendors, sex workers, scrap collectors, unregistered taxi services and suppliers of clean water and electricity. For the informal workers, who may make $1–2 a day, the only habitation is 'wild housing' – makeshift shanties constructed overnight on squatted land without electricity or water. The zone is extensively contaminated by toxic wastes both emitted by factories and dumped on the island by 'a well organized smuggling industry' (Wulandari 2011: 27–31), which also makes it an alleged transhipment point for illegal African ivory trade (Fadli 2013).

An estimated 300 women and children are sold in or from Batam every week by crime rings immune from police action. The island is also a site for sex tourists, especially men from the Singaporean working poor for whom Indonesian sex workers have 'bargain basement' prices (Ford and Lyons 2008).

After hearing an explanation of the place of Batam FTZ in the electronics industry supply chain, an Indonesian worker quipped: 'All this time we might have worshipped the wrong God. It is the global supply chain that put us here in Batam. It is the one who rules and determines our lives. It is the God' (Wulandari 2011: 27). What this God gives can also be taken away. In recent years organizing by BBK workers succeeded in raising the minimum wage in the zone. This encouraged the departure of electronics companies to rival locations in Vietnam, Thailand, Malaysia and above all, Shenzhen. The Indonesian government now contemplates abandoning the SEZ's electronics orientation in favour of low-cost shipbuilding (Gabriel 2012), a strikingly illustration of the chronic insecurity of the electronics assembly proletariat.

Sales

Heather Horst and Daniel Miller describe how in Jamaica pre-paid phone cards have generated 'thousands of "parlor style" micro-retailers that have permeated into the pores of Jamaican society in a manner that is probably only matched by the local informal trade in marijuana' (2006: 2018). Broadly similar conditions seem to govern cell phone credit sale in other parts of the world.

It is widely reported that mobile phone operators generate a significant number of jobs across the developing world: in 2008 the World Bank reported that the mobile phone industry had created 3.5 million jobs in Africa (Bhavnani 2008). It also notes, however, that 'mobile operators themselves only create limited employment' – jobs 'highly paid and sought after'. The major source of work is in retail, 'through the sale of airtime, handsets, and SIM cards'. Pádraig Carmody suggests that these jobs constitute a new 'hybrid (in)formal economy':

> sellers of phone credit work in the 'unregulated', or popular economy, but are articulated to the formal economy because they are effectively employed by major cell phone companies – either as 'indirect employees' for whom they do not have to pay payroll taxes or as

nominally self-employed entrepreneurs who are in actuality the sales arm the these companies (Carmody 2012: 8).

A more recent report (Foster and Heeks 2011) bears out this perspective. Acknowledging great difficulties in estimating mobile phone jobs in low-income countries, it suggests that the sector 'provides sizeable employment for those close to poverty' amounting to 'at least tens of millions worldwide' and is likely to continue to grow. Comparing data from Kenya, Pakistan, Bangladesh and Sudan, it again notes the predominance of airtime and SIM vendors (75 per cent in Kenya, 81 per cent in Pakistan), followed at some distance by handset sellers; these categories combined dwarf 'technical' jobs. Most vendors are 'microenterprises' with less than ten employees, and often only a solo self-employer, frequently 'jumping' and 'juggling' across activities, connected to formal companies without contracts only as informal outsourcers. With a sobriety unusual in mobile development literature, the report emphasizes that such informal employment is 'highly unstable', vulnerable to changes in the supply chain, technology or regulatory setting, and remarks that 'contextual instability and uneven power relations' often make 'upgrading in the value chain impossible' and that 'too much instability will lead to reduced viability of such enterprises in the long run'.

Support

Unlike SIM card phones, smartphones, once sold to affluent consumers, require support; 'telecommunications companies that charge for access ... offer accessibility, responsiveness, and personalized attention, but such promises are expensive to deliver' (Brophy and de Peuter 2014). The solution is 'the same as that adopted in a range of industries since the 1990s – the call centre'. Telecommunications firms are, along with the financial sector, the largest call centre employers in the world. Working at the 'interface' between communicative capitalism and the high-value customer segment, call centre workers 'address billing complaints, resolve technology failures, sell services, and collect on overdue accounts' (Brophy and de Peuter 2014).

In the global North, call centres started to proliferate in the 1990s as part of the digital New Economy, accompanied by an encouraging rhetoric about an educated workforce (i.e. students) and flexible hours (Friends of Kolinko 2012). Combining a post-industrial office environment with assembly-line techniques, work in call centres is technologically mediated, but also 'affective', involving dealing both with computer orchestrated calling systems and customers' enraged outbursts, practising techniques such as 'smiling with voice' while subject to advanced surveillance techniques such as 'emotion detectors' (Poster 2011). These conditions generate conflicts between labour and management, and, as Brophy and de Peuter write, 'the terrain for these conflicts ... is global, with companies seeking to ... play workforces in different countries off against each other' (2014).

After the New Economy crash of 2000, call centre work from Europe and North America was often sent to Asia to cut costs and/or avoid labour strife. India was a particularly important destination, with call centres constituting a second tier of the 'shining' IT sector – not as well paid as programming, but still making wages considered 'middle class', and, unlike programming, relatively open to women as well as men. In Gurgaon, an industrial suburb south of Delhi, call centres handling work from large US and European corporations are located alongside Toyota car plants, Honda motorcycle factories, and garment making sweatshops. Some are enormous, with as many as 2,000 or more workers, others in 'hidden backrooms with six people on the phone' (Friends of Kolinko 2012).

Workers are recruited from students or graduates, transnationally multilingual, accent-trained. They can make '12,000 to 14,000 Rupees for normally 50 hours of night-shifts' – over ten times as much as an unskilled construction worker, three or four times that of service workers, and more than senior permanent car plant employees:

> The money, the night-shifts, the contact with the 'western world' creates a kind of call centre culture ... the technological control and general pressure, the shared flats, the purchasing power, the expensive food in the neighboring shopping malls, the long hours in cabs, the frequent job changes, the more open gender relations at work, the burn out, the difficulty to keep the perspective of an academic career or to find jobs as academics ... are experiences of a new proletarianized middle-class generation. (Friends of Kolinko 2012)

The pressure of work and demand for flexible hours produces churn as, or higher, than in the global North. Indian call centres have raised wages, but for workers who hang in, a major concern is the risk of 're-shifting': 'They know that they were at the receiving end of global re-location (although they are also aware that they earn only about 20 per cent of the US-workers), but they also know that the boom is temporary, that capital/work might move on' (Friends of Kolinko 2012). And indeed post-2008, competition intensified between Gurgaon call centres and rivals in the Philippines or South Africa, or in remoter (often conflict wracked) areas of India – or even in rustbelts of the global North as global precarity turned full circle.

Disassembly

If call centre work is at least several notches above the most brutal levels of mobile proletarianization, at the final stage of the circuit we descend again into an abyss. At the end of the cell phone's life cycle, billions of them swell toxic e-waste dumps, 'scoured by scavengers seeking recoverable metals and components' (Brophy and de Peuter 2014). According to a recent UN report, e-waste, including not just mobiles but all computers, monitors, TVs, phones, appliance components and e-toys, is the world's fastest growing waste stream; by 2017, its annual volume will 'fill a 15,000-mile line of 40-tonne lorries' (Vidal 2013). We have to imagine these trucks heading from the populations of North America (30 kg per head of e-waste) and Europe (over 20 kg per head) to dumps in, again, China (which at 5 kg per head still generates most in absolute volume) and also in India and Africa (which have some of lowest per person rates of e-waste on the planet).

A glimpse of these destinations comes from journalist Afua Hirsch's account of Agbogbloshie, Ghana's vast e-dump outside the capital of Accra. Titled 'This is not a nice place to live', her report describes a site where computers from every period 'lie haphazardly on large mounds in the dump, which stretches as far as the eye can see'. Everything is 'smeared and stained with mucky hues of brown and sooty black'; 'huge plumes of foul-smelling smoke' and 'head-pounding fumes' rise from 'large fires where the dismantled items are burned to remove traces of plastic, leaving the metal behind'. Here again are the familiar features of extreme proletarianization: teenage boys, migrants from north Ghana, making the equivalent of between 60c and \$1.30 a day, sending funds back to their family; women and girls wandering the site 'hawking peeled oranges, water sachets and cooked food' with 'tiny babies wrapped in cloth tied tightly to their backs'; children trawling the site with 'magnets tied on to the end of a piece of string, picking up any tiny scraps of metal left behind in the dirt'; and thousands living in shacks on the site, carrying on lives 'in the midst of its filth and fumes' (Hirsch 2013).

Moments of Appropriation

The effects of mobiles on proletarian life around the planet cannot, however, be accounted for solely by their conditions of production. Where they touch the majority is as an everyday communication device. Indeed, most champions of mobile-led economic development would probably say that however bad conditions might be in coltan mines, electronics factories or e-waste dumps, this is more than made up for by the benefits mobiles offer to low-income users in terms of an unprecedented, affordable scope of communication. It is, however, possible to look critically at the purposes that mobiles fulfil within the context of capitalist globalization. So to complement Brophy and de Peuter's cartography of the moments of exploitation in mobile production we draw on the work of ethnographers of cell phone adoption to add a discussion of moments of mobile 'appropriation' by global proletarians. To describe some of the most common ways mobiles are integrated into the lives of the poor and dispossessed we present a mnemonic, five 'M' list: eMployment, eMergency, Migration, Money and CriMe. In this mapping we see how the mobile is used to cope with the many exigencies of life in global zones of poverty and precarity. These daily proletarian appropriations of mobiles are, however, ambivalent, for 'coping' with conditions of deprivation may also be a way in which such conditions are reproduced and maintained, so that proletarian appropriations of the mobile are also often moments of continuing expropriation by capital.

eMployment

Proletarians work producing mobiles, but mobiles are also a 'platform for labour' (Brophy and de Peuter 2014), a means of finding other sorts of work. The major reason cell phones have become a necessity in the developing world is because work is 'informal': insecure, transient and low-waged jobs or self-employment. In neoliberal discourse this informality is represented as a matter of intrepid and promising entrepreneurialism, and there are indeed instances of such success. But for every 'slumdog millionaire' there are billions simply trying, and often failing, to survive. We have already glimpsed some of the innumerable faces of informal precarity, from artisanal mining to selling cell phone cards or scavenging e-waste, but similar labours pervade all sectors of the economy in impoverished zones.

In a reply to a politician who suggested that the rapid spread of cell phones amongst the population of India was a sure sign of increasing affluence, the journal *Sanhati* (2010) observed that 'given the low cost of buying a mobile phone and cheap tariff, it is possible for a person living on Rs. 20 a day or less to own and use a mobile phone', and presented the following analysis:

> Most of the workforce in India (around 93 per cent) is in the unorganized sector and the overwhelming majority of them have an extremely precarious economic position apart from their being poor … The fact that informal sector workers have to use mobile phones only means that the precarious nature of their employment forces them to spend a substantial amount on mobile phones to mitigate uncertainty. It does not mean that workers are having a good time talking to each other over their mobile phones and that this is an indicator of the growing wealth among the working class in India. It is merely an indicator of the growing costs of obtaining and retaining a job in a scenario marked by growing informalization … a cell phone in India today is no longer a luxury item … it has become one more item that a worker needs to spend on if she/he has to cope with the work-lives in the rapidly expanding informal economy. (Sanhati 2010)

The author goes on to suggest that, for the poor, informal employment has made the cheap cell phone an 'inelastic' commodity – that is, one they cannot afford to do without. The portrait of mobile-aided prosperity fades and 'in its place a frightening picture emerges':

> Consider a family consisting, say, of five in an urban slum, that is, a woman, a man, two children and one elder grandparent. The family is earning around Rs. 2000 per month. There are two mobile phones in the family: one for the man and the other for the woman. The family has to spend Rs. 200 per month for their mobiles. The woman perhaps waits at the phone for information about prospective domestic labour on offer by a middle-class homeowner (e.g., washing or house-cleaning). The man, too, waits perhaps for information about work

that has become available. And for retaining this connection, they are having to cut down their expenses on food further. (Sanhati 2010)

While this analysis is specific to India, there are similar reports from other countries of the compelled necessity of mobiles for the poor in conditions where subsistence has become dependent on fluctuating and unpredictable wage labour. In their study of cell phone use in rural Jamaica, Horst and Miller (2006: 103–4) were surprised to find a world, not of entrepreneurial opportunities, other than selling phone cards or drugs, but just a juggling of 'occupational multiplicity', in a context where, to get by, women had to circulate between work as domestics, barmaids, shop workers, agricultural labourers and household labour. Carmody reports on a study of cell phones in rural Uganda that found those without mobiles feared missing opportunities for work, as employers would first contact those with mobile phones, so that the mobile became a necessity for those involved in casual labour, and many homes reduced their purchases of store-bought groceries to pay for airtime. He suggests we think of this as 'negative adoption', in which 'the costs of exclusion from social networks would be too great to not have them' and hence 'some people have mobile phones, even if they find them expensive to run' (Carmody 2012: 6).

eMergency

Precarious lives descend into crisis because of lack of work, ill health, accident, domestic disturbances, natural disasters, and war. Horst and Miller (2006: 165) observe that in poor regions of Jamaica they were dealing with people in 'an almost constant state of crisis' because there is 'simply no surplus funds available'. Alarcón similarly notes that in El Salvador 'emergency' was one of the most 'pervasive concepts' he encountered in his interviews and 'came up every time I asked about the importance of cell phones in everyday life', adding that the 'normalization of emergency' also justifies the 'almost complete lack of participation by the state in most social issues' which has been 'a constant in Salvadoran history', only recently somewhat alleviated since the election of an FMLN centre-left government in 2009.

The growing centrality of mobiles to everyday existence in the low-end zones of capital occurs in societies that are undergoing massive transformations because of the slow collapse of subsistence economies and the influx of people into cities, where state welfare provisions are absent, or scanty, and often rolled-back by privatization and structural adjustment programmes. It is in such contexts that one well-known positive effect of cell phones, the strengthening of social networks of kin or community, assumes a crucial importance. These networks, with their intricate ties of reciprocity and obligation, are communal mechanisms of survival, where state and capital fail. They are the means of circulating scarce resources, which today include money, amongst the poor.

In this sense, mobiles actually help download the costs of socially reproducing proletarian life away from capital and onto proletarians themselves; as Carmody observes, mobile adoption may often represent part of a 'defensive livelihood strategy, given widespread poverty and the importance of extended family networks to survival' (2012: 7). Thus Horst and Miller (2006: 166) report that, contrary to developmentalist discourse of mobile-enabled business success, what they discovered in Jamaica was a cell phone economy of 'amelioration' rather than 'entrepreneurialism' – 'not a way of making money, but of getting money'. Mobiles are, they conclude, means not of techno-boosted bottom-up indigenous capital growth, but of 'low level redistribution', circulating resources from 'those who have little' to 'those who have less' by 'gifting, trading and begging' (Horst and Miller 2006: 119).

Migration

One way in which proletarians attempt to escape constant crisis is by migration – 'a process of forced mobility for capitalist purposes (to do waged or unwaged labour where capital needs it), [that] also includes elements of autonomous proletarian mobility to escape misery, exploitation, and patriarchy in the areas of origin' (Friends of Gongchao 2013b). The World Bank economist Branko Milanović argues that while 'inequality between world citizens in the mid 19th century was such that at least a half of it could be explained by income differences between workers and capital-owners in individual countries', in the early twenty-first century, 'more than 80 per cent of global income differences is due to large gaps in mean incomes between countries, and unskilled workers' wages in rich and poor countries often differ by a factor of 10 to 1' (Milanović 2011a). Milanović's blunt distinction between class and spatial divisions – and hence between 'proletarians' and 'migrants' – is naive, for many of the territorial inequalities to which he refers are the product of capital's imperial segregation of core and periphery in the world system.

However, his suggestion that 'a new global political issue of migration has emerged because income differences between countries make individual gains from migration large' (2011a) is obviously correct.

In the next chapter we will look at the changing scale and scope of twenty-first-century migration. Mobiles are one of the factors that have changed it. They make it easier for transnational families to stay in touch; to get help with visas; to seek out information about new destinations; to reach relatives, friends and communities in strange places. Mobiles are likely to be crucial for finding work – often, of course, in the new country's version of the precarious or informal labour sector, as we saw, for example, in the case of service workers in the IT industry, from San Jose to Hyderabad – although as Cara Wallis (2011) found in her study of young female migrant workers, mobiles can also provide employers with a means of surveillance and harassment. They help with legal and illegal border crossings, and keeping ahead of raids and sweeps by immigration authorities. In a study of asylum-seekers in Australia's detention camps, Linda Leung looked at the use of cell phones as detainees attempted to keep in communication with families and friends and obtain legal help while negotiating a labyrinthine approval process, and concluded that 'for refugees, the mobile phone is not a technology of choice but instead, a technology of necessity and survival' (Leung 2007).

Remittances from those who have migrated from low to higher wage zones, either from rural areas to cities or internationally, are particularly important to proletarian communities. An International Monetary Fund report estimates that officially recorded remittance flows to developing countries reached $338 billion in 2008 (Barajas et al. 2009). Mobiles make it easier to send back remittances and support packages, either directly or by e-money transfers or by communicating about other transfer methods. One reason cell phones are so important in El Salvador is because remittances represent some 16 per cent of GDP. Horst and Miller (2006: 117) estimated that in 2004 the amount sent through a cell phone enabled remittance system for Orange County, Jamaica, was equivalent to two months' low-level income for everybody in the area. Migration and remittances epitomise the ambivalent nature of proletarian choices: survival often leaves little choice but to leave a homeland, for economic or political reasons, and seek to support oneself and family, friends and community from somewhere else; at the same time, such mobility confirms the zonal divisions of global capital, which, for reasons usually deeply etched in colonial and imperial history, ensure that for millions wealth resides abroad.

M-Money

Remittances are only one aspect of mobile financialization. The Kibera slum in Kenya outside Nairobi has become emblematic of the strange encounters between mobiles, immiseration and money:

> Raw waste carves gullies along the ragged ribbons of bare earth that serve as side streets and alleys, where children crawl and play in dirt you wouldn't step in unless you had to ... Forests of twisted aerials sprout from the roofs of shacks raised up from the mud and topped with sheets of metal. The main streets are full of the hustle and bustle of the ultimate free market, the sort of anarchic community libertarians beg for, but would beg to be rescued from. AirTel signs and M-PESA logos compete with butchers and charcoal-sellers, bombarding the senses with a barrage of colour that still can't quite match that smell. (Robbins 2012)

M-Pesa is the most famous of several mobile financial systems – generally referred to as 'M-money' or 'M-banking' – that since 2005 have emerged in various developing countries, involving applications that may include 'transmitting airtime, paying bills and transferring money between individuals' (Aker and Mbiti 2010). M-Pesa began as a mobile phone microfinance loan programme, but in 2007 expanded into a money transfer system. The project was assisted by the monopoly position, governmental connections and skilful marketing of its owner, the Kenyan telecom Safari. com. Decisive in its success, however, were Kenya's post-election riots of 2008, when thousands were trapped in Kibera and other Nairobi slums, or did not wish to use banks implicated in ethnic conflicts. By 2013 over 17 million Kenyans, more than two-thirds of the adult population, had used the system; reportedly around 25 per cent of the country's gross national product flows through it and it has spun off a number of e-start ups that have become the basis for Nairobi's hopefully named 'Silicon Savannah' (Economist 2013c).

M-Pesa has become a flagship for notions of poverty relief through 'inclusive', 'bottom up', or 'empowering' capitalism, which not only feature prominently in 'ICT4D' (ICTs for Development) thought but are promoted by figures such as Bill Gates, who views M-Pesa as exemplary. The idea is that mobile phone money will provide financial services to the roughly 2 billion people who have the use of a cell phone 'but no bank account' (Economist 2009b: 13). The World Bank estimates that 'the unbanked' include almost 60 per cent of adults in developing countries and 77 per cent of adults making less than $2 a day (Economist 2009b: 13). M-money is intended to provide these populations with 'financial inclusion' – that is, allow them to save, tide over crises and improve their economic situation, in particular by entrepreneurial activity. Based on these hopes, and the apparent success of M-Pesa, similar schemes have been launched in India, Tanzania and Nigeria, but with much less uptake.

There is no doubt M-Pesa has become an important part of Kenyan life. However, it is not clear that it provides the opportunities for the poor promised by its promoters. Although it is associated with the image of the Kibera slum, many of its subscribers are more affluent, and it appears to be these who use it as a bank (Greely 2013). When it is used in slum or rural communities, rapid, previously non-existent transfers of money are indeed 'a boon', but not necessarily for saving or entrepreneurial activity. Rather users 'cash in and out quite quickly' to contribute to ceremonies, kinship networks, or in numerous small transmissions: on average users reported they kept about 300 Ksh. (about $4) on their phones (Greely 2013). In other words, it sustains communal existence in conditions of informal, vulnerable employment but does not necessarily transform those conditions by creating grassroots capitalism.

On the other hand, where M-Pesa undoubtedly does build capitalism is at its top end. Safari.com has become an integral part of Kenyan capitalism's aggressive neoliberal state-private enterprise nexus, which is marked by high concentrations of wealth and notorious corruption. In 2014 Safari.com's profits rose 31 per cent, largely because of M-Pesa growth (Mumo 2014). Although the company is an icon of Afro-capitalism, it is in fact 40 per cent owned by the multinational Vodafone (which recently undertook to extend M-Pesa to Rumania). So while M-Pesa may or may not help make money *for* its proletarian users, it certainly, by fees on its service, makes money *from* them; M-Pesa is a poster-child of market-oriented developmentalism, but it is also an example of transnational financial expropriation, in a way no strategy of 'financial inclusion' is likely to disturb.

CriMe

Horst and Miller (2006: 1) start their study of Jamaican cell phone use with an urban legend about the hold up of a bus in the suburbs of Kingston: the youthful, AK-47-armed robbers, having been given 26 cell phones, angrily demand an additional three because the stated capacity of the bus is 29: they get them. The story is told to illustrate the widespread diffusion of mobiles; hijackers can correctly assume everyone has them. It also, however, suggests something else; that in a world of general mobile use certain underlying conditions of hazard, such as robbery, and the impoverishment that makes robbery commonplace, remain. Our point is not to suggest that mobile phones create crime; that would be ridiculous. It is rather, to point out that mobiles are absorbed into and reproduce the structures of criminality on which many global proletarians depend for survival. Crime is not something to romanticise. Some of it may be Robin Hood activity, and some of it is victimless. Nonetheless, much crime, including virtual crime, is itself shadow capitalism organized in petty rings or massive cartels that are themselves violently exploitative of their workers and their communities. Human trafficking and drug wars are salient examples; in these cases our fifth 'M' should read Mafias.

Alarcón reports that most of the people he interviewed in El Salvador wouldn't answer a call unless they recognized the number, because extortion via cell phones is 'one of the main postwar criminal activities' in the country. Transnational Salvadorian gangs such as La Mara Salvatrucha and La Mara 18 'use cell phones to threaten people, sometimes randomly and sometimes based on a significant amount of knowledge about the victim's income'. Such extortion is mainly committed 'from inside Salvadoran and even Guatemalan prisons'. The practice led the authorities to make registration of cell phone numbers obligatory; nonetheless, large numbers still have unknown owners, with many of these lines presumably used in criminal activities. Extortion is a commonplace; transport workers are frequent victims, but 'in other cases, relatives and members of the community attempt to extort their neighbors' (Alarcón 2014: 5–6). El Salvador is not unique: mobile extortion is, if anything, yet more vicious in Mexico.

An even more striking criminal example is the maritime pirates of Somalia. In Somalia, since the 1990s wracked by war, famine, invasion and terror, to a point where civil authority has disintegrated, there has been 'extraordinary demand for telecoms services ... in the wake of state collapse'

(Collins 2009: 204). Somalia is one of the highest users of telecommunications in East Africa, driven by a huge diaspora and the 'astounding' amount of money it remits each year (Collins 2009: 203). One consequence is that Somalia's major telecommunications companies, most of whom have their origins in the seizure of the state's facilities after its collapse in 1991, have become some of the most influential institutions in the country. This is not least because of their capacity to supply Somalia's 'pirate' economy of ship-hijacking and ransom demands with the sophisticated satellite phones, navigational systems and data banks on which it depends, and to shield these systems from foreign intervention (Jamaa 2011; Liddle 2014). Again, our point here is analytic, not moralistic: pirate and other criminal uses of mobile phones are an outcome of their introduction into conditions of deep societal collapse, conditions that cell phones may help people to adapt to and survive, but which such technologies do not in any way by themselves reverse.

There is sometimes a point when crime transmutes into political resistance. Criminal acts of looting and violence become communal acts of protest and rebellion, and demonstrations and assemblies are outlawed by authorities. The mobile is present in these moments, transmitting the call to action, monitoring the security forces, keeping tabs on the chaos of street fighting and arrests, photographing the violence. Mobiles are used in marches against workplace exploitation or protesting the murder of friends and comrades by the police, and in the crowds that storm the residences of corrupt elites, even as state forces seek to deactivate and disrupt the mobile networks, breach their anonymity, and cull evidence for retaliation.

In 2010, for example, there were major riots in Mozambique against a rise in the price of grains: 13 people died, 400 were arrested (AP 2010). Cell phones were widely used by rioters; the state attempted to block text messages, claimed the riots were organized by criminal gangs, and afterwards legislated an end to mobile subscription anonymity (Anderson 2010). The price rise was however rolled back. This was a recurrence of the much wider round of food riots that between 2007 and 2008 ran from West Africa to Bangladesh to Egypt (where they set the stage for the later uprising of 2011), precipitated by a variety of factors including speculative futures trading in basic food commodities. Interspersed in reports of these riots are repeated references to the use of cell phones by 'the angry poor' (Economist 2010). In Chapter 8 we will examine more of such events, and see how in these contexts mobiles can have a radical valence. Such moments are, however, often mobile-enhanced transgressions *against* the logic of markets, not examples of markets' mobile amplification. With this in mind, we now tally up our travels around the global circuit of cell phone capitalism.

Virtual Paupers

In what is, for a World Bank economist, an unusually sceptical look at the claims of mobile-driven global economic development, Milanović observes:

> If one lives in a shack, in insalubrious conditions, with a volatile income that is barely above subsistence, and is unable to send his kids to school or offer to his family decent health care, it makes no sense to classify him as part of some imaginary 'global middle class' because he can dial a cell-phone. (2011b: 174–5)

In such a context, the cell phone figures as a way of enduring, not abolishing, proletarianization. It is a technology rapidly adopted by an insecure, nomadic global workforce, continually coping with crisis, largely lacking basic social services, threatened by war, civil disorder and natural disaster amidst frail infrastructures, dependent on familial and communal networks offering support provided neither by capital nor state. Mobiles have become a necessity in these contexts because conditions of life and labour are precarious. In this respect, they manifest a cybernetic circularity. Digital globalizing processes have fatally disrupted subsistence economies – via electronic value chains, high-technology agribusiness and speculative electronic commodity markets – and drive huge migrations from rural to urban areas and across transnational frontiers in socially chaotic conditions. These conditions require further everyday use of cybernetics for people to survive proletarianization, the insecurity of which mobiles in many ways actually intensify by allowing capital ever wider and more fine-grained activation of 'informal' and insecure waged work.

There are, from capital's point of view, many promising mobile paths to such activation. As Brophy and de Peuter (2014) point out, the concept of a widely distributed online work has evolved rapidly since it was pioneered by Amazon.com's Mechanical Turk in 2005, an experiment that effectively demonstrated the capability of cybernetic global wage-bidding systems to drive down compensation floors. Its success is now extended by new contenders such as Microtask or ClowdCrowd, specialists in using software to 'carve a given task into microscopically small pieces', stripped of information about the larger context, and simplified for execution at minimal skill levels (Stross 2010). Extending such techniques to the huge labour pools of low-income countries via mobiles is the new frontier of cybernetic piece work, pioneered by companies such as Jana (formerly txteagle), a Boston company founded in 2009 to dispatch 'simple info-tasks via text message' to what it perceives as an 'untapped work force in developing countries'. The project was piloted by recruiting bi-lingual Kenyans to 'use their mobiles to receive and translate words to regional dialect for a multinational telco localizing a handset interface' with these 'txt-workers' and 'in a recursive loop, compensated in airtime' – that is, in paid minutes of cell phone use (Brophy and de Peuter 2014).

Such experiments are an extrapolation from current tendencies in mobilizing precarious and informal work to better serve global capital. In a discussion of what he terms the 'informationalization of poverty' (2012) in Africa, Carmody argues that mobile phone coverage of the continent has made no noticeable alteration to its research and development activity, nor changed the traditional dependency on agricultural and fuel and mineral exports, and may even effect an upwards extraction of value from the poor to the transnational owners of mobile companies (Carmody 2012: 6). He and his co-authors suggest that though ICTs such as mobile phones do assist small enterprises in terms of communication and logistics, this remains a 'thin' integration that leaves populations excluded from higher levels of the value chain untouched, and has done little to ameliorate the challenge facing 'hypercompetitive markets, increasing levels of import penetration, and human capital limitations' and is 'enabling foreign firms and importers to capturing more value as a result of their ability to enter African markets' (Murphy et al. 2014: 279).

More important than merely casting doubt on the promises of mobile development, however, is to recognize such 'thintegration' (Murphy et al. 2014: 279) as a component of a new phase of capitalist subsumption. This phase is characterized by a deepening digital envelopment of the planet, simultaneously enabling selective access to and disconnection from the vast labour reserves furnished by globalization. Alarcón writes of an 'electronic social-formation' constituted by 'uneven development of a subordinated digitization in which Third World countries and popular classes all over the world are being incorporated into a new kind of social synthesis under capitalistic commodity form' (2014: 2).

We can approach this 'new synthesis' through Marx's discussion of 'surplus populations' – the vast pool of permanently superfluous labour created by capital through its own globalizing and automating momentum. Marx observed how this means that many proletarians become chronically excess to system requirements, and hence live as 'virtual paupers' for whom waged work is always contingent, constantly liable to unemployment (1973: 604). Mobiles suggest both a concretization and reversal of the 'virtual pauper' concept. Such technologies create a situation where surplus populations, still excessive to capital's needs, can nevertheless be intermittently summoned to on-call virtual work at globally arbitraged rates, and in this way systemically 'included via exclusion' (Theorie Communiste 2011).

This is a prognosis at odds with the dominant optimism about global mobiles. It is, however, not without a developmental perspective, albeit one rather different from that of 'ICT4D'. According to conventional wisdom, mobiles bring modernity and its benefits – capital, wage work, commodification – from the core of the world system to the periphery. It may be, however, that the new subsumption moves in an opposite direction. The conditions of work and daily life normalized in the periphery – informalization, precarity, vanishing state supports, vulnerability to disaster – flow from low to high zones of the world economy, carrying with them the daily practices, such as mandatory mobile connection, necessary for cybernetic proletarianization.

7

Globe

Prelude: The Content Moderator

In an office on the 'second floor of a former elementary school at the end of a row of auto mechanics' stalls in Bacoor, a gritty Filipino town 13 miles southwest of Manila, a woman is watching streams of violent and pornographic imagery pass across her computer screen (Chen 2014). She is working. As the hours of her shift clock down, she swiftly, repeatedly, marks each feed for deletion, acceptance, or further evaluation by the social media company that hires her. Her labour is contracted and insecure. In North America it might be paid $20 an hour, although it is also performed for less; in the Philippines it earns between $500 and $300 a month.

Some 100,000 people around the world perform such 'Commercial Content Moderation' (CCM) for social media and digital entertainment companies (Chen 2014). Until recently it was a relatively secret work, hidden by employers reluctant to reveal trade practices and disturb social media's attractive appearance of direct, spontaneous interpersonal communication; CCM workers are frequently bound by non-disclosure agreements. Yet, as Sarah T. Roberts (2015) makes clear in her groundbreaking study of CCM, this form of digital labour is essential to its corporate employers, for without it their platforms would be deluged with user-generated content so shocking as to repel other users, and perhaps expose companies to litigation. As Roberts shows, CCM is performed in a variety of settings – in-house, outsourced to boutique third-party operators or mass call centres, or as piece-work microlabours. Conditions and wages vary. In general, however, the work is contracted, precarious, 'low status and low wage' (Roberts 2015). It is also 'rote, repetitive, quota-driven, queue based', and 'vacillates from the mind numbingly repetitive and mundane' to abrupt, repeated encounters with 'violent, disturbing, and at worst, psychologically damaging' material (Roberts 2015). Employers usually provide little or no assistance to moderators dealing with trauma.

CCM is global work, in a twofold sense. First, it is performed around the world, from the United States to the Philippines to India and Bangladesh. Some companies 'run dual level operations, sending broad level screening offshore and retaining US workers to assess content that needs culturally specific assessments' (Chen 2014). There appears to be a growing tendency to seek out low-wage locations. Some aspects of content moderation can be automated – for example the identification of text strings or even of videos showing large expanses of human skin, a likely indicator of pornography, and there are increasing efforts to harness sophisticated artificial intelligences in identification of problem material (Roberts 2015). For the moment, though, human judgements are indispensable, and digital capital strives to cheapen the price of this cognitive and affective labour by the same offshoring process through which industrial capital slashed the costs of factory work.

Second, the content CCM moderators scan comes from around the world: bombings and beheadings from the Middle East, drug war violence from Mexico, spam from Nigeria, pornographic and paedophiliac images from globally exploitative industries, suicidal messages and screams for help from everywhere. And while a proportion of this can perhaps be ascribed to some irreducible component of human disturbance and pathology, its volume is also a testament to the immiseration and anxiety, desperate survival practices and exploited labour of people dependent on low wages and precarious livelihoods – the user-generated content of a planetary unhappiness factory. Indeed, from 2008 on, as the social media boom gained momentum, mounting numbers of CCM moderators were also to face an increase in disturbing content, as the consequences of a giant economic crisis of 2008 spilled into increased suicide levels, social revolts, street violence and war. CCM is thus, both in its immediate labour conditions and in the miserable material it processes, a manifestation of global proletarianization.

Planet and Zone

Over the last 50 years automata and networks have been instruments of the violent transformation of capital's working class into a 'global proletariat' (Roth 2010). In the previous four chapters we tracked some of the episodes in this transformation. We now attempt a planetary overview of the process and the role of cybernetic technologies within it. To reiterate the definition offered in Chapter 1, 'proletariat' names the class that must live by labour within capital. Although there has been a tendency to equate the proletarians with waged workers, Marx himself was clear that to be a proletarian was, by definition, a condition of precarity, constantly liable to ejection from the 'filled void' of workplace exploitation to the 'absolute void' of unemployment and social 'non-existence' (1964: 122). 'Proletariat' thus includes not only the human material that has been picked up by capital's vortex and is whirled around in its core as waged work, but also that which has been plucked off the land by mechanization, without necessarily being able to find employment, or has been ejected from production by cybernetic automation and communication and is forced to find unwaged subsistence in various forms of dependent labour, or is just dropped to the ground as so much living debris.

This overview therefore follows Roth's broad view of the 'global proletariat' as constituting a 'many-layered multiverse' composed of 'those classes and layers which have to sell or divest their labour power to the capitalist machinery of accumulation and regulation in order to survive' (2010: 219). Its portrait of cybernetic proletarianization includes the world-historical exodus of agrarian populations from the land as automation and biotechnologies disintegrate peasant cultures; the consequent formation of vast surplus populations engaged in informal and subsistence labour; the electronic supply-chain-enabled transfer of manufacturing work from the global north-west to Asia; the growth of a diffuse 'service sector' involving wage labour in the spheres of circulation and social reproduction; the mobilization of women both for wage work and unpaid domestic labour; and the escalation of unemployment, under-employment, and insecure labour and unpaid work.

These developments have to be set alongside de-proletarianiz-ing tendencies such as the expansion of professional and technical intermediate strata, and of capital's managerial sector, both of which fuel the worldwide boom of university and college 'edu-factories' (whose students would, however, in the crisis of 2008, face a scenario of abrupt re-proletarianization). Finally, the expansion of both proletarian segments and intermediate strata has to be understood as subordinated to the vertiginous ascent of capital's info-tech-armed '1 per cent'. The chapter concludes by suggesting that capital's very success in deploying high-technologies to decompose the mass worker formations of the planetary north-west and create a labour force of low-wage and precarious labour was a victory that set the scene for the crash, recession, and a new series of struggles.

These struggles would, however, be waged under conditions markedly different from those Marx and Engels imagined in *The Communist Manifesto* when they invoked the 'workers of the world'. They assumed an emergent proletarian solidarity was assured by the very processes of capital itself, as it disciplined and organized workers sharing a common experience of factory production, and connected them by the railway, telegraph and steamship. In retrospect, it is clear they massively underestimated the difficulties of this project of global class composition. Although in other writings Marx observed tendencies towards the segmentation of the working class, into fractions such as 'aristocracies of labour' amongst skilled workers or chronically unemployed 'lumpenproletariats', many consider that he never gave sufficient attention to such divisions, or to the possibility that they would become as deep as they have today.

In the 1960s and '70s a number of Marxist world-systems theorists took up this issue. They analyzed the relation between capitalism's industrial 'core' and a 'periphery' of formerly colonial possessions condemned by the 'development of underdevelopment' (Frank 1966) to serve as an apparently perpetual reservoir of raw materials and cheap labour. Samir Amin (2010) spelled out the radical conclusion: there was not one but two proletariats, one in the global North, the other in the South, divided in their condition, antagonistic in their interests, those in the North bought-off by various social-democratic settlements permitted by the affluence extracted from the super-exploited South, in whom alone revolutionary potential resided. This analysis informed a number of Third World Marxisms, and has recently been trenchantly revived by Zak Cope (2012).

During the 1970s and '80s, however, capital's supply-chain-driven restructuring disrupted the map of 'core' and 'periphery'. The rise of Asian 'dragons' or 'tigers', such as Singapore, Taiwan, Hong Kong and South Korea, followed by the emergence of Special Economic Zones in Asia and Latin America, and then the emergence of China as the 'workshop of the world', broke up the unity of the undeveloped global South. Some areas developed industrially, others slid into deepening misery. Although the economic dominance of the advanced capitalist powers of the United States, Europe and Japan remained in many respects remarkably stable, the conditions of proletarians in the South itself began to fracture.

By the 2000s a ruling discourse on 'globalization', usually celebratory, sometimes apprehensive, asserted that all traces of a colonial post were becoming insignificant in what Thomas Freidman (2005) declared 'the flat world' of universal capitalism. This view was strangely mirrored by Hardt and Negri's *Empire*, according to which a capitalism 'with no outside' constitutes an entirely 'smooth' space, with divisions between core and periphery holding little significance as workers of both become part of a common 'multitude' characterized by the diffusion of 'immaterial labour' – a view that attracted scathing criticism from African, Asian and Latin American Marxists (including Amin) for its fast airbrush of the continuing concentrations of capitalist power in the US, Europe and Japan, and sharp differences in living standards between global North and South.

Neither Third World-ism nor Empire-theory seems adequate to the situation produced by the cybernetic capital. The historical process of colonial expansion (itself driven by the need of capital to escape internal class conflict) produced a planetary core/periphery structure that was now, at a higher level of subsumption, thrown into confusion as the manufacturing capacity of the former industrial heartlands, and even some high-tech operations, were offshored. What activated this movement was precisely the wage and regulatory differentials between the former capitalist core and their one time periphery – the opportunities for cheap labour, cheap land and unprotected ecospheres. Conversely, however, outsourcing and offshoring also set in motion a reverse dynamics in which some supply-chain destinations attain sufficient critical mass of domestic industrialization to upgrade themselves as subsidiary or even rival centres of capital accumulation, with the 'BRICS' – Brazil, Russia, India, China and South Africa – often being cited as a case in point.

One way to conceive the new arrangements – although so far only partially theoretically developed – is through concepts of a 'zonal capitalism'. Theorie Communiste (2011) speaks of three geographical zonings of the world market:

> capitalist hypercenters grouping together the higher functions in the hierarchy of business organization (finance, high technology, research centers, etc.); secondary zones with activities requiring intermediate technologies, encompassing logistics and commercial distribution, ill-defined zones with peripheral areas devoted to assembly activities; third, crisis zones and 'social dustbins' in which a whole informal economy involving legal or illegal products prospers.

For TC, the critical point is that 'Although the valorization of capital is unified through this zoning, the same is not true for the reproduction of labour power.' In the first zone, 'high-wage strata' with privatized risk protection mesh with fractions of the labour force where 'certain aspects of Fordism have been preserved' while others struggle through precarious work and welfare. In the second zone, precarious low-age employment is the norm, with 'islands of more or less stable international subcontracting, little or no guarantee for social risks and labour migrations'. In the third, proletarian survival depends on 'humanitarian aid, all kinds of illicit trade, agricultural survival, regulation by ... various mafias and wars on a more or less restricted scale, but also by the revival of local and ethnic solidarities'.

This account of 'zones' recall Amin's 'worlds' – and it is important to note how much its hierarchy traces the legacy of colonialism and thus of a deeply racialized division of global labours. However, 'zoning' can be taken as designating a more porous and volatile process than the previous demarcations of first, second and third worlds. The zones are both repeatedly traversed by new proletarian migrations and subject to constant realignments of capital. Thus, for example, as wages rise in China's manufacturing sector, it becomes a core for its own peripheral low-wage zone in South East Asia and Africa, while conversely, deindustrialized sections of the former core slide sharply into second or third rank zones. In these zonal arrangements, class is both fractal and fractioned; fractioned in so far as the overall conditions of social reproduction vary sharply from one zone to another, fractal in that the basic relations separating capital, intermediate strata and proletarianization manifest across all of them in self-similar patterns, albeit in different mixes and ratios. It is better, usually, to be a proletarian in Canada than in China, and better in China than Chad, but in each zone capital leaps ahead of all other classes, while intermediate classes pull ahead of workers, who, depending on their permanent, part-time or precarious relation to capital, in different registers repeat patterns of lack of control over working conditions, relative impoverishment, and chronic insecurity. Thus we could say with *Gurgaon Workers News* that there is a planetary proletariat, but 'in local [or perhaps zonal] formation' (2010a).

A Note on Sources

Our whirlwind tour of the cybernetic vortex so far has drawn accounts of its currents and conflicts from a variety of sources, including militant inquiries by workers, participant-observer scholars, and reports by frontline-struggle organizations. To get an aggregate global picture, however, there is little choice but to rely heavily on capital's own great statistical agencies – the World Bank, various offices of the United Nations, the Organization for Economic Cooperation and Development (OECD), and the International Labour Organization (ILO), especially its *Key Indicators of the Labour Market* reports – and also some well-resourced corporate research ventures, such as those of the McKinsey Group, or the global wealth reports of Credit Suisse.

As all these agencies acknowledge, there are major difficulties in collecting and collating data on different types of work and worklessness, especially from the poorer and more devastated areas of the planet, many of which appear only as blank spaces in statistical series. There are also considerable problems in reconciling their varying definitions of categories as basic as 'work' or 'income'. Beyond this, however, there are also major problems in using these sources, arising from their ideological commitment to the success of the world market project, which often colours their categories and measures in such a way as to present an exaggeratedly rosy portrait of a globe subsumed by capital.

The boast of neoliberal capital is that it has lifted millions out of poverty. The internationally accepted definition of extreme poverty, at the time of writing, is an earning of $1.25 a day or less. Using this official standard the United Nations announced that the first objective of its Millennium Development Goals, halving world poverty between 1990 and 2015, was achieved early, in 2010. The share of total population in developing countries in extreme poverty fell from 43 per cent to 21 per cent. Much of this was due to the plunging of rural populations into the urban inferno of industrialism: China was responsible for three quarters of the achievement (Economist 2012: 11). There is little doubt that proletarian incomes have increased in newly industrializing zones around the planet. However, there should be some deep scepticism about the degree to which this amounts to an elevation 'out of poverty'.

Measures of increased income in the developing world partly reflect the transition of populations from subsistence economies largely independent of money to a cash economy (Leech 2014). Moreover, even within a monetary metric, the $1.25 day measure is, as Benjamin Selwyn, author of the important book *The Global Development Crisis* (2014a), notes, 'inhumanely low' (2014b). Selwyn observes that the author of this measure, World Bank economist Martin Ravallion, admits that it is 'extremely conservative', and goes on to note that if applied to Britain, $1.25

a day would be equivalent to '37 people living on a single minimum wage, with no benefits' (Selwyn 2014b). To this we can add that the US's official poverty line in 2013 was $63 a day for a family of four (Economist 2012: 11). This does not means that the poor in the US or other rich areas of the planet do not suffer egregiously, or that they are precisely 12.6 times better off than those in the planet's crisis regions: it does indicate both capital's zonal differences and the low-balling of the official poverty measure. Selwyn points out that many development experts contend that much higher income figures would be more reasonable: 'The London-based New Economics Foundation argues for $5 (US) a day. World Bank insider Lant Pritchett advocates $10 (US) a day.' Even by the current official measure, of some 7 billion alive today, 1.1 billion still live in extreme poverty, while a vastly largely number – the merely poor – are scraping by on less than $2 a day; by the $10 a day measure, '88 per cent of humanity lives in poverty' (Selwyn 2014b).

A similar scepticism is warranted in relation to the many claims about the size and wealth of an emerging global middle class. In two important articles discussing the global class formations revealed in the 2008 crisis and the 2011 revolts, Goran Therborn (2012, 2014) makes a cool appraisal of these claims. As he points out, mainstream economics and policy literature determines membership of this group almost entirely by income. It has become fashionable to declare that anyone who makes some small surplus over bare subsistence, and thus can become a 'consumer', is also 'middle class'. By these standards, the bar for membership of the middle class is an income anywhere between $2 and $13 a day. As Therborn observes, this is very far indeed from capital's utopian dream of 'boundless consumption, of a middle class taking possession of the earth, buying cars, houses and a limitless variety of electronic goods, and sustaining a global tourist industry' (2012: 17). In many cases, it signifies no more than possession of a reasonably stable job with a very modest standard of living. Therborn acknowledges the emergence of a new diffuse middle strata throughout Asia, Latin America and Africa, with an 'indeterminate' and 'heteroclite' position vis-à-vis capital, but suggests that the 'consumer dreams of liberal academics and marketing consultants are still largely projections into the future' (2012: 16).

The biggest difficulty in interpreting the official documentation on work and worklessness is, however, that the questions these agencies seek to answer are not ours. Class composition is a militant concept, aimed at an assessment of power and struggle, ultimately with a 'communist horizon' (Dean 2012). Such a horizon is one which official agencies either have no interest in, believing it vanished for good, or, if they suspect it persists, actively wish to suppress. They have other concerns: advising policy makers, informing investment decisions, promoting market-driven development, or, in the best of cases, such as the ILO, supporting social-democratic gains by organized labour. Their documents do not use class concepts, defining conflictual relations between groups occupying different positions in the relations of production. This is not to deny that important knowledge can be gleaned from these sources. They supply crucial data – providing it is always remembered that using these records to understand class composition requires reading against the grain and between the lines.

Labour Force

From 1980 to 2010 capital's planetary 'labour force' expanded from 1.2 billion to approximately 3 billion. This increase was not just a function of population growth, but also of deepening market penetration of the planet: the capitulation of the socialist bloc alone is estimated to have doubled the number of workers available (Dobbs et al. 2012: 3; World Bank 2013b: 3–4). Of course, capitalism has always drawn on worldwide labours: the slave trade, super-exploited colonial workers, and the peasantry of the periphery all attest to this usually brutal truth. What gives the idea of a 'global working class' (Mason 2007; van der Linden 2008; Struna 2009), or rather, we will argue, a 'global proletariat' (Roth 2010), credibility is not just the possibility of aggregating the sum of all labours directly and indirectly mobilized by capital, a reckoning that could have been made at any time in the last 300 years, but rather the systematic organization of this labour, in coordinated systems of production and circulation of a scope, flexibility and granularity that would have been impossible without cybernetic technologies, creating what capital's own analysts began to discuss as an emergent 'global labour market' (Dobbs et al. 2012: 1). Within this overarching process, we select seven main proletarian currents, and briefly note their relation to class and cybernetic technologies, and then proceed to a discussion of intermediate strata and capitalist composition (for a comparable listing of class composition tendencies connected to digitization see Fuchs 2008).

1) *The end of the global peasantry.* The subsistence farming that over millennia supported the largest part of the world's people in Asia, Africa and Latin America has for decades been eroding under a variety of pressures: the 'urban bias' (Lipton 1977) of capitalist and socialist modernizers; monocultural food export policies; the automated harvesters and genetically modified seeds of high-technology agribusiness plugged into the supply chains of the global food industry; land expropriations for urbanization or extractive industries (Weis 2007). Increasingly unable to sustain itself by farming alone, and dependent on periodic or permanent wage labour, the global peasantry is slowly disintegrating, in a process combining the coercive push of poverty and violent dispossession with the pull of wages and urban modernity (Wildcat 2008). To become proletarian is both emancipating and immiserating; the vortex blasts people free from local famine and parochialism, and into limitless insecurity and new subordinations; for young women in particular, flight from the land can be a liberation from traditional patriarchal repression, but in exchange for factory exploitation. This exodus fuels a new phase of the primitive accumulation that provided capital's early proletariat. In 1980 agricultural labour accounted for nearly half of global work, but three decades later it was closer to 35 per cent (Dobbs et al. 2012: 3). In 2010 for the first time more than half of all people lived in urban areas, compared with 1990, when less than 40 per cent of the global population did so, and representing an epochal break with the situation a century ago, when only 2 out of every 10 did so (WHO 2010; World Bank 2013b: 6).

2) *New migrations.* Workers are always nomads of the wage, but now in new ways ever more intensely regulated by capital's global labour market needs (Mezzadra and Neilson 2013). There are more than 200 million international migrants worldwide – some 3 per cent of the world's population, many temporary or seasonal workers, others moving permanently (World Bank 2013b: 14, 52). Remittances sent home by migrant workers amount to more than three times the world's total foreign aid, and in several countries for more than a quarter of the gross domestic product (DeParle 2010). There is debate as to whether populations are today more mobile than ever before. In the nineteenth century 10 per cent of the population may have migrated, largely on transatlantic routes to the North America 'new world'; in comparison, it is suggested, today's supply-chain globalization is actually more friendly to the mobility of capital than of people (Solimano and Watts 2005). However, if one takes

into account migration within national borders, the picture changes: the movement off the land in China alone over recent decades is often considered the largest in history. Today's migrations are certainly different from those of previous centuries. They follow new routes; they involve more women, many leaving families at home that they support by working to care for others abroad, or caught up in massive global sex trafficking operations; and they move at tempos shaped, on the one hand by new means of transportation and communication, such as the mobiles we examined in the last chapter, and on the other, by the barriers of smart borders and detention camps. These latter use the new technologies to scan, evaluate and filter different grades and types of migrant labour power (skilled/unskilled; entrepreneurial/refugee; permanent/temporary) with increasing precision according to national policies geared to the fluctuating priorities of the most locally influential sectors of capital.

3) *Informal toil.* Millions wash into the shanty towns of the vast conurbations of Asia, Africa and Latin America, creating what Mike Davis (2007) termed 'the planet of slums'. We have mentioned the 3 billion or so people now held to constitute capital's labour force, spoken of in official reports as enjoying 'jobs' and 'work'. However, contrary to what 'jobs' and 'work' might seem to suggest, not everyone in these categories is being paid. Far from it: of the 3 billion workers the World Bank numbers, only slightly over half, 1.6 billion, receive a wage or salary; the other 1.5 billion are engaged in either (or both) subsistence activities, still within or on the fringes of decomposing agrarian societies, or 'self employment'. The balance between waged work and unwaged self-employment differs both quantitatively and qualitatively and between developed and undeveloped sections of the capitalist world economy: wage work predominates in Europe at 80 per cent, versus 20 per cent in other categories, but these ratios are reversed in Africa (World Bank 2013b: 5). Even in the global North, self-employment does not necessarily mean a well-capitalized store or a business consultancy. Rather, it is often a fragile web-based micro-sales enterprise or nominally independent contracting work, utterly dependent on corporate supply chains or franchises – activities that can fairly be described as auto-exploitative forms of proletarianization. In the global South, self-employment generally means the survival strategies of street-vending, day hire, begging and huckstering. In India nearly three out of four working people are 'informally 'employed, either doing day to day piecework or buying and selling (Clifton and Ryan 2014). As we have

seen, this is the world in which the cheap cell phone becomes a crucial technology of urban survival.

4) *Neo-industrial proletariats.* Contrary to many information-society claims, the overall share of industrial work in global employment has been relatively steady over recent decades. What is more, total manufacture output more than tripled over the four decades from 1970 to 2011, increasing from \$2.58 to \$8.93 trillion measured in constant 2005 US dollars (United Nations 2013) during a period when world population did not even quite double. This is very far from fantasies of a 'weightless' or 'immaterial' digital economy. While large amounts of manufacturing work have been offshored from Europe and North America, significant tranches of industrial and other conventionally working-class labours survive, but increasingly in non-unionized, wage-tiered, casualized and deregulated forms. These are often crucial to capital's 'information-era' infrastructures; for example, the construction industry is now central to the creation of the wired, and wireless, built environments. Miles of cable are laid in building the giant data centres that send computing into 'the cloud', while construction of cell phone towers, often under pressure for rapid completion, is one of the most dangerous occupations in North America, with a terrifying incidence of falls, death and injury (Knutson and Day 2012).

However, industrial work *has* been transnationally reorganized, shifting from the former core of the capitalist system to its one-time periphery – declining by roughly one-third between 1970 and 2008 in what had been considered industrial countries but increasing steadily in East Asia, especially China. Exceptions are Japan, considered one of the old industrial countries, and South Korea, which industrialized early in the 1970s and 1980s, but from the early 1990s saw its share of manufacturing in employment and GDP decline (World Bank 2013b: 237–8). This generates new proletarian formations such as those we have already seen in electronics assembly in Mexico, Shenzhen and Batam. These formations in some ways resemble those of the mass worker, but are positioned in far more precarious conditions, both because of the agility of digital supply chains and the new intensities of automation – including robots – that can be bought into play by capital if worker organization puts upward pressure on wages.

5) *The multiplication of labours.* Across almost all regions the expansion of a diffuse 'service sector' outstripped both agricultural and industrial work. 'Service' is a notoriously amorphous category, encompassing a complex 'multiplication of labours' (Mazzadra and Neilsen 2013) including everything from high-end professional accountancy and consulting services to security guards, janitors and fast-food workers. Some service work is an adjunct of industrial operations, but much of it is describable in Marxist terms as an expansion of employment in the spheres of circulation (retail, advertising and promotion, sales, communication and entertainment), finance (or more properly 'FIRE' – finance, insurance and real estate) and social reproduction (health care, education, cultural production). Because of this heterogeneity there are huge differences in how cybernetics has touched different kinds of service work: some remains resolutely 'in person' – hairdressing is the conventional example – but others are now intensely mediated by information technologies and consequently in principle both globally re-locatable and increasingly subject to automation. An appropriately eclectic selection of instances includes not only the online content moderation discussed at the start of this chapter, but also virtual sex work, 'gold farming' in online video games, or the labour of digital scanning of various sorts, from bodies at airport security checks to books copied by Google.

6) *The 'feminization of work'.* This is a deceptive term, as women have always performed both waged work and the unwaged labour in the home that is the basis of the formal economy. It does identify an apparent long-term global tendency for more women to enter the commodified labour market (Elder and Schmidt 2004), though this trend slowed in the 2000s, and in some regions even reversed after the financial crisis of 2008 as women assumed responsibility for social caring activities cut by austerity regimes (ILO 2012). Part-time and vulnerable employment is common. Gender wage gaps between men and women persist; globally, women do twice as much domestic work as men; and, when all work – paid and unpaid – is considered, work longer hours (ILO 2012). The relation of this change in the gender composition of waged work to cybernetics is complex. On the one hand, it seems spurred by the machinic transformation in the labour process, as digital changes in the labour process remove requirements for physical strength that were at least the ostensible reason for men monopolizing certain industrial jobs, and by the accompanying expansion of the service sector. At the same time, however, the positions that women

enter in cybernetically transformed workspaces are often low wage and routinized. In high-technology industries themselves, the main levels of design and management remain predominantly male, with women entering mainly in service and support tasks.

These tendencies are especially pronounced when they are combined with the racialized zoning of the global economy. We have already discussed the gendering of the labourer on the global assembly line, with millions of young women in *maquiladoras* and export zones acting as the shock force of the value chain. There is another, related aspect of this, emphasized in Huws' original account of the 'cybertariat', which is the offshoring of predominantly female clerical work – the old Fordist typing pool – under new conditions of digitally enhanced Taylorism, now to a non-white but still largely feminized labour force. Such 'lift-and-shift' offshoring of back-office work, whether to independent third parties or 'captive' operations of large corporations, enables capital to fraction its costs, often to a degree where it can afford to solve problems such as checking of documents by a 'brute-force' employment of additional labour power, while at the same time benefiting from time-shifts to maintain round-the-clock operations (Dossani and Kenney 2003). Credit card processing for the US market has been done in Latin and Central America and the Caribbean for more than two decades. Business processing in fields such as payroll records, insurance claims, medical transcription, map digitization, and document entry and conversion, has been a third element, alongside software programming and call centres in India's IT industry (Dossani and Kenney 2003), creating what business ethnographer Shehzad Nadeem (2011: 4) does not hesitate to describe as a 'white collar proletariat' whose cheap and subordinated insertion into the value chain reactivates the legacies of colonialism.

7) *The rise of the edu-factory.* The increasing techno-scientific demands of capital are reflected in the global growth in the education sector, driven by a flood of aspirants striving for upward mobility, or at least to maintain class position:

> Families everywhere are trying to send at least one of their children to school ... This applies both in the developed world and in the global south. Since 2000, the global participation rate in higher education has grown from 19 to 26 percent; in Europe and North America,

a staggering 70 percent now complete post-secondary education. (Endnotes 2013: 34)

Such enlargement means, as Endnotes goes on to point out, that during the 2000s post-secondary institutions were being filled with the children not only of capitalists and the intermediate strata, but also (even if usually in different institutions) with the offspring of proletarian families, working their way through school or racking up massive student debts.

This was accompanied by the adoption of the 'edu-factory' style of post-secondary education, with an explicitly vocational mission, increasingly corporate management models, tight linkages to the corporate sector – to which an endless stream of unpaid interns were now supplied as free labour – and favouring STEM disciplines integral to technology development, for which the university now functions as both an incubator and a market (Edu-Factory Collective 2009). This development would also make the education sector a major service sector employer. In its sharp division between full-time, tenure-tracked faculty and legions of part-time, contract instructors and graduate teaching assistants, the university mirrored the wider fissures of cybernetic capital between diminishing groups of relatively secure workers and the growing mass of low-wage precarious proletarians (Bousquet 2008). This toxic educational class composition would explode in many places during the 2011 cycle of struggles, but before arriving at that point we should consider the relation of cybernetics to new forms of the intermediate strata that many students either aspired to enter or to reproduce their familial position within.

Intermediate Cyborg Strata?

The issue of intermediate strata, aka 'the middle class' has always been problematic for Marxism (Nicolaus 1967; Poulantzas 1973; Carchedi 1977; Wright 1978), and perhaps particularly so for its 'workerist' branches (but see D'Angelo 2010). Without pretending to resolve all the issues attending analysis of these intrinsically 'fuzzy' groupings, we will here just recall that in Chapter 2, our machinic approach to class defined such strata as those capital relies on to design the new means of production, or to supervise, train and socially reproduce workers adequate to this machinic apparatus, and therefore tends to place relatively highly in its wage hierarchies. Cybernetics has both created and destroyed such strata.

Global employment is conventionally categorized in three main sectors – agriculture, industry and services. Ever since the announcements of a post-industrial era, attempts to identify a fourth, specifically 'information', sector have been plagued with definitional problems, for today it is in fact hard to think of a job not in some way touched by digitization. The OECD recently adopted two measures of 'ICT employment'. One was 'narrow', comprising 'specialists whose job is directly focused on ICT such as software engineers'. A 'broader' measure included 'jobs that regularly use ICT but are not focused on ICT per se', including 'scientists and engineers, as well as office workers' but excluding others, such as teachers and medical specialists for whom, apparently, 'the use of ICT is not essential for their tasks'. In 2010 the narrow definition (specialists) accounted for between 2 and 5 per cent of employment in OECD countries, and the broader group for over 20 per cent of total employment (OECD 2011), with both on a rising trend; there seems to be no comparable data for countries outside the affluent OECD group.

These reports do not distinguish line-workers and supervisory labour. Nonetheless, they confirm the widely reported and observable emergence of new layers of workers strongly linked to cybernetic systems, growing from the early computer hackers of the 1970s into programmers, software engineers, application developers, network experts, web designers, systems administrators, security specialists and telecommunications workers, and spreading through the entertainment, advertising, administrative and financial sectors, and beyond to new cultural or 'creative' industries. The growth in technology-related work is often identified with a growth in jobs with 'middle class' salaries and status; this is a narrative that now has a global purchase, the promise of an IT based 'shining India' being a salient example. As we have already seen, this story is far from the whole truth. Huge numbers of jobs that involve direct work with networked technologies are routine, subordinated, precarious and poorly paid.

Nonetheless, the ILO suggests that over the last decade the number of 'professionals and technicians and associate professionals' in employment has increased in 'the large majority of economies'. In European economies these occupations accounted for more than a quarter of the employed in 2000, and developing countries, just below 15 per cent, and grew by 2 to 3 per cent over the subsequent decade, though faster in the developed than the developing group. The ILO ascribes these shifts to 'more employment in service sectors, automation and the increasing impact of information and communications technology' (ILO 2011).

ILO reports also show a ballooning category of workers involved in 'management' activities; in some advanced economies this purportedly accounts for as much as 15 per cent of the workforce (ILO 2011). This contradicts the common claim that information technologies have created 'flatter' and less hierarchical business organizations. One of the supposed benefits of computerization was to thin out not only Fordist industrial workers, but also costly middle managers, as personal computers gave a reduced number of higher executives digital access to vital command and control data. Apparently, however, the post-Fordist, Toyotist devolution of management processes has created a different dynamic. Supposedly 'flat' or 'nimble' information-age organizations generate huge numbers of team leaders, project coordinators, special consultants and in-house gurus, so that capital's elaborate management apparatus has not so much been abolished as reconstructed at a lower 'molecular' level.

It does therefore seem that the growth of cybernetic capital has been bound up with the rise of new intermediate strata assuming technical and supervisory responsibilities for capital. This does not, however, necessarily carry with it the connotations of either prosperity or security often associated with the term 'middle class'. Although it may do so in some contexts, in others it can mean a large number of professionals, technicians and lower-level managers experiencing stagnation or downward pressures on wages and conditions. This has been extensively documented in the literature on the sorry condition of the US 'middle class' (Warren 2014), which, while rife with confusing terminology, paints a plaintive picture of overworked and stressed families, with incomes sustained only by double-income households, shrinking benefits, increasing expenditures on child care and house work performed by proletarian nannies and domestics, and for their children's education, and chronic fear of the loss of jobs to automation or offshoring. (In 2013 a report circulated that a software developer at the US corporation Verizon had been discovered outsourcing his own $250,000 a year job to China for $5,000 while continuing to pull his full salary and passing his working hours browsing cat videos on social media; 'his' product was impeccable, and he was considered his company's 'best employee' [BBC 2013a].) In other wage zones the issue is not so much fear of falling as the inability to move up, to enjoy prosperity, autonomy and influence considered commensurate with the skills and training. The expansion of the intermediate classes with their contradictory locations and loyalties is thus constantly haunted by possibilities of re-proletarianization, so that in the crisis these strata generated radical movements of both left and right.

The Victory of the 1 Per Cent

In a notorious memo of 2005, the investment bank Citigroup affirmed that 'the world is dividing into two blocs – the Plutonomy and the rest'; this gave the name to Chrystia Freeland's *Plutocrats* (2012: 5), a study oscillating between voyeurism and critique as it paints a picture of the predominantly male, globally nomadic, super-achieving, banal-idea-oriented, philanthropic alpha-geeks, disproportionately drawn from the worlds of finance and high technology, owning shares and investments but also, to a much higher degree than past generations of robber barons, frenetically working as super-salaried executives to enlarge yet further the corporations they own stakes in (a situation in which one could truly say that capital owns the capitalist). This class is divided between mere millionaires, of whom there are about 29.6 million, less than 0.5 per cent of the global population, and the Ultra High Net Worth Individuals, with assets of over \$50 million, of whom there are 84,7000 (Credit Suisse 2011).

Silicon Valley's top tech magnates have regularly occupied Forbes' annual list of the richest people on the planet: Microsoft's Bill Gates clambering in and out of top spot, Oracle Corp.'s CEO Larry Ellison reporting a 2013 net worth of \$43 billion, Google co-founders Larry Page and Sergey Brin around \$23 billion each, Facebook CEO Mark Zuckerberg with a paltry \$13.3 billion, and Steve Jobs, and then his widow, Laurene Powell Jobs, with an almost trivial \$10.7 billion. In the minor leagues, one in five Americans with a net worth above \$30 million lives in California, stoked by the 'wealth-generating cluster' of the Silicon Valley (Mendoza 2013).

This, however, is not the most important measure of the importance of cybernetics to capital. Nor is the fact that a variety of ICT related companies – Apple and Hon Hai Precision in electronics, AT&T, Nippon Telegraph and Telephone in telecommunication, IBM and Hewlett Packard in information technology – can be found in a list of the 63 global companies with annual consolidated revenues over \$100 billion. Nor is it that a slightly different group of companies – Microsoft, AT&T, China Mobile, Apple, IBM, Google – have at various different times since 2008 been numbered amongst the top ten global companies in terms of market capitalization (i.e. share price multiplied by shares issued). Nor is it that a *Financial Times* ranking of the ten most profitable corporations includes Apple, Vodafone and Samsung. In fact, important as all these reckonings are, they show that ICT capital, while a significant sector of global capital, is in general nowhere nearly as weighty in its own right as finance, food, oil and energy, retail or several other groupings.

The real significance of ICT capital is what it has done for capital in general. The period of the rapid adoption of cybernetics – from the 1970s on – has been a period when the tendency to a reduction of global inequalities was not only halted, but sharply reversed (OECD 2011). As *The Economist* (2011b) observed: 'Globally, the rise of many people out of poverty has reduced income inequality, though many people in informal and illegal work have not benefited. But within most counties inequality ... has increased in recent decades. In most countries inequality seems bound to keep growing.' However, these divisions are in part internal to labour. As the classic mass worker of the global north-west declined, capital's labour force not only spread out across the world, but also bifurcated, like some amoeba splitting into segments, separating intermediate strata of professionals and technicians, a diminishing group of protected workers with full-time wages and benefits, and a sea of chronically insecure proletarians. Most extreme, however, was the gap between capital and everyone else. By 2013 the richest 1 per cent of the world controlled $110 trillion, or 65 times the total wealth of the poorest 3.5 billion people (Oxfam 2014): 'This concentration of wealth is based, in part, on the immiseration of the world's poor. The latter have seen their share of global wealth reduced over the last 30 years through falling wages, reduced social protection, rising unemployment and the privatization and despoliation of natural resources' (Selwyn 2014b).

According to the ILO (2011), labour's share in 16 developed countries dropped from about 75 per cent on average in the 1970s to 65 per cent just before the financial crisis. The shrinking labour share is even more remarkable because it is evident across 'rich' and 'poor' economies alike. The labour share of China's GDP dwindled to less than 50 per cent in 2008 from nearly 65 per cent in 1992. Although the explanations offered by various mainstream agencies for this growing inequality vary, these nearly always implicitly or explicitly emphasize the role played by capital's new cybernetic powers. The ILO estimates that 46 per cent of the fall in the labour share was caused by the financial sector since the 1980s, accompanied by an emphasis on maximizing short-term shareholder returns. As we have seen in Chapter 5, finance is amongst the most highly cybernetic sector of capital, now utterly dependent on algorithms, computerized risk modelling and high-speed network trading. The OECD, in contrast, attributes 80 per cent of the shrinkage in the labour share to growth in productivity and 'capital deepening' made possible by new information and communication technologies, which have led to 'unprecedented advances in innovation and production processes that boost productivity' and the replacing of workers by machines, especially in routine jobs (Wheatley 2013). Whichever of these two explanations is most correct, the message is the same: cybernetics enterprise has been capital's armourer in a relentless class war waged from above.

The Crisis of Surplus Humanity

The crash of 2008 arose from the very success of capital in decomposing its class antagonist. The defeat of the mass worker in the factories in the global North, and the erosion of the old Fordist welfare state that managed and administered the social programmes the mass worker had won, created a problem at the consumption end of capital's circuit. Wages and social costs in the centre could be held in check by automation and outsourcing, but a global low-wage economy also limited the purchasing power available to buy the goods streaming off the cheap-labour supply chains, causing over-production and a shortage of investment opportunities. At the same time – and in a reciprocal relation with this over-production problem – the growing costs of technological investments in increasingly complex cybernetic systems were beginning to cancel out whatever remissions computerization had given capital from its falling rate of profit tendencies.

Finance capital filled this void with bubbles of debt and speculation. Debt, via credit cards, mortgages or micro-finance, created the consumption power the global proletariat lacked – debt to be paid back with interest over lifetimes. Derivatives and other speculative instruments enabled capital to make money without actually producing and selling commodities, by gambling on the risks of its own circuit, as if independent of labour. However, the success of this flight from the source of value proved temporary: the bubble burst in the sub-prime mortgage crisis that disrupted the entire world market, setting off waves which, moving in complex and contrary directions, manifested simultaneously in the terrible slowness of US welfare lines and the speed-up of Chinese assembly lines.

When capital's contradictory need for low wages and high consumption collided in the sub-prime mortgage collapse that destroyed the US housing sector and disrupted the entire world market, cybernetic systems of exceptional scope and speed created the conditions for this runaway breakdown. Finance capital's 'money grid' distributed esoterically packaged 'securitized' sub-prime mortgages primed to explode like mailed time bombs. Once these started to go off, financial markets responded at speeds dictated by algorithmic trading programs sensitive to time-arbitrage possibilities existing for milliseconds. Thus the house of cards fell fast and hard, as defaults on sub-prime mortgages spread to a general credit crisis, paralysis of industrial capital, government bailouts, and fiscal crisis of the state.

It is reported that in 2008 President George Bush, confronting a tsunami of financial collapse set in motion by the failure of sub-prime mortgage bonds, and the news that his own Republican Party might nix the bailout frantically pulled together to avert the crisis, responded with the immortal words: 'If money isn't loosened up, this sucker could go down.' At the same emergency meeting, Treasury Secretary Henry M. Paulson Jr. 'literally bent down on one knee as he pleaded with Nancy Pelosi, the House Speaker, not to "blow it up" by withdrawing her party's support, prompting her to remark "I didn't know you were a Catholic"' (Herszenhorn et al. 2008). At this dramatic moment, as the leaders of global capitalism contemplate the possible collapse of the world market and suddenly acquire religion, we will leave this ruling class *tableau*, and, turning to those who would actually pay for their antics, attempt to summarize the situation of the global proletariat in zonal formations as the world slid into crisis (Roth 2010).

Within cybernetic capital, the proletarianizing process of incessant absorption into and ejection from waged work, in which different populations fluctuated in altitude above an ever present abyss of immiseration, had continued to provide the basic process of accumulation. Around the world proletarians emerging from peasant communities were, at least in monetary terms, better off than their parents. Everywhere, however, they were separated by a greater gulf from the condition of their class masters than ever before, and in ways more visible thanks to advanced media. They also inhabited a world in which the close coupling of cybernetically integrated systems meant that turbulences created an immense insecurity, so that improvements in living conditions could be dashed within the space of a few months by an alteration in technological conditions, or in a day by the millisecond fluctuations of financial markets.

The sudden paralysis of the key sectors of the capitalist economy following the Wall Street crash of 2008 intensified and threw into a terrible clarity the underlying problem of cybernetic capital – its vast 'over-supply' of labour relative to what capital was willing to wage (Alpert 2013). This over-supply was generated by the automation which replaced work of all kinds; by the networked supply chains, which, while they delivered jobs to the end of the earth, could as swiftly snatch them back again; and by the electronic financialization that severed accumulation from production. Cybernetics had at once enlarged the pool of workers on which capital could draw, and enabled capital to disassociate itself from these workers. It was the existence of a great, cybernetically created pool of un- and under-employed labour that was at the heart of the global proletarian condition.

In an important study at the peak of the crisis, John Foster et al. (2011) reanalyzed ILO figures depicting the global workforce; 1.4 billion were wage workers; 218 million unemployed; and 1.7 'vulnerably employed' – that is, labouring in informal, subsistence and unpaid work. Foster and his co-authors included their best estimates for the 'economically inactive' aged between 25–54 (students, criminals, and the chronically unemployable). Adding up these categories gave a figure of some 2.4 billion unwaged or unemployed labourers, compared to 1.4 billion in the 'active labor army' (Foster et al. 2011: 20). Two years later, the World Bank (2013: 6) would describe youth unemployment as 'still alarming' in many countries – above 40 per cent in South Africa since early 2008 and above 50 per cent in Spain in 2012. Even in countries where youth unemployment was lower, it remained twice the national average or more. In addition, 621 million young people were 'idle' – not in school or training, not employed, and not looking for work. Foster and his co-authors discussed their findings in terms of the classic Marxist category of the 'reserve army' of the unemployed. Even this category may be inadequate to the scale of the problem their work identifies, since it is clear that many of those in the reserve would never be called for active service: they were rather what Mike Davis defines with a yet bleaker term, 'surplus humanity' (2007).

The proletariat that was plunged into the 2008 crisis was both more segmented and more fluid than that envisaged by Marx and Engels. It was segmented in so far as its basic condition – exploitation in the work on which it must nevertheless depend for survival – had been divided and recombined in various packages, whose proportions and intensity of exploitation and exclusion varied, with different mixes for the secure worker, the various forms of precarious and informal labour, unpaid domestic housework, bonded toilers and slaves and the outright unemployed. These forms existed all around the world, but their distribution varied according to the zonal arrangements into which capital divides the planet. The segments were made fluid by various processes of de-proletarianization in which specific layers of workers, by their expertise or organization, had gained in security and prosperity, and even edged into various intermediate positions ambiguously situated between capital and labour. Yet these apparent gains were always subject to re-proletarianization, in which they could be lost to capital's new technical or organizational offensives, so that – as the 2008 crisis revealed – the floor might suddenly drop out from beneath apparently stable life conditions.

As austerity and depression unfolded, the urgent question was what, if any, political recomposition could arise out of the new class formations. Several different types of struggles around proletarianization were unleashed. Some had to do with diverse *new* proletarianizations, in the neo-industrial centres of Asia, the flows of un-and under-employed workers into urban centres in the Middle East, or in migrant communities in Europe. Others, however, arose from a '*re*-proletarianization' in which 'intermediate strata' – and students hoping to enter these strata – were abruptly blocked in their upward path (Rocamadur 2014), or even thrown back or trapped into a world of precarious wage labour: this is the line of the 'graduate student without a job' (Mason 2012) from Tunisia to New York, but also of other sections of the edu-factory, of precarious cultural industry workers and of hacker networks filled with laid-off or never-hired techies. The complexities of the 2011 uprisings arose from the interactions of these 'upward and downward' moving proletarians. As Roth observed: 'In the various global regions these segments stand in very different [and, we would add, often antagonistic] relations to each other', but between them there were also 'fluid transitions and networks' (2010: 220) – including the cybernetic networks of cell phones, the internet and social media, to whose role in the crisis we will now turn.

8

Cascade

In Front of the Office of the Governor

On 17 December 2010, following an altercation with police who had for years humiliated and harassed him, Mohamed Bouazizi – an indebted vegetable vendor, a toiler in the informal economy who, despite his poverty, was putting money towards his sister's university degree – stood in front of the office of the governor of Sidi Bouzid, a provincial town in Tunisia, North Africa, and shouted 'How do you expect me to make a living?' He then doused himself with gasoline and set himself on fire. Over the following months across the Middle East and Europe, over a hundred attempts at self-immolation in response to poverty and unemployment would be described as copies of this act, and these were a mere fraction of the wave of suicides and domestic violence attributable to the hardship of recession (Endnotes 2013; Alpert 2013; Taylor 2014; Gallagher 2014). Severely burned, Bouazizi remained in a coma until his death 18 days later. Almost immediately, however, angry protests broke out in Sidi Bouzid. News spread by media and internet inspired demonstrations across Tunisia which grew in scope, until on 14 January 2011 the corrupt and authoritarian government of Ben Ali fell.

Within a few days, the Tunisian Revolution catalyzed other uprisings throughout the Middle East. In neighbouring Egypt, on 25 January 2011 two million people converged on Cairo's Tahrir Square in the culmination of long-simmering revolt against the dictatorial regime of Hosni Mubarak. As the authorities blacked out social media, internet services and mobile phones, demonstrators fought pitched battles with security forces and regime supporters until two weeks later, with ten million protestors on the streets and strikes added to demonstrations spreading across other cities, and after over a thousand deaths and 12,000 arrests, Mubarak resigned. Together, the fall of the Tunisian and Egyptian regimes marked the beginning of what would become known as the Arab Spring, a decisive moment in the new cycle of struggles.

The austerity measures and bailouts with which US and European states responded had inspired a ragged series of resistances, winding from the US university blockades, to Iceland's ejection of a government in the pocket of 'banksters', French strikes, and British student occupations and urban riots. In Greece, where a debt crisis had been raging since 2007, youth battling police in the tear-gas-soaked streets of Athens posted photos of the confrontations on social media with the eerie message 'we are an image from the future' (Schwarz et al. 2010). The Arab Spring revolts thus extended to North Africa a crisis seething across the Eurozone, with its origins in the US.

The uprisings in Tunisia, Egypt, Libya and elsewhere had their roots in decades of popular struggle against repressive governments waged under conditions particular to each region, and to each country within it, but the economic convulsions released by the 2008 crash brought these to a boiling point. Popular unrest was intensified by the rising food prices caused by the globally inflationary effects of the Federal Reserve Bank's emergency dollar-printing policies, intended to stimulate a frozen US economy back into life. At the same time, contracting export markets for North African products, especially in the Eurozone, relayed the effects of the crisis to countries such as Egypt, where they pushed chronically bad un- and under-employment levels yet higher (Maher 2011). Thus although the North African revolts had their own very distinctive features and were propelled forward by their own sub-cyclical dynamics, they were also catalyzed by the wider turbulences of the capitalist vortex. In turn, the Arab Spring leapt back across the oceans: on 15 May 2011 it crossed the Mediterranean when Spanish *indignados* protesting youth unemployment took inspiration from Tahrir Square and occupied Madrid's Plaza del Sol in a massive encampment.

Then the Take the Square movement leaped the Atlantic. North American proletarians had confronted the near collapse of the system in a depoliticized condition, precariously employed, heavily indebted, saturated in hedonic media and frenetically speeded up by life in the heart of the cybernetic vortex. Union and social movement organization had suffered massive wear-down. Thus at the very moment when it seemed capital might annihilate itself, anti-capitalist networks went silent. Indeed, in the US and elsewhere, because of the left's silence, opposition to corporate power travelled right, to tea parties and militias denouncing big government, bankers and black presidents in a brew of right-wing populism.

In February 2011 the occupation of the Wisconsin state legislature by public sector workers and their allies protesting the revocation of collective agreements in the name of austerity seemed about to reverse this pattern, but then fizzled out. Then, on 17 September 2011, a few thousand people responded to an internet call to Occupy Wall Street, or, as it actually turned out, Zuccotti Park, a small plaza adjacent to New York's financial district. Modelling their assemblies on those of the Spanish *indignados*, and wearing 'Fight like an Egyptian' buttons, 'the 99 per cent' denounced inequality, debt and unemployment. At first a tiny protest, Occupy propagated rapidly across North America and beyond; on October 15, a Global Day of Action saw occupations or protests in 951 cities in 82 countries.

Meanwhile thousands of miles away and apparently a world apart, another wave of defiance was boiling. The speculative bubble that burst in 2008 had been pumped up with the investments generated in China. In the factories where this surplus was accumulated, labour unrest had pulsed since at least 2003. Although the first impact of the 2008 economic crisis threatened Chinese manufacture, and damped strikes, massive government spending ensured that economic growth continued, but also simultaneously intensified work pressure and tightened labour markets. During the summer of 2010, as Chinese workers struck at Toyota and Honda car plants, at the Shenzhen factory of Foxconn, the world's largest electronics assembler, 18 workers committed or attempted suicide, leaping from factory dormitories in protest against alienating conditions. As the labour turmoil continued into 2011, Occupy protestors received only a few messages of support from China, but the circulation of news, photos and videos about Foxconn certainly meant they knew where and how their computers and smartphones were made.

Time nominated 'The Protestor' as 2011's 'Person of the Year', with a cover portrait of a generic, internationally hybridized and androgynous figure wearing either a hijab or a balaclava-bandana combo. Yet even as this cover story appeared, the tide seemed to ebb. In the US, after two heady months Zuccotti Park was cleared by police and other occupations evicted. In Europe, Greek elections put the protest-aligned party, Syriza, within sight of victory, only to lose to the forces of austerity and face an increasingly vicious neo-fascism that turned the discontent against migrants. In Spain, Italy and France the agony of youth unemployment continued without respite. In the Middle East, the Egyptian and Tunisian revolutions yielded electoral victories for Islamists whose fundamentalism contradicted the aspirations of many activists. Protests in Bahrain were repressed, and in Libya and Syria spun into vicious civil war stoked by foreign interventions. If 2011 was an *annus mirabilis* for revolt, 2012 was its *annus miserabilis*, in which, as Mike Davis had foreseen (2011), 'Spring confront[ed] Winter'.

And then, in 2013, the squares and streets lit up again, in unexpected places. The plan by the Turkish government to build an Ottoman-barrack-themed shopping mall over a park next to Istanbul's Taksim Square hurled thousands into weeks of running battles with security forces. In Brazil, a campaign against the costs of public transport suddenly escalated into a wave of street protests that also took aim at political corruption and state expenditures on sports spectacles. In Sweden, haven of social democracy, violent conflicts exploded between immigrant workers and police in days of rioting. And in a horrible reprise of the self-immolation with which this chronology started, in Bulgaria five people incinerated themselves in suicidal objection to unemployment and corruption, setting off a wave of demonstrations and confrontations with police. And it went on: in 2014 the Turkish and Brazilian revolts flared up again, with deaths in the streets; regions of Bosnia were paralyzed by uprisings; and in Ukraine, in the largest and bloodiest 'take the square' uprising after that of Cairo, the occupiers of Kiev's Maidan (Independence Square) topple a kleptocratic government, precipitating geopolitical crisis as Russia then annexed Crimea and supported a counter-uprising in the Donbas region.

The social unrest that culminated in 2011 suddenly illuminated cybernetic capitalism's new class composition: the layers of surplus populations (dramatized by Bouazizi's suicide); the youth in the edu-factories, now suddenly re-proletarianized as 'the graduate student without a job' (Mason 2012); the neo-industrial proletarians who leapt from dormitories in Foxconn plants; and the myriad precarious, low-wage workers who filled squares from Cairo to New York. They displayed the divisions and confluences between secure and precarious workers, and the contradictory class positioning of the intermediate strata of professionals and technicians, who at some times and places marched and demonstrated together, or at least in parallel, with proletarian strata, as in moments in Egypt and Europe, and in other times and places mobilized against them, as in later turmoils in Thailand and Venezuela. These events showed the complex connections across and rifts within the global proletarian multiverse. And, as we have already seen, they raised the question of whether the same cybernetic technologies that brought this new class composition into being might be turned against capital.

Circulations, Cascades and Uneven Dynamics

The theorists of worker autonomy contrasted the circulation of capital, involving the realization of value in market exchange, with the circulation of struggles, involving the connection of resistances, creating networks of opposition to capitalist accumulation. In the mid 1990s the emergence of the anti- or alter-globalization movement coincided with growing access to the internet, open source software and creative commons production. The digital dissemination of the Zapatista call for resistance to neoliberalism galvanized a movement whose summit-busting manifestations, from Seattle to Genoa, included a central role for indie-media centres, weaving what Harry Cleaver (1995) termed 'an electronic fabric of struggle', circumventing the ideological filters of media capital. But as the tide of alter-globalization ebbed in the wake of 9/11, so too did the cachet of cyber-activism, whose speedy communication seemed to contribute to the movement's evanescence. As oppositional energies declined, capital recuperated radicalism in a commodified Web 2.0, fuelled by the free cultural labour and surveilled self-revelation of its users, apparently confirming Jody Dean's (2009) diagnosis of a 'communicative capitalism' capable of assimilating everything digital militants threw at it.

The uprisings of 2011 added another twist to this story. They occurred within populations and generations for whom the virtual was increasingly commonplace, even if access continued to be stratified by class, fraction and zone. The International Telecommunications Union (2013) estimates that in 2010, although 67 per cent of the population in the 'developed' world used the internet, only 21 per cent of that in the developing world did so, meaning that of the world population 30 per cent was internet connected and 70 per cent was not (these figures had by 2013 changed to 77 per cent, 31 per cent and 39 per cent respectively). A more significant development, as we saw in Chapter 5, was the mobile phone, which was ubiquitous, with 77 subscriptions per 100 people globally in 2010 (115 in the 'developed' world and 69 in the developing); three years later there would be 96 subscriptions per 100 globally, with 89 per 100 in the developing world (ITU 2013). Broadband service was a major marker of class and zonal division; in 2010, the 'developed' world had 43 mobile broadband subscriptions per 100 people, and the developing world 4, for a world total of 11; change was rapid, however, and by 2013 those figures were 75, 20 and 30 respectively (ITU 2013). The new struggles unfolded in contexts where, as Jack Qui (2009) puts it, the division of digital-haves and have-nots was giving way to gradations of digital 'haves' and 'have-lesses'.

The changes were qualitative as well as quantitative. With Facebook, YouTube, Flickr and Twitter, information capital seemed to have captured the radical practices of participatory user-created commons. In the pacified political climate of a US preoccupied with housing booms and infinite credit card debt, it seemed this corporatization of 'social media' would only contribute to consumerist subjectivities and capitalist revenue streams. What became apparent in 2011, however, was that when introduced into more explicitly authoritarian political contexts, such as Egypt, these platforms, even in the hands of a relatively small number of activists, recovered their subversive charge. This radical recovery was then relayed back up capital's zonal hierarchy of regions to Europe and North America, where these platforms were much more widely distributed (a Pew Research Centre [2012] survey found 28 per cent of Egyptian respondents used social media, 42 per cent in Spain and 53 per cent in the United States) in a new set of cyber-agitation practices, such as the repeated internet calls to 'take the square'.

The significance of this digital agitation in the new cycle of struggles is difficult to discuss because it has been so thoroughly fetishized in media reporting – as if, for example social networks, not unemployment, rising food prices and authoritarianism, caused the uprisings in Egypt, or no popular uprisings had ever been possible before Twitter. This 'Facebook revolution' trope does indeed, as Dean argues, vindicate high-tech capitalism by diverting critique of its problems to celebration of its gadgets, and often locks attention on the digitally well-connected, social-media-visible intermediate class strata, usually at the expense of manual labourers and the unemployed. To try and better understand the contradictory and uneven consequences of digital networks in the uprisings, this chapter suggests thinking not so much of a circulation as of a *cascade* of struggles.

The idea of a communicational 'cascade' originates in information science, mainly in rational agent theory, behavioural economics and network analysis with an individualist orientation, to explain 'contagion' effects in a 'collective action' such as a political protest (Lohmann 1994, 2000). It informs some liberal commentary on the 2011 protests (Fischer

2013; Shirky 2011). We appropriate the concept for class composition analysis to articulate how networks both link and separate vertically stacked class segments in a cycle of struggles. A 'cascade' of struggles is less smooth than a 'circulation', more chaotic and contradictory. It does not connect parts of a relatively homogeneous working class, as might have been imagined in the time of the mass worker, but traverses proletarianizations that are segmented, fractalized and fractioned.

The communisation theorists Woland/Blaumachen (2014: 7) argue that the 2011 cycle of struggles shows an 'uneven dynamic', with various forms of outbreak, each displaying differing class compositions. We will address three of the forms they identify – 'riots of the excluded', 'mass public space occupations', and workplace conflicts, or what they term movements for the 'revindication of the wage' – and add one other, 'leaks and hacks', to include the activities of Wikileaks and Anonymous. In this schematic approach, however, it is important to emphasize, as Woland/Blaumachen do, that there are many moments in the cycle when these different types of struggle overlap or combine, but then may separate again. This is precisely what makes a 'cascade' of struggles. With this caveat in mind, for each of these categories we will review the form of their struggles, their underlying class composition and their various cybernetic appropriations.

Riots of the Excluded, with Cell Phones

As Rocamadur (2014) observes, in the global North the break up of the old 'working class' has resulted in various forms of class fission. For many it leads to the 'the pauperisation of the wage', precarious deskilled services positions, chronic unemployment, unravelling of welfare provisions, and proliferating petty crime. These tendencies are often strong in old and/or new non-white migrant and minority communities, where 'new waves of immigrants [are] typically channeled into those very neighborhoods where opportunities and resources have been steadily diminishing' (Rocamadur 2014: 102). These areas effectively become segregated 'urban prisons' under heavy police control, in a 're-drawing of the social map of the cities and the penalisation of poverty' that creates a 'diffuse ghetto' inhabited by 'the new dangerous classes' (Rocamadur 2014: 101).

The 'riots of the excluded' involve minorities, migrants and those at the extremes of proletarianization, penned in segregated areas of cities or, in the case of migrants, in detention camps. An early example was the rioting by migrant communities in the impoverished sectors of Paris suburbs – the *banlieues* – in 2005. After the crash, austerity conditions, subtraction of benefits and intensification of policing worsened the conditions of these groups, and led to further outbreaks – often sparked by police killings: examples would include the 2008 riots in Greece, in 2013 in Sweden, the riots in migrant detention camps in France and Italy, and, in a situation unfolding as this book goes to publication, in 2014, in the US in Ferguson, Missouri.

The violence of these revolts resulted in condemnation not just from authorities but also from the left, who, while recognizing their social causes, lamented the lack of explicit political objectives. However, Woland/Blaumachen argue that this lack is intrinsic to the conditions of 'those who are radically excluded from the official circuit of surplus value', or, more accurately, integrated into it via 'inclusion by exclusion' as a 'carcerally confined form of cheap labour':

> They asphyxiate in a 'prison without bars' (when you cannot afford to leave your neighbourhood and you are constantly cornered by the police, you are imprisoned) ... by attacking the prison, by attacking all state institutions that define them as prisoners for life, they challenge in their revolt their social roles within the 'prison' they find themselves in. (Woland/Blaumachen 2014: 8–9)

Riots are not Facebook revolutions. The British riots of the summer of 2011, ignited by the police shooting of a young black man, Mark Dugan, started in Tottenham in North London, and then over four days spread throughout the capital and to other cities across the country, involving 'upwards of fifteen thousand people' in looting, burning of public buildings, and battles with police (Trott 2013). During and after the riots, British media and politicians excoriated what were variously described as 'Twitter mobs' or 'Blackberry mobs'. There was a grain of truth in this.

The major academic study of the riots found there was hardly any use of Twitter or Facebook to incite or organize rioting (Lewis et al. 2011). The very few people who did use these public platforms to do so were easily arrested and harshly sentenced. There *was* however extensive use of the Blackberry cell phone network, whose low cost recommended it to marginalized young people, and whose encrypted network provided a degree of security. As some rioters travelled quite long distances to get to the sites of conflict, and were operating on unfamiliar territory, such communication could be very useful for identifying targets, evading police, etc. (Lewis et al. 2011).

Fuchs is quite right to state that 'social media panics are a new element in the history of moral panics ... an ideology that abstracts from the societal causes of problems and inscribes these problems into technology' (2012: 385). Here they obscured the roots of the riots in police violence and harassment, poverty, inequality and the austerity regime elimination of social programmes and educational benefits (Lewis 2011; Trott 2013). It is also true, however, that rioters used the mobile as a weapon with which to take on the cybernetic apparatus of security – video surveillance, computerized profiling, predictive and pre-emptive policing, high-tech prisons – against which they struck back.

The London riots occurred at the same time as an extensive British student mobilization against university tuition increases, including militant demonstrations and campus occupations, which certainly did use social media. To some observers it seemed there was no communication between these two uprisings, though others find interaction along a seam of resistance to social cuts and police violence (Endnotes 2013b). The two do seem to have been largely separate in regard to media; student activists sympathetic to the rioters write of being appalled by the general torrent of condemnation on Facebook. Most of the social media traffic about the riots was from witnesses trying to find out what was going on, secure their safety, deplore what was happening, or to volunteer for the massive government-supported city repairs (Lewis et al. 2011). As one journalist observed, 'social media has its own class divide': 'Twitter as the "good" social network, used by upstanding citizens to mobilise cleanup operations', contrasting with 'BBM, a secretive tool for rioters' (Ball 2011).

Wage and Workplace Struggles: Exceptions and Rules

Steven Colatrella (2011) argues that up to Winter 2010, when the sequence of 'take the square' occupations began, the main obstacle to state austerity programmes was a 'global strike wave'. Thus he notes that in 'the single two-day period of October 21 and 22, 2010, while France was still largely paralyzed by massive strikes opposing President Sarkozy's attempt to change the retirement age', widespread strikes and actions were occurring all around the globe. His account of what was going on during these 48 hours includes strikes by workers at the Acropolis and the Piraeus port in Athens; Spanish air traffic controllers; firefighters in the UK; public servants and teachers in Trinidad; entry-level professors in Italian universities; workers in docks, jute plants and garment factories in Bangladesh; Turkish United Parcel Service workers; Chilean public sector workers; and workplace protests and demonstrations, several resulting in arrests, at Foxconn factories in India, Romanian docks, and in Egypt, South Africa and Central Europe.

Noting that this brief period was only the culmination of several years of intensifying global worker unrest, Colatrella identifies four main vectors of the strike wave: strikes by workers in newly industrialized zones; by workers in the logistics and transportation sectors, 'at docks, on railway lines, truck routes, shipboards, at customs and border crossings, at post offices, delivery services and on airlines'; by workers in the agricultural and extractive industries, reacting to price rises in the commodities they produced; and by public sector workers opposing austerity programmes.

In this very wide and heterogeneous range of global actions, some strikers were definitely using digital networks. One of the most telling instances came from the largest sequence of wage and workplace struggles, in southern China. Here the composition of the Pearl River workforce had changed significantly from that of the 1990s and early 2000s. A new generation of migrant workers had higher aspirations and better education: there were many students doing mandatory 'internships' in the Pearl River plants who hoped for something better than a factory future (Friends of Gongchao 2013a). Already in 2004–5, numerous strikes had occurred in factories in Shenzhen, forcing up the minimum wage. In 2008, at the start of the financial crisis, there was another outbreak of labour unrest. In the spring of 2010, as the Chinese government's massive anti-recession stimulus programme tightened labour markets, and hence improved conditions for activism, a new wave of unrest swept the area. Unrest that began at a Honda factory in Foshan spread to other automobile factories, and then to other industries.

The initial strike on 17 May at Honda was called through the sending of text messages, and it was also through such messages 'that certain workers persuaded their co-workers not to go back to work until their demands were met' (Beja 2012: 5). The strikers were part of what Qui (2009) has described as China's 'working-class network society', habituated to mobiles, online games and cyber-cafes, and keeping in touch with friends through the QQ instant messaging service and other social networks. In a strike situation, this resulted in a high degree of 'contagion' (Beja 2012: 5).

This was especially important because the workers struck outside of, and in defiance of, capital-compliant state-organized trade unions; in this context 'exchanges via Internet, weibo (the Chinese Twitter), and SMS made up for the absence of organisational resources' (Beja 2012: 5). Workers launched discussions and information exchanges about strikes on internet sites, and circulated mobile phone videos both of their working conditions and of attacks by thugs paid to break up strikes. They also displayed a strong awareness of the tactics of repression used by the government against other Chinese social movements, and 'used QQ accounts to circulate information to journalists, lawyers and human rights organizations' (Beja 2012: 5–6). All this contributed to a succession of victories in auto-plants and other industries.

As these strikes unfolded, the outbreak of worker suicides at the Shenzhen factory of Foxconn, where iPhones and other mobiles, laptops and game consoles were manufactured, seized global attention. The Shenzhen plant was vast, employing over 230,000 workers. It was characterized by all the negative features of electronic assembly work we have already met, raised to a new intensity in a combination of authoritarian, indeed 'militarized' management style, high-speed, high-intensity labour, high-risk machinery, toxic materials, body searches of workers, harsh punishments for 'offences', and crowded company sleeping quarters that separated workers with common backgrounds (Friends of Gongchao 2013a). These conditions appear to have been so severe as to preclude the organized militancy of the workers at Honda, leading instead to a form of protest by self-destruction (Chan and Ngai 2010; Chan, Ngai and Selden 2013).

Digital media and cell phones were also important at Foxconn, both in circulating the news of suicides within the vast plant – producing its own fatal contagion effect – and communicating it to first Chinese and then international media. Foxconn workers became objects of the 24/7 news cycle, generating searing investigative reports into their working conditions by the *New York Times*, and earning Steve Jobs widespread condemnation for his company's relation to Foxconn. This process was, however, then compromised by the fiasco of Mike Daisy's self-indulgently inaccurate radio dramatizations of the Foxconn workers' plight, in which it was revealed he had fabricated interview material. Partly as a consequence of the international scandal, the protest suicides did result in pay rises. But they also resulted in a grotesque public relations counter-offensive by Hon Hai, in the form of a carnivalesque party thrown at the Shenzhen plant to assure the world all was now well: workers in cheerleader costumes held up huge posters of CEO Terry Gou, reading 'Love me, love you, love Terry'. The falsity of this message would be revealed later in riots rather than suicides in Foxconn factories.

It is, however, important to recognize that the degree of media attention won by the Foxconn worker suicides was quite exceptional. The pathos of these youthful deaths; the brand fame of Apple, the company that indirectly drove its iSlaves to this end; the Chinese government's willingness to allow the exposure of scandals at a foreign, Taiwanese, factory; the existence of established anti-sweatshop networks; and perhaps even a subtle Sinophobia in the Western media's outraged response to rising Chinese industrial power – all these factors made Foxconn a very special case. Compared with the auto-sector strikes, where the use of networks for militant organizing was arguably far more practically effective than the tragic events at Foxconn, the latter garnered far more global attention.

Indeed, if we look at the scope and scale of the global 'strike wave' in the years Colatrella documents from 2007 to 2010, it is perhaps remarkable how little news of this seething unrest circulated. The youthful Shenzhen proletariat may, in fact, have been far more digitally adept at using networks than many, or most, other sectors of the global labour that struck or protested over this period, and were sometimes killed or imprisoned as a result. Although media coverage of strikes varied enormously from region to region, neither collectively nor individually did this mass of actions circulate and claim the global attention in the same way as Foxconn, which in some ways became an exception proving the general indifference of global media to labour struggles. As Peter Hall-Jones (2010) suggested, remarking on the indifference of media in the surge in actions by workers that included massive strikes in India, Egypt and Greece, many times outside of the framework of official trade unionism, it seemed that this response to the general crisis following 2008 was barely considered newsworthy. This contrasts sharply with the far greater publicity afforded other components of the post-crash austerity movements, illustrating the unevenness and contradictions that emerge in a cybernetically mediated cascade of struggles.

Mass Occupy Movements: New Assemblages?

Mass occupy movements assumed prominence from 2011 on with the sequence of 'take the square' protests running from Tahrir, to Puerta del

Sol, to Zuccotti Park, and then on to Taksim/Gezi Park and the Maidan. Woland/Blaumachen associate such protests with a 'fluid middle class':

> A middle strata [that] rebels because they are a collapsing middle strata (Greece, Spain) or because they are not allowed to constitute themselves as such (Arab Spring) or because they are much more repressed and economically squeezed compared to the pre-crisis period (Turkey), something that involves not only their lower-than-what-it 'should' be income, but also all other social relations, the commodification and enclosure of public spaces, gender, politics or politics-and-religion. (Woland/Blaumachen 2014: 9)

According to this analysis, the main participants in occupations were members of intermediate class strata undergoing or fearing re-proletarianization, and demanding remedy: 'By "occupying" they claim the right to their material existence as a subject facing the state, which they believe to be attentive to their needs' (Woland/Blaumachen 2014: 11).

There are, however, some important qualifications to this characterization of the Occupy movement's class composition. In its 'peak' manifestation, in Cairo, the 'take the square' movement became a mass insurrection, in which the re-proletarianized sectors of the Egyptian middle class – as Therborn (2012: 7) notes, 'largely composed of unemployed or underemployed graduates' – was, temporarily, alongside other strata. The interaction of the *shabab al Facebook* (Facebook youth) and the *shaabi* – 'lower classes' – was recognized by activists as a problem of the anti-Mubarak movement, and they went to some lengths to try and bridge it (Gerbaudo 2012: 48).

This included labour solidarity; Tahrir Square was prefaced by a long arc of strikes that middle-class activists of the April 6th Movement had actively supported. The renewed outbreak of strikes in the course of the uprisings in Cairo and Alexandria may have placed the last nail in the regime's coffin. Additionally, the occupation also involved, not riots, but street fighting, in which football fan clubs played a big part, so that 'the commune is defended against the police mostly by the young, male and poor part of the proletariat, which is experienced in fighting the cops' (Woland/Blaumachen 2014: 11). It also engaged 'hacktivists', such as those of Anonymous, working around the internet blackout with which the Egyptian government sought to damp down protest. Thus at its moment of crisis the occupation combines within or around it nearly all the elements of the 'uneven dynamics' of struggle.

Even occupations that did not attain this level of intensity were heterogeneous. In many North American Occupy Sites the homeless became part of the encampment (and a pretext for the 'hygienic' eviction of the occupation by police). Moreover, even though the very form of assembly protests tended to favour those who didn't have full-time jobs, some sections of organized labour played a supporting role, a circulation that developed furthest in the brief Portland docks strike in association with Occupy Oakland. The Maidan occupation, one of the longest lasting, seems to have undergone several recompositions, starting off as a student protest, then attracting more and more professional and technical workers and intermediate strata, and then drawing in proletarians from smaller cities outside Kiev (Ischenko 2014).

Nevertheless, the widespread involvement in occupations of precarious cultural, intellectual and technical workers, and students with or without jobs, meant that the frequent press description of such activists as 'media savvy' was fairly accurate. These are the forms of struggle for which the 'Facebook [or Twitter] revolution' designation is most credible. In these movements there is high degree of transfer between the net and the square. Writing of the Spanish *indignados*, Victor Sampedro and Jose Sánchez Duarte (2011) claim that '*La red era la plaza*' (The net was the square) – that is, the horizontalism of assembly organization was an embodiment of online social media practices. In contrast, Gerbaudo (2012) insists that the net was *not* the square, precisely because protesters recognized the need to get off social media and 'take it to the street'. Between them, these counterpoint opinions catch the two sides of the repeated interaction between bodies and networks characteristic of mass occupy movements.

In the cycle of occupations a recognizable sequence to these net/square interactions gradually emerged. First came an internet call to occupation: in Egypt the summons on the *We are all Khaled Said* blog, commemorating a young man killed outside a cyber-cafe by security police – 'each one … forget[s] the fear and goes down from his house on January 25th with one goal'; the 'Tomme la calle!' (Take to the streets) with which *Democracia Real Ya!* (Real Democracy Now) launched Spain's 15-M *indignado* encampment; the *Adbusters* blog posting of the hashtag #occupywallstreet with an exhortation for '20,000 people to flood into Lower Manhattan'.

This is followed with a descent to more terrestrial community organizing, either before or in the early stages of the occupation, during which leadership elements may shift significantly.

As the occupation begins, there is circulation of news about the protest on, in varying proportions, Facebook, Twitter, YouTube and blogs, and more calls for support. Meanwhile the daily life of the commune, including protection from or negotiation with security forces, and arrangements for food, sleeping, washrooms, security, is organized, with much of the coordination via social media and mobiles making it an alternative centre for 'social reproduction' (Thorburn 2015). Net sites become the place for the issuing of demands and manifestos, or of insisting no manifestos or demands be issued. Interaction with other media become critical; the interactions of Tunisian and Egyptian protesters with Al-Jazeera, and of OWS with the New York media, showed that if protest could even briefly hegemonize digital space there was a possibility of reversing the vicious spiral of media silencing dissent, generating instead a virtuous spiral of amplification. As the 'take the square' movements spread internationally, they learned from each other about the choreography of struggle; the *indignado*'s manual for holding general assemblies was distributed in the initial calls of OWS; young people fighting police in Taksim Square messaged to supporters that they had watched other occupations and 'knew what to do'; in Ukraine, where Jehane Noujaim's film about Tahrir, *The Square* (2013), was banned at the time of the Maidan protests, occupiers nonetheless 'organized a public screening of the film right on the square among the barricades' (Matviyenko 2014: 28).

A subset of mass public occupations is the anti-austerity student movements such as those in Chile, Canada, the UK and France, which combine elements of assembly and riot (Woland/Blaumachen 2014: 9–10). In these movements of youth 'who find all the doors closed, who are not going to climb the ladder of social mobility', but are not totally excluded in the same way as those from urban ghettoes, there is an exceptionally high degree of networked sophistication and activity. Thorburn (2014) reports on the use by Quebec students in the anti-cuts movement of roaming teams of videographers transmitting live stream video to student-run television stations, operating both as a form of counter-surveillance against police violence and as a means of building and maintaining support of the movement. It is instances such as the mass occupations and student blockades and protests that perhaps provide the best case for seeing elements of the 2011 struggles as involving not only assemblies but also a new 'assemblage' of protestors and network technologies expropriating the forces of cybernetic capitalism (Thorburn 2014).

By the same token, however, the class composition of the occupations, with their important intermediate strata components, set the limits to how far this new assemblage would go in struggle. Woland/Blaumachen suggest that the major horizon of the mass occupy movements was 'a better management of the bourgeois state' (2014: 12) – expressed either in the demands for a change of government, or in a chaotic medley of reform proposals.

As the cycle went on, there were increasing tendencies for sections of the intermediate strata to take to the streets not against capital, but for it. In Brazil, a movement that shook the centre-left government of the Partido dos Trabalhadores (Workers' Party) – reportedly involving a 'gigantic quantity' of protestors 'working in telemarketing, with college degrees' – began with progressive demands for reducing the price of public transport and increases to social services, then became mixed with right-wing anti-corruption activists in a chaotic street melange of 'déclassé youth', 'inflation hit middle classes' and 'new proletarians' (Singer 2014; see also Saad-Filho and Morais 2014). In Venezuela and Thailand, Occupy-style tactics become the preferred practice of middle-class movements trying to roll back the gains of the poor.

In Spain and North America, the physical occupations were eventually evicted, and their social media flows dissipated, with some transplantation of energies into other projects. Elsewhere, in Cairo or Kiev, occupations declared as victories the securing of a change in government, broadly within the frame of liberal electoral democracy. These were outcomes which often fell short of the more radical aspirations raised in the struggle. In Egypt, the liberal and secular elements were defeated in elections by the fundamentalist Muslim Brotherhood, and then reversed this decision with the support of a military coup that fully restored the army to power. In Ukraine, an initially liberal-nationalist movement against state corruption opened itself, in the midst of the struggle to hold Kiev's Maidan, to the combat power of a small but well organized far right – whose presence provoked a counter-uprising in the Donbas, and then Russian invasions (see Ischenko 2014; Radynski 2014a, 2014b). In both Egypt and Ukraine, 'the fall of the government marks the end of the movement' (Woland/Blaumachen 2014: 12).

Leaks, Hacks, Masks, Arrests

The 2011 cascade also included a subset of cybernetic actions, digital leaks and hacks, virtual exploits with ramifications 'on the street': these included the disclosures of Wikileaks; the retaliatory actions of the US state; the counter-strikes by Anonymous, and, in turn, its targeting by the security apparatus; and then, some years later, Edward Snowden's disclosures about the scope of US national and international surveillance.

Wikileaks grew from Julian Assange's situation at the intersection of hacker movements with the alter-globalism of the late 1990s. Manning, its most famous and most severely punished informant was, like Snowden later, a defector from a relatively low rank but high security clearance position in the US cybernetic military-security complex. Wikileaks also involved journalists, lawyers and parliamentarians professionally committed to freedom of speech and information, alienated from the post-9/11 US security state, and/or active in anti-austerity struggles. Its major sequence of leaks started with the release in April 2010 of the Collateral Murder footage of American helicopter attacks on civilians in Iraq and proceeded with the disclosure of more secret military documents in the Afghan and Iraq War Logs. It culminated on 10 November 2010, the date international newspapers cooperating with Wikileaks published major stories about the 'Cablegate' leak of thousands of US diplomatic messages. The overlapping of Wikileaks with the 2011 street movements was in part a coincidence, but its revelations resonated with their protests against systemic corruption, and sometimes fed directly into the revolts, as when release of unflattering US communiqués about the Ben Ali regime stoked the Tunisian uprising.

Anonymous arose from the transformation of 4chan, an amorphous network of internet pranksters, into a political assailant of internet restrictions and abuse (Deterritorial Support Group 2012). This politicization proceeded by way of an epic battle with the Church of Scientology, but directly confronted US capital when at the end of 2010 Anonymous came to the defence of Wikileaks, whose network access and funding sources were now threatened by a US state-prompted corporate blockade. Anonymous' 'Operation Avenge Assange' launched or attempted denial of service attacks against PayPal, Visa, MasterCard and Amazon. In 2011, Anonymous members assisted Tunisian and Egyptian movements in defying internet bans or evading surveillance, and there may also have been Anonymous denial of service attacks against the Turkish government at the time of the Taksim Square occupation. Anons participated in the early organization of Occupy Wall Street, and attempted cyber-attacks on the New York and London stock exchanges. Although the class composition of Anonymous is intrinsically opaque, and is almost certainly very heterogeneous, it clearly represents a proletarianization of the hacker tradition through the access to relatively easy to use hacker tools available to young people socialized in virtual games, chat rooms and music piracy.

The Anons also, however, provided a wider iconography for the 2011 cycle of struggles. The Guy Fawkes mask from the film V for Vendetta showed up on streets and squares from Cairo to New York to Istanbul. Some of those wearing it were Anons, but others were just ordinary protestors. Masks as symbols of resistance to observation and identification by power run from Zorro to Subcommandante Marcos, but the Anon mask may also have a wider set of connotations. In a discussion of the 2011 cycle, Endnotes (2013: 51–52) suggest that in an era of surplus populations and precarious labour, when capital can swap out its human components almost at will, there comes to be something profoundly disposable, fungible and inter-changeable in conditions of contemporary identity. The Anon mask can perhaps be taken as defiant adoption of this 'facelessness' of contemporary proletarianization as a marker of revolt.

The hacktivists connected in an uneven way with the other parts of the struggle cascade. They wielded arcane technical expertise, sometimes from the shadows, sometimes with a manifest elitism, which in the case of Assange's charismatic vanguardism became problematic in several ways. Their specific concerns with freedom of internet speech didn't directly correspond with the issues of jobs, evictions and debt that drove many people to the streets and squares – nor did they attempt to formulate a political horizon that included such matters. Nonetheless there was a general articulation with popular outrage at an unaccountable, venal power.

The hacktivists were, however, themselves vulnerable to the cybernetic wars they unleashed, and were largely quelled by the digital apparatus they took on. In the battle of surveillance against sous-veillance, the leakers and hackers ultimately could or would not maintain anonymity, and once identified the retaliation was implacable. By the end of 2011, the US attack on Wikileaks had paralyzed its activities; Manning was awaiting trial, snitched out by hacker friends, and Assange had sought asylum in London's Bolivian embassy. Anonymous also seems to have been disrupted by the informant penetration that followed its anti-corporate activities, with dozens of arrests. After these events, what rendered Snowden's revelations about the extent and scope of the surveillance apparatus particularly heroic was that they were made with a clear recognition that he could only hope for a brief window of time before he faced arrest or flight (and even this clarity could not save him from the paradox of finally seeking refuge in authoritarian Russian klepto-capitalism).

Ultimately capital's cybernetic dominance – despite its many short-term reversals and skirmish defeats – afflicted all parts of the 2011 movements. 'Twitter protests' were followed by 'cyber-crackdowns', whether by subpoenas from social media and cell phone companies, pre-emptive police hacking of activist accounts, or the scanning of media and security camera video feeds to identify rioters and protestors. Cybernetic capital may have turned everyone into so much anonymous labour power, but when that labour power stepped out of line, or even near to the line, the police could digitally identify the perpetrators. As the wave of insurgencies gradually ebbed, everywhere that regimes had not fallen (and sometimes where they had) movement participants became increasingly aware of this vulnerability, with chilling effect.

Over the Cliff

The most powerful influence of cybernetics on the movements of 2011 was capital's preceding deployments of technology to slice and stratify what was nonetheless a global labour force. This created initial conditions of proletarian decomposition and weakness but also possibilities of connection. The reappropriation of commodified social media offered a way of countering divisions, but also in some ways replicated those fractures. Circulation of struggles occurred within the forms characteristic of particular class segments – notably amongst the mass public occupations, and between them and hackers and leakers, and also within strikes in China and perhaps elsewhere – but not so much between riots, wage struggles and occupations. Occupiers were aware of rioters and strikers, though practical links were few or non-existent, and suspicions and antagonisms were often high. Certain moments cut through this, as at the peak point of struggles in Egypt. At an overall level, the simultaneous visibility of different levels of struggle gave a sense the whole system was breaking down.

It is this coexistence of circulation and segmentation that characterizes a cascade of struggle. Cascade suggests a stepped process, as when a flow of water tips over a rugged cliff, here making small falls from one prominence to another, there pooling in declivities and going nowhere, in other places hurtling off long falls with incredible velocity. In one sense, however, cascade is not a good term, because it names a trajectory from above. Although this might be true in so far as the 2008 Wall Street crash was precipitated by capital, it is deceptive in so far as once the crisis was underway its momentum came from below, as an uprising. We might, therefore, think of the 2011 uprising as an inverted cascade: a fountain, perhaps – but a fitful one.

The struggles of the cycle were fought on the basis of a divided proletariat's 'uneven dynamics', segmentary subjectivities, limited horizons and fractioned class capacities. Thus the 'riots of the excluded' proceeded largely outside of any articulated political horizon, flared up and went down – until next time. Wage struggles, where they were not simply defeated, as they usually were, could be contained by ... wage increases; in China, strike waves subsided as the price of labour rose. Leakers and hackers, however startling their exploits, paid a very heavy price for them. Occupy movements generally failed to extend themselves out of the squares, to the mass of service and industrial labour and pauperized communities; they did not go, at best, beyond regime change, and usually fell far short.

Proletarian movements against capital must make use of cybernetic communication, because they are in a profound way inside such systems, and indeed of them, formed under conditions of technological subsumption that have for a generation shaped workplaces, worker subjectivities and popular cultures: it would be extremely difficult to riot effectively, organize dispersed and intermittent workers, or occupy not just a square but anywhere else for any time without using networks. That uprisings in the past proceeded without such technologies is largely irrelevant, because the effect of cybernetic subsumption is to remake the structure not just of labour but of everyday life within the digital medium, so that to step entirely outside is to be invisible – which may from time to time be tactically advantageous, but is a long-term strategy of oblivion.

At the same time, cybernetics, perhaps to a greater degree than any other technological system, has been designed and implemented for capital's vortical dynamic of abstract value. Digital technologies such as the internet 'annihilate ... space with time, to turn over capital in the "twinkling of an eye"' (Marx 1973: 538–9). They offer near real-time global communication that can be scanned, stored and replicated. These features, introduced in a military context, have been enhanced by capital to accelerate, amplify and intensify the circulation of commodities. The reappropriation of such technologies in struggles therefore circulates news quickly, but without building trust; enables the fast start-up of struggles, but also their ephemeral fragmentation; can give an extraordinary visibility to anti-capitalist militancy, but also subjects it to omnipresent surveillance. Wide in scope, weak in ties; fast but evanescent; unstoppably viral but surveilled; these cybernetic properties mean that proletarian movements can and must use such systems even while working against their bias to develop the longer term strategies, solidarities and safety that cybernetics tends to nullify (Pietrzyk 2010). This paradox is, however, part of a larger conundrum: to overcome the force that exploits it, a proletariat segmented by the operations of supply chains, internet markets and financial algorithms must destroy the very divisions of which it is made – and in doing so abolish its own identity. Can the global proletariat use cybernetics against capital? Yes, but only by simultaneously being against what it uses. This is only a subset of a larger question: can the global proletariat be against capital? Again, yes, but only by being against itself.

9

Aftermath

Better than Ever?

Some seven years after the Wall Street crash, it seemed the crisis might be safely narrated as the survival story of a system that had taken a near crippling blow, but marshalled its resources for a massive effort of containment, sealed off the most acute danger zones, and rode out the peril. Struggles continued to circle the globe, as a version of Occupy hit Hong Kong, or burst up out the streets of racialized deprivation zones like Ferguson, Missouri. In Greece, the anti-austerity party, Syriza, again seemed to have a chance of electoral victory, though only at the cost of damping down its radicalism. But 2011, the 'year of dreaming dangerously' (Žižek 2012), when revolts were everywhere, had passed. In many places, squares or streets that had been filled with occupiers, tear-gas, or blazing police cars, were again fully normalized locations for shoppers and panhandles. Memories of revolt seemed falsified, as if they never really happened at all – a testament to the power of 'capitalist realism' (Fisher 2009) to erase all traces of disruption. Elsewhere, in a contrary but complementary oblivion, the hopes of revolt were also overridden, but by catastrophe. In Ukraine as well as Syria and other areas of the Middle East, rebellion was followed by military interventions and civil wars, so that the optimistic images on social media of thousands thronging the squares against tyranny were replaced with real and simulated atrocity videos. Regimes had fallen, but nowhere had they been replaced by an alternative to the rule of global capital. Observers such as Philip Mirowski (2013) suggested that the neoliberal forms that brought on the crisis emerged from it even stronger than before.

How far this apparent resilience went was, however, uncertain. In the crash of 2008, the bottom dropped out of the continued expansion of wage labour in the advanced sectors of global capital. The immediate effects in terms of job-loss were dramatic. Even more telling were the longer

term problems of the period of so-called recovery, in which employment
in some key wage zones ominously refused to return to pre-recession
levels. In the 1980s and '90s there had been a spate of speculation about
how computerized automation would result in 'the end of work' (Rifkin
1995), including from Marxists such as Ramin Ramtin (1991) and Stanley
Aronowitz (1994). Within a decade, these speculations seemed to have
been disproved by capital's globalization of its labour market. The option
of replacing workers with expensive robots was dissipated and reversed by
that of finding cheap labour at the end of networked supply chains. The
growth of media, communication and internet industries – all accelerating
the circulation of capital – seemed to negate the work-destroying aspect of
computerization and rather incite whole new fields of 'immaterial labour'
involved in an explosion of networked human to human interaction.
Capital's separation from labour *tout court* was replaced with disassociation
from any *particular* labour, in any specific place – that is to say, by the
making of a global proletariat.

   The possibility that the vast pool of workers was surplus to capital's
requirements was partially hidden by precarity and informality. When the
consequences of a low-wage global economy became apparent in terms of
inadequate consumption and stalled investment opportunities, the slack
was taken up by financialization and credit at individual and national
levels, so that debt, personal or collective, becomes a feature of proletarian
existence. Once that bubble burst, however, unleashing a torrent of global
unrests, the automating option reappeared. Everywhere cheapened labour
has revolted the option of technologically eliminating it returns to the
table, enhanced by new generations of robots emerging from early twenty-
first-century wars, and increasingly directed not just against manual
work, but at the white-collar jobs of intermediate positions once imagined
as secure. With the growth of social media – the greatest part of which
has come since 2008 – the destination of the internet is revealed as a
vast harvesting of algorithmic data to codify, predict and even machine-
delegate consumption activities, while post-crash finance exhibits a
renewed determination to leap directly from money to more money by
means of high-frequency trading and other network exploits, by-passing
both production and consumption. Globalization's planetary cheap labour
market, the apparent remedy to capital's cybernetic drive to automate
workers out of existence, has not cured this compulsion, but merely
generated a set of baroque complications overlaying the initial condition,
which now explodes again with incubated virulence. Cybernetics'

combination of networks and robots exemplifies capital's process as a 'moving contradiction' that absorbs labour, technologically transforms it, and then ejects it. This simultaneous attraction and repulsion of labour by capital continues, but its apparently circular process is not a symmetrical, equilibrium process, with job losses and gains balancing; rather, an initial period of high absorption (the globalized search for cheap labour) is being followed by an accelerated ejection. In this chapter we will look at three instances of this tendency – automata, apps and algorithms – and at their implications for class composition.

Robots

At a closed retreat in late July 2011, shortly after the worker suicides at Foxconn, Terry Gou, the chief executive of the company, unveiled a plan to 'hire' 1 million robots by 2013, claiming that the company would move its human workers 'higher up the value chain' and into 'sexy fields' such as research (Markoff 2012). *The Economist* was more to the point, observing that 'Robots are easier to manage'; they 'don't complain. Or demand higher wages, or kill themselves' (2011b). According to China's official Xinhua news agency Gou himself was franker on a later occasion, when speaking of his more than 1 million employees worldwide, he said: 'As human beings are also animals, to manage one million animals gives me a headache' (Markoff 2012).

Foxconn subsequently appears to have had difficulty in meeting this automation target, with only limited numbers of 'Foxbots' so far deployed for electronic assembly. It continues to pursue the option of finding labour in other low-wage locations, such as Western China, Indonesia or Brazil, less in the global spotlight as those at the now notorious Shenzhen plant (BBC 2011; Kan 2013; Xuena 2013). Nonetheless, Gou's plan was indicative of a broader trend. China's apparently unlimited supply of cheap labour was becoming too expensive. Worker struggles drove up wage rates; peasant protests compelled the government to improve conditions in rural villages, decreasing the flow of migrants; youth started shunning factories. One result was that Chinese capital itself started to 'globalize', investing for example in areas of Africa such as Ethiopia – 'where factory wages of about $40 a month [are] less than 10 percent the level in China' – Tanzania and Senegal (Hamlin et al. 2014). At the same time, however, it also started pouring funds and talents into machinic options – becoming the world's largest market for industrial robots (Durfee 2012); in a 'man-bites-dog' scenario during the 2010 Pearl River strike wave, one of the factories affected was the Chinese plant of Japan-based Denso, the world's largest manufacturer of small assembly automata.

There were 3,000 industrial robots in the world in 1973, 800,000 in 2003 and 1.1 million in 2011 (IFR 2012). Worldwide shipments of robots grew more than threefold between 1994 and 2012, rapidly rebounding from a post-crash slump in 2009. In 2013, about 179,000 industrial robots were sold worldwide, again an all-time high and 12 per cent more than in 2012, a previous record year. Asia was the largest site for robotics (in 2013, every fifth robot sold in the world was installed in China), but sales were also high in the United States where between 2008 and 2013 annual sales of industrial robots increased by 12 per cent on average per year (IFR 2014). The main sectors for robotics introduction were in automobiles, metals and machines, but sales were also high in pharmaceuticals, electronics and foods. In addition to industrial robots, there is a growing category of service robots, which unlike industrial robots are 'not defined as having to be fully automatic or autonomous, but may assist a human user or be tele-operated' (IFR 2014); these include domestic servant robots, personal mobility assistance robots, pet exercising robots, cleaning robots for public places, delivery robots in offices or hospitals, fire-fighting robots, rehabilitation robots and surgery robots. In 2012, about 3 million service robots for personal and domestic use were sold, 20 per cent more than in 2011, but the largest single category was defence-related service robots (IFR 2014).

From 2001 on, the war on terror spurred military robotic development, particularly in the area of autonomous vehicles, both aerial and terrestrial: the US forces deployed in Afghanistan and Iraq were indeed 'robot armies', because of their dependence on such vehicles for drone reconnaissance and attack, bomb disposal and transportation (Singer 2009). In 2012 DARPA, the same agency that financed the early internet experiments, announced a competition aimed to encourage US capital to 'build and demonstrate high-functioning humanoid robots' by the end of 2014 (Brynjolfsson and McAfee 2014: 33).

Post 2008 a distinct US robotics complex was forming, centred in the Boston region, initially driven by military contracts, but increasingly funded by massive information corporations such as Amazon and Google, and connected to academic programmes such as Harvard's Self-Organizing Systems Research Group. A driver of this growth was 'the ongoing trend to automate production in order to strengthen American industries on the global market and to keep manufacturing at home, and in some cases, bringing back manufacturing that had previously been sent overseas' (World Robotics 2014). The US robotics revival is focused around robots 'more flexible and far cheaper than their predecessors' (Rotman 2013), often described as 'adept' or 'humanlike and cage free' (Markoff 2012; Anadan 2013). While US robot companies are exploring a wide variety of sectoral applications, they display a particular interest in the logistical operations that have become so integral to cybernetic supply chains.

The flagship company is Rethink Robotics, the maker of 'Baxter', a machine which has been the subject of some careful public relations thinking. Designed with an endearing, or at least benign, appearance and nicknamed the 'the Blue Collar Robot', Baxter recommends itself to capital by being much cheaper than all but the most temporary industrial employee at a cost of under $25,000, and suitable for a variety of assembly and light industrial tasks (Grant 2014). Since 2005 Rethink Robotics has taken in $73.5 million from Boston-based venture capitalists and Bezos Expeditions, the personal investment fund of Jeff Bezos, the owner of Amazon – a company that has shown a sustained interest in advanced automation. In 2012 Amazon bought, for $750 million, Kiva, a company building automatons that 'look like metal ottomans' and operate in the warehouses central to its globe-spanning logistics systems in conjunction with software that tracks 'all the products, shelves, robots and people' (Brynjolfsson and McAfee 2014: 32) The robots deliver shelves of merchandize to workers, indicate the item to be picked off and placed in box, and then take it away. Amazon announced in 2013 it was testing drone delivery (BBC 2013c).

The drones and robots are clearly intended to cut down the company's $4 billion per year shipping expenses, but it also seems that, as so often, automation is rushed in at the first hint of labour troubles. Amazon had already been accused of endangering the mental and physical health of its warehouse workers after an undercover BBC crew videotaped work in a system where digitally monitored workers were expected to walk as many as 11 miles per shift and to find a product for shipment every 33 seconds (BBC 2013b). The humans on which Amazon's current cheap delivery system depends were also showing signs of revolt. Amazon's products are often delivered by companies that define their drivers as 'independent contractors', avoiding payroll taxes, workers compensation and health benefits, responsibility for breakdowns and the risks of unionization. In

2014 some of these drivers launched a legal action on grounds of 'mis-classification', claiming they were *de facto* employees of the couriers and eligible for minimum wage and overtime protections, potentially raising Amazon's supply chain costs (Jamieson 2014).

Amazon's rival in acquiring human-shedding technologies is Google, which in 2013 purchased Boston Dynamics, a builder of 'self-balancing humanoid or bestial robots' such as its 'Big Dog' – designed to support American troops in the field by carrying heavy loads (Gibbs 2013). This was only one of seven companies purchased by Google to support a self-described robotics 'moonshot':

> Schaft, a small Japanese humanoid robotics company; Meka and Redwood Robotics, San Francisco-based creators of humanoid robots and robot arms; Bot & Dolly who created the robotic camera systems ...; Autofuss an advertising and design company; Holomni, high-tech wheel designer, and Industrial Perception, a startup developing computer vision systems for manufacturing and delivery processes. (Gibbs 2013)

Though consumer-oriented robot products were expected in three to five years, Google's plans seemed initially aimed at manufacturing and industry, and in particular the company's own operations, 'automating portions of an existing supply chain that stretches from a factory floor to the companies that ship and deliver goods to a consumer's doorstep' (Markoff 2013). Google's owners, Sergei Brin and Larry Page, have also invested in automated mobile telepresence systems, designed for office and medical environments, and in the self-driving-vehicle system which, as mentioned in Chapter 3, has massive implications for the elimination of labour in the transportation business.

Apps

If bots and robots are manifestly job threatening, cybernetic capital continues to promise that it will provide rewarding work. The latest version of this pledge is the 'app economy' (Macmillan et al. 2009). Even as Occupy Wall Street was seizing city squares at the height of the recession, rumours that apps were 'where the jobs are' were sweeping North America (Mandel 2012). The idea that micro-programs for mobiles were the panacea for recession had been building ever since Apple opened its App Store in 2008. 'App making for dummies' manuals proliferated, alongside media stories of young men abandoning day jobs or school to make millions developing apps. These were amongst the very few sparks of light in the general darkness of the post-crash slump. By 2012 it was estimated there were half a million software application workers in the US (Streitfeld 2012). There are two aspects of app development that we will highlight here: the networked crowdsourcing by which capital drives down labour costs at the heart of the cybernetic design process, and the way in which apps themselves are often a form of automation.

When in 2007 Steve Jobs announced that Apple would open the iPhone to outside app developers this was hailed as a radical democratization of software development – a gesture, one journalist remarked, akin to a virtuoso violinist 'letting a toddler play with his Stradivarius' (Streitfeld 2012). Third-party software development was a long-standing feature of the computing industry. Apple's crowdsourcing strategy, followed in short order by Google's similar Android Market (rebranded in 2012 as Google Play), implemented it on a wider basis than ever before.

This was enabled by two factors – one technological, the other subjective. Technologically, it was enabled by the falling costs and increasing power of computing. These tendencies produced smartphones themselves, but also low-cost devices with which to program apps for smartphones. Platform providers can distribute Software Development Kits, downloadable to a Mac or PC, for free or less than $100, including authoring tools, libraries, debuggers and handset emulators; supplemented from other third-party business-to-business sources, providing instruments for cross-platform adaptation, ad networks, user analytics, crash reporting and back-office functions that can transform the home into a virtual app-factory. App crowdsourcing also, however, depends on a certain subjectivity, a special stratum of labour power always integral to the computer software industry: youthful, predominantly male, technically wizard, sceptical towards suits, outside the union traditions, and ideologically in varying proportions, libertarian, entrepreneurial and idealist.

In the 'mobile application distributed development process' ('MADD') (Bergvall-Karebon and Howcroft 2011), developers build apps for a platform, such as Apple's iPhone or Google's Android, using a kit made available by platform providers. The app is then published on an internet portal, which may be uncontrolled, with developers freely uploading and distributing apps, or, more usually, run by platform providers, who act as middleman, set policies, and charge fees or take a cut of revenues.

The customer downloads the app – free or paid for – to their mobile. Developers get revenues either directly from the sale of apps, indirectly from advertising for which their app serves as a vehicle (the most popular, but least lucrative, method), or from fees for 'in-app' sales.

Notwithstanding talk of apps as a democratization of production, when asked about the point of the App Store, Steve Jobs replied, 'Sell more iPhones' (Streitfeld 2012). Smartphones are sold in a 'two-sided market', characterized by a 'feedback loop' in which a commodity's successful circulation produces effects that further intensify its circulation: a popular smartphone attracts app developers, who create app libraries that attract more consumers to buy yet more handsets. While platform providers and app developers need each other reciprocally, power is very much with the former. If the platform providers charge a fee to place an app in the store, or take a cut of sales, this is a form of technological rent. Even where entrance to the store is free, the platform developer benefits because the app increases the use value of the smartphone, and hence enhances the potential exchange value the platform provider can extract from it – either directly, by increased sales of a proprietorial operating system (Apple), or indirectly, from increased advertising revenues (Google).

The sheer volume of app production (with some 1 million apps available in 2014 from both the Apple and Google stores) means app developers face a massive problem of 'discovery' – that is, of making their apps visible and easily available to users. Appearance on a branded portal, such as the App Store or Google Play, is all but vital for survival. This makes apparently independent app makers, 'in a sense, another arm of platform providers' research and development program' (Streitfeld 2012). Apple and Google only create some key apps in-house. The crucial difference between the small number of software engineers employed by Apple at its Cupertino campus or by Google at its Googleplex and independent app developers is that while the former make salaries in the $100,000 range, the latter are paid nothing by platform corporations – and, indeed may pay for the privilege of appearing in their store.

It *is* possible to make living, even a fortune, at it, because app workers *do* receive incomes, not from platform providers, but as either wages from app development companies or from the revenues of their own micro-enterprises. The actual earning and conditions of app workers are, however, highly variable. Reports of 'appillionaires' (Stevens 2011), like Nick D'Aloisio, the teenage designer of top-selling news app *Summly*, clash with tales of virtual pauperization by aspiring developers who give up jobs and cash-in assets to set up an at-home app businesses, and end up indebted and impoverished, clinging pathetically to the dream by maxing-out credit cards to buy the latest iPhones. App development has created a handful of rags to riches stories, and a layer of well-paid jobs, predominantly for salaried employees and skilled freelancers at the handful of commercial app development companies that dominate the successful offerings in the Apple and Google app stores. Washing around the basis of the app economy is, however, a sea of aspirant independents, small start-ups, and their employees, for whom software development, far from providing a secure livelihood, rather offers yet another variant on the themes of precarious, intermittent, unprotected and low-wage work that have come to characterize cybernetic capital.

Surveys of independent developers repeatedly show that only a tiny percentage make fortunes, and a somewhat larger group the equivalent of modest living wage, while the majority make low or zero profits from their efforts (Dyer-Witheford 2014a). Although independent developers generally own the apps they make, they do not own the distribution channels to sell them. They are therefore subject to the discipline, and the vagaries, of the platform providers. This is particularly aggravating for iPhone app developers, for whom Apple's control over app acceptance is a source of 'great frustration', but problems over issues 'of control, transparency and consistency' are, however, general (Sithigh 2012).

In 2011 an 'Android Developers' Union' website (Andevuni), with the slogan 'sharecroppers unite', targeted Google's Android App Market, demanding a bigger cut of app payments, better app promotion and payment options, public bug tracking, removal appeals, improved liaison with the platform provider, and 'algorithmic transparency' about how apps appear in searches. The following year another website, 'App Developers Union', listed grievances against Apple including the company's toleration of cloned applications and its inadequate response to a 'patent troll' company which threatened developers with law suits, and called for a reduction in Apple's cut of each app sale (Arthur 2011). These initiatives gained very little traction. App crowdsourcing encourages developers to compete, rather than collaborate against the platform providers. It ensures they identify as freelance entrepreneurs who work 'for themselves'. An alternative understanding would be that platform providers' control over app distribution places independent developers in the increasingly large category of nominally self-employed contractors who, in fields ranging from software to plumbing and food services, actually constitute a floating proletarian labour force for large companies dominating supply chains and distribution networks.

In February 2014 Facebook purchased the company What'sApp, a cross-platform instant messaging subscription service, for $19 billion in shares and cash. The deal incited widespread comment, not on account of the price, but because of the jobs involved – or rather, the lack of jobs. What'sApp served some 500 million customers, but had only 55 employees. Noting that Facebook had acquired this staff for 'almost $350 million per head', reporter Eric Reguly (2014) wondered 'if any company has ever had fewer employees relative to its market value ... or fewer employees relative to its customer base'. He went on to suggest the deal was a weathervane for the effects of digitization on employment, remarking on how sites such as Instagram had contributed to the 'gutting' of Eastman Kodak, the former photography giant, a company that as late as 1990 had '141,500 employees and vast profits' but went into bankruptcy in 2012. Other media reports struck a similar note about the What'sApp sale, making it a brief flashpoint for a series of North American anxieties about employment.

Despite the hopes attached to the app economy, apps are not counter to capital's tendency to drive humans out of the production process. Rather, they are an ancillary part of this drive. Apps download to 'prosumer' mobile users those functions within highly automated production and distribution systems that still require human decision, thereby removing the waged worker even from a linking function. As Manzerolle and Kjøsen (2014: 152) observe, they provide 'the anchor points in the "last mile" that makes individuals part of a high-speed feedback loop fueled by a torrent of extracted, transmitted, stored and processed information about the tethered individual and its behavior'. In some cases, apps directly link to factory or office automation processes previously performed by workers. In others they indirectly feed into this dynamic: in-app purchasing – via which 'capital can launch its digitized commodities directly at the consumer' in a way 'similar to how anti-aircraft batteries try to intercept planes or missiles by tracking them in real time' – is the extension of an e-shopping boom now laying waste to retail jobs throughout North America (Manzerolle and Kjøsen 2014: 153).

Despite – or indeed because of – attempts to put a human face on these operations by the fabrication of cybernetic personae, such as Apple's Siri, apps help eliminate humans from economic activity. As Benjamin Bratton puts it, the most important, viable and effective apps and app market platforms serve 'non-human users', in ways that 'modularize, link or de-link the technical capacities of component machines working in concert':

> The rhetorical prioritization of the human user as somehow piloting the work of the app is ... really an alibi protecting an essential opposite effect, namely that the mammal user is only a provisionally necessary mechanism for dragging Gigaflop tracking devices through the avenues of cities, and re-monetizing ... these routes as the spatial career of algorithmic capital (and its successors). (2014: 15)

Algorithms

Within both robots and apps lie algorithms – mathematical processes that allow machines to learn and improve their performance, 'rapidly executing repetitive tasks, logically evaluating between multiple choices, predicting the future, evaluating the past, and finding the overlooked' (Saffer 2014). Algorithms are far from new, but increases in computing power and the extension of networked environments supplying big data have recently made them far more ubiquitous and effective (Steiner 2012). Algorithms determine Google page rankings, Facebook feed content, Netflix recommendations, and the advertisements accompanying Gmail. Impressed by this proliferation of apparently intelligent cybernetic agents, one journalist suggested that 'we don't have to go to other planets to find aliens. They live among us as algorithms' (Saffer 2014).

If there is anything to this, it is only because algorithms as alien life represent an extension of the process of alienation, in which workers' knowledge is first routinized, then codified and transferred from its variable (human) component to its fixed, machinic form (Terranova 2014; Pasquinelli 2014a). Robots are fabled and often visually impressive demonstrations of this alienation process, and apps an alluring one. Algorithmic automation is, however, often far less perceptible, embedded in invisible software operations. But it is at the root of what *The Economist* terms an 'onrushing wave' of digital automation of mental labour of the sort previously thought to be immune to machinic usurpation:

> The combination of big data and smart machines will take over some occupations wholesale; in others it will allow firms to do more with fewer workers. Text mining programs will displace professional jobs

in legal services. Biopsies will be analyzed more efficiently by image-processing software than lab technicians. Accountants may follow travel agents and tellers into the unemployment lines as tax software improves. Machines are already turning basic sports results and financial data into good-enough news stories. (Economist 2014)

As the report goes on to observe, even jobs apparently not easily automated may be algorithmically transformed as data-processing technology breaks them down into smaller and smaller cognitive chunks that can either be outsourced to networked micro-labourers or fully automated. All this persuades many observers that, while the robots may be carving into assembly lines and logistics centres across the globe, the bots are also about to decimate the intermediate strata in their offices (Steiner 2012).

The forward frontier of algorithms still, however, remains in finance, and it is here that they are linked to perhaps the largest disruption of human economies. We already looked at the algorithmic automation of finance capital in the run up to the sub-prime meltdown. Here we will focus on two further points: the new intensities this automation has attained since 2008, and the scale of the processes it facilitates, a scale that must, from capital's point of view, throw into question the conventional distinction between the 'real' and 'fictitious' economies.

Although high-frequency trading (HFT) had emerged prior to the crash, it was only some two years after that a major financial perturbation was specifically attributed to it. In the 'Flash Crash' of 6 May 2010, the Dow Jones Industrial Average fell 600 points in five minutes, and made the biggest one-day decline, 998.5, in its history. An investigation into this event by the US Security and Exchange Commission attributed it to 'hot potato' high-frequency selling which massively amplified the triggering effect of a single major sell order (Bowley 2010). As much as 55 per cent of all US stock trading is executed with HFT, using algorithms 'whose lifespans can be as short as a few weeks', effecting trades on the basis of a statistically identified correlation between movements of different stocks. These practices include 'momentum' trading – buying a rising stock expecting the rise to continue, and 'mean-reversion' – expecting it to fall, but also now taking into account anticipated responses from other 'algos' operating in a massively self-reflexive competitive environment (Adler 2012).

Leading HFT companies spend millions on infrastructures to attain trading speeds that give them an edge. In 2012 trades were executed over distances between 700 and 1,000 miles in a round-trip time of between 14.5 and 13.1 milliseconds over buried fibre optic cable, and 9–8.5 milliseconds via microwave beamed through the air. This need for speed spurs plans such as accelerating trades between New York and London with 'unmanned, solar-powered drones carrying microwave relay stations [that] could hover at intervals across the Atlantic' (Adler 2012). In this context, publicly posted quotes for stock prices are obsolete before they are seen by human traders, 'like looking at a star that burned out 50,000 years ago'; HFT competitors have already acted on them, and conventional orders will have been recognized and preempted by algos that effectively 'know' market movements 'in advance' (Adler 2012; Lewis 2014). HFT generates robo-sub-industries, such as automated 'news analytics' services turning up to 100,000 news articles a day into trade-ready algo-actionable data. Financial trading is thus dominated by autonomous machines, a game in which human interference spells loss, and one that is increasingly 'an end in itself, operating at a remove from the goods-and-services-producing part of the economy and taking a growing share of GDP' (Adler 2012).

This automated arena dwarfs the human economy in the scale of value transactions. HFT is generally considered most advanced in derivatives markets, where the purchase of rights to buy or sell a specific commodity at a specific time, at a specific price, trades on risk. In many cases, what is wagered on in such futures markets are currency fluctuations – that is to say, the conditions under which money itself will trade (Valladares 2014). Estimation of the size of derivatives markets is difficult, because much is clandestine, conducted in the 'dark pools' of special electronic exchanges, and contested, because the relation between the real and notional values involved – that is, between the amount of money put down in a deal and the amounts potentially at stake – is highly esoteric.

In 2013 *The Economist* reported the Bank for International Settlements' (BIC) estimate of the size of the derivatives market as somewhere between $600 and $700 trillion in notional terms; it noted 'for perspective' that the World Bank estimates the combined market capitalization value of every listed company on Earth at about $50 trillion (Economist 2013a). The next year the BIC reported figure went up to $710 trillion, some 20 per cent higher than before the 2008 crash (Snyder 2014). Others estimate the value of all derivatives outstanding tops a quadrillion (1,000 trillion) dollars, more than 14 times the entire world's annual GDP (Sivy 2013).

Whatever the precise figure, 'since the recession, the value of derivatives outstanding has grown, and they remain very risky with the potential for large, unpredictable losses' (Sivy 2013).

Although Marx in Volume II of *Capital* wrote about financial capital's attempt to leap from M to M', and later, in Volume III, about the role of credit in the crises of the business cycle, he clearly never imagined the scale this would attain in the early twenty-first century. And while autonomists discussed finance as a means by which capital attempts to escape the working class, they have not fully reckoned with the scope of the alternative realm capital has built in the attempt to by-pass its own production processes, about which it can be truly said 'another world is possible'. Capital commodifies money itself, and then it commodifies the very moment of exchange in a gamble on risk. One might envisage it as a process by which the circuit curves round recursively on itself, spiralling up to a higher level in a sort of capitalist 'overworld'.

Bryan and Rafferty describe this overworld as one of 'meta-capital'. They draw a distinction between 'basic, or simple, commodities (wheat, iron, cars, etc.)' and '*meta-commodities*', with the former being 'historically prior and the products of labour' while *meta-commodities* 'come historically later, with the initial purpose of hedging the conditions of production and circulation of simple commodities' (2006: 13). They suggest that the 'meta-commodities' have 'grown in importance, particularly since the 1980s'. The essential characteristic of these meta-commodities – that is, derivatives, is 'that they are *products of circulation*, not significantly of labour' and are 'therefore always "capital", for they never "leave" a circuit of capital'. 'In that sense, they are more intensively capitalist commodities than simple commodities, for the latter are merely *produced within* capitalist relations, while meta-commodities are *products of* capitalist relations' (2006: 154). The creation of this meta-capital spiral – 'separated from ownership of physical assets in which an exchange of derivatives rarely if ever involves the actual exchange of the underlying asset' – gives capital an extraordinary 'fluidity and self transforming capacity' (2006: 66). This is not to say that it is caused by technological advances: the phenomenal expansion of finance capital had its genesis in the disparities between production and consumption caused by globalization. But electronic communications provided the conditions of possibility for this hypertrophy. This realm of meta-capital – we could call it capitalist heaven – is now fully machinic.

Futuristic Accumulation

In a piece for the prestigious business consultancy, the McKinsey Institute, Brian Arthur prefaces his reflections on the state of technology with two examples. The first is that of his boarding an aircraft. Instead of presenting a ticket to an airline worker as he might have done less than a decade ago, he now scans a credit or frequent flier card into a kiosk machine. In three or four seconds its spits out a boarding pass, receipt and luggage tag. Arthur remarks that in those three or four seconds a 'huge underground conversation' is conducted 'entirely among machines', as computers check your flight status, travel history, seat choice, frequent flier status, and security listings, with

> multiple servers talking to other servers, talking to satellites that are talking to computers, and checking with passport control, with foreign immigration, with ongoing connecting flights [and] also starting to adjust the passenger count and seating according to whether the fuselage is loaded more heavily at the front or back. (Arthur 2011)

His second example concerns 'shipping freight through Rotterdam into the center of Europe'. Again he observes that in the not so distant past, this would have involved humans: 'people with clipboards would be registering arrival, checking manifests, filling out paperwork, and telephoning forward destinations to let other people know'. Now, however, 'such shipments go through an RFID [Radio-frequency identification] portal where they are scanned, digitally captured, and automatically dispatched'. The RFID portal communicates digitally with the 'originating shipper, other depots, other suppliers, and destinations along the route, all keeping track, keeping control, and reconfiguring routing ... to optimize things along the way'. Arthur then concludes:

> So we can say that another economy – a second economy – of all of these digitized business processes conversing, executing, and triggering further actions is silently forming alongside the physical economy. If I were to look for adjectives to describe this second economy, I'd say it is vast, silent, connected, unseen, and autonomous (meaning that human beings may design it but are not directly involved in running it). It is remotely executing and global, always on, and endlessly configurable. It is concurrent – a great computer expression – which means that

everything happens in parallel. It is self-configuring, meaning it constantly reconfigures itself on the fly, and increasingly it is also self-organizing, self-architecting, and self-healing. (Arthur 2011)

That capital's drive to machine innovation might eventually all but eliminate wage labour was not an idea foreign to Marxism. It finds its most famous (or notorious) expression in a short passage from Marx's 1857 notebook, *Grundrisse*, known as 'The Fragment on Machines' (1973: 690–712). Contemplating the industrial factory of his era, Marx sees the emergence of a 'mechanical monster':

> the means of labour passes through different metamorphoses, whose culmination is the *machine*, or rather, an *automatic system of machinery* (system of machinery: the *automatic* one is merely its most complete, most adequate form, and alone transforms machinery into a system), set in motion by an automaton, a moving power that moves itself; this automaton consisting of numerous mechanical and intellectual organs, so that the workers themselves are cast merely as its conscious linkages. (Marx 1973: 691)

This would seem to mark the ultimate victory of capital over labour. However, Marx suggests, it would be a pyrrhic victory. Capital's automating drive is ultimately self-destructive, for its very success in substituting ever cheaper, more capable machines for human workers subverts the propellant energy gradient of the vortex, the transfer of surplus value to capital through wage labour. By undermining the need for the sale of labour power, advanced automation would undo the most basic institution of capital, the wage, creating 'the material conditions to blow this foundation sky-high' (Marx 1973: 705) and clear the ground for a new, communist, society.

A straightforward reading of this passage suggests an increasingly automated system collapsing under the stresses of mounting unemployment. The renewed attention given to the passage, however, has been inspired by an almost diametrically opposite interpretation. The post-*operaismo* analysis emphasizes that increasing automation requires what Marx terms 'general intellect' or the 'social brain' (1973: 705). It envisages this as composed of the 'immaterial labour' involved in various types of intellectual, affective or communicative work, which becomes the basis of a 'multitude' capable of reappropriating the fruits of the general intellect (Virno 1996; Hardt and Negri 2000).

In contrast, our analysis suggests that immaterial labour is itself now being cast out of the system it has created. The 'general intellect' is now in the process of automating itself, as it moves on from decimating assembly lines and routine office labour to replacing journalists with news aggregators, translators with translation programs, lawyers with precedent-searching expert systems, photographers with photo-bots, pop stars with virtual holographic performers and stockbrokers with swarming artificial intelligences. This interpretation of 'general intellect' emphasizes, not the empowerment of immaterial labour, but the explosive proletarianization and re-proletarianization that arises as huge tranches of the global population are rendered surplus to requirements by an increasingly automatic capitalism.

Capital too can see this possibility. Having painted his picture of a 'vast, silent, connected, unseen, and autonomous' machinic economy, Arthur (2011) admits there is 'a downside' in the 'adverse impact on jobs', one 'dwarfing' the effects of globalization. He then suggests that 'short workweeks and long weekends', subsidized job creation, and even a change to 'the very idea of a job and of being productive' may be necessary, and blithely concludes: 'The system will adjust of course, though I can't yet say exactly how.' His is only one of a number of similar reflections. In the face of North America and Europe's slow recovery from recession, both scientists and economists express concerns about the effects of automation on jobs.

The most common proposal for dealing with this is more education – as if this could summon corporate investment in human capital, rather than just intensify competition for what jobs exist. Some, however, go further. Google CEO Larry Page has expressed the opinion that the economy could easily function, and would actually benefit, if we ended the 40-hour workweek and had more part-time jobs (Fiegerman 2014). Mexican telecom magnate Carlos Slim, the world's second richest man after Bill Gates, is reported as advocating reducing the workweek to three days to increase productivity and quality of life for workers (Davidson 2014). Neither of these billionaire's statements made it clear how much these reduced or precarious positions should earn (and indeed Slim seems not to envisage any reduction of hours).

Others are yet more daring. In their acclaimed study of the exponentially automating tendencies of computing, *The Second Machine Age* (2014),

MIT professors Eric Brynjolfsson and Andrew McAfee foresee a potential employment crisis. Recognizing that the orthodox economic response to such fears is an assurance that surplus labour will be absorbed into new forms of work in a 'march through the sectors' that proceeds from agriculture to industry to services, they nonetheless suggest that this time automation escalation may be too fast and steep for this to happen again. Brynjolfsson and McAfee suggest a 'basic income' for all citizens, regardless of whether they work or not, or a 'negative income tax' that 'combines a guaranteed income with an incentive to work' (2014: 232–8), though they are vague as to what levels these should be set at. They also favour a 'sharing' or 'peer to peer' economy, with lots of opportunities for internet-coordinated micropayment-fuelled exchange of services. Their book even includes a 'wild ideas' section which includes providing citizens with dividends from corporate profits, paying people for non-profit service activities, or even – wild indeed! – mass government public work programmes of the kind instituted at the time of the 1930s Great Depression to undertake tasks such as 'cleaning up the environment' (2014: 247).

Some of these sound like radical proposals. The idea of a 'basic income', for example, has been vigorously promoted by post-*operaismo* thinkers, and I have advocated it myself (Dyer-Witheford 1999). There are, however, two major caveats to make about such proposals. First, the political significance of a basic income depends entirely on what level it is set at: if it is low, at near-poverty rates, it becomes a way of streamlining untidy welfare systems and managing mass pauperization better: this is why the political right sometimes favour such schemes. Second, none of the plans enunciated by Brynjolfsson and McAfee (or, of course, Page and Slim) say a word about depriving capital, or its human personifications, 'the 1 per cent', of control over production or command of the preponderant part of the value it generates. It is in fact possible to envisage all the ideas put forward in *The Second Machine Age* as relatively low-cost ways to 'park' increasingly superfluous proletarians, under intensifying levels of policing, while machinic capital gets on with the business of accumulation.

In actuality there is little or no sign of advanced capitalist regimes adopting such 'reform' measures. Rather, the dominant post-crash line continues to be a full-out assault on the living standards and security of proletarians under the banners of debt repayment and austerity, with increasingly degrading and impoverishing workfare conditions for the unemployed, and relentless cuts to public services and public employment for nations – such as those of southern Europe – unable to live up to the expectations of finance capital. Nonetheless, what Brynjolfsson and McAfee propose can be understood as a 'plan B' for cybernetic capital if the going gets rough.

In the aftermath of the crash, there will probably be eventual rebounds in employment numbers, but the real test for their durability will come when this results in upward wage pressures – for example, from low-paid service workers – or in the next major financial fluctuation. At this juncture we may see a further emergence within the cybernetic vortex of a nascent 'futuristic accumulation'. This can be contrasted with the previous phases of 'primitive accumulation' – when the whirlwind of capital first tears dispossessed labour off the earth by destroying peasant societies – and 'expanded reproduction'– in which the cycle of waged labour and commodity consumption simultaneously reproduces both capital and its working class. In futuristic accumulation, capital would learn to function, not while drawing populations into production, as in primitive accumulation, but while ejecting them from it. Humans would continue to provide the 'conscious linkages' required by cybernetic systems, but in increasingly unimportant and unremunerated ways. The bands dividing the planet into high- and low-wage zones will continue to rotate and shift alignments as the global search for low-wage labour persists. However, precarious labour, on-call as and when machine systems need it, will become a norm.

Indeed, it is already: a 2013 Gallup Poll investigation, based on 136,000 interviews in 136 countries showed that only one in four adults worldwide – or roughly 1.3 billion people – worked full-time (defined as 30 or more hours a week) for an employer: the percentage of full-time jobs varied from 43 per cent in North America and 42 per cent in the former Soviet Union to 19 per cent in the Middle East and North Africa and 11 per cent in Sub-Saharan Africa (Clifton and Ryan 2014). For this intermittent labour force, work will be increasingly tightly coupled to cybernetic systems in forms of symbiant union that are 'mindless' (Head 2014), intensively measured and monitored in the ways familiar to Foxconn, Wal-Mart and Amazon employees, and in some cases, geared not even to conscious decision making but to autonomic nervous responses, such as those already invoked in some forms of big data processing operations (Andrejevic 2015). In the high-wage zones, some type of 'basic income' scheme may complement the pauperization of wages; elsewhere, the so-called 'informal economy' will constitute the nexus for a range of survivalist and hand to mouth practices. In futuristic accumulation, capital's priority becomes the reproduction not of human workers and consumers but of cybernetic systems. In production, workers are placed in direct competition with new generations of adept robots across a widening spectrum of occupations; circulation is increasingly automated, through online b2b (business-to-business) and big-data-driven market prediction and recommendation; and both production and circulation are subordinated to finance, simply generating the fluctuating movements – akin to those of a ball on a roulette wheel – that speed-of-light trading can take as its speculative object. This would be the culminating stage of the cybernetic vortex.

10

Front

Lightning and Thunder

Vortices have histories; they come into being, grow in power, scope and complexity, develop eddies, turbulences and counterflows, begin to lose coherence, collapse. Though vortex breakdown is poorly understood, in at least some cases it occurs when chaotic internal turbulences make the vortex's circulation reverse: within the system, flows fold back on themselves, forming a knot or cell around which other currents start to move in a direction contrary to the main rotation, and the vortex then disintegrates (Lucca-Negro and O'Doherty 2001). In capital's value vortex, this inversion would involve resistance arising from changes in class composition and accumulation dynamics. The current cycle of struggles marks an incipient stage in such an inversion. Its development remains uncertain; it may suddenly intensify, or falter and fade out. Historically, at every point in its unfolding, the vortex has been propelled to higher energy levels by its inter-strata stressors and frictions, whose overcoming only drives it further on its 'flight into the future'. So we ask the question every hurricane-watcher and tornado-chaser asks of the object of study: where is this going?

The perspective of this essay derives from what is called autonomist Marxism, and its antecedent school of *operaismo*. Autonomist Marxism champions the autonomy of workers, their capacity to resist and find alternatives to capital. To that end, it has always focused on struggle, and working-class capacity. Today, however, capital is autonomizing itself from workers, albeit by a circuitous path. The conjunction of cybernetics and globalization raised to a new intensity the fundamental dynamic of the capitalist vortex: the 'moving contradiction' of its simultaneous induction and expulsion of labour. This now manifests as, on the one hand, the encompassing of the global population by networked supply chains and agile production systems, making labour available to capital on a planetary scale, and, on the other, as the drive towards the development of adept automata and algorithmic software – robots, networks, networked robots and robot networks that render that labour redundant, the useless capacity of a surplus humanity.

The 'moving contradiction' simultaneously inducts and ejects labour, but not in an equilibrating, self-balancing process. Rather, it ramps up in a spiralling path towards ever higher machinic intensities. Increasingly, the huge volumes of labour sucked into the cybernetic vortex are put to work to create, directly or indirectly, the systems – industrial robots, self-guided transportation, automated calling systems, and algorithmic finance bots – that are vaporizing capital's dependency on the human. The labour of a myriad proletarians – extracting rare earths, laying fibre cables, constructing cell towers, assembling computers, servicing techno-savants – is building a world of automatic semiconductor factories, robot assembly lines, cloud computing data-centres, drone-delivered commodities and high-frequency financial trading. A period of high labour absorption, global and networked, is followed by accelerated ejection, as new levels of automation, in both production and circulation, combined with algorithmic financialization, increasingly disassociates capital from workers.

Let us look for a moment at some photographs. Here in Sebastiano Selgado's *Worker: An Archeology of the Industrial Work* (1993), recording 'a time when men and women at work with their hands provided the central axis of the world' (Selgado 1993: 6–7), are those who worked the land and now are leaving: sugar-cane cutters in Cuba and Brazil, replaced by the robotic harvesters of biofuel; Sicilian fishermen and women in Galician fish canneries, put out of work by giant trawlers and freezing plants; labourers on the island of perfume, Reunion, near Madagascar, renting vats by the day to distil scents of 'geranium, vetiver and vanilla' soon to be rendered obsolete by the wonders of synthetic biology. Here too are the industrial and extractive labourers, from Ukrainian car workers to Caspian Sea oil-crews, Chinese steelworkers, masters of a machine age, but themselves staring into the cybernetic maw, like the workers who from each end of the Eurotunnel connecting England and France set in motion automatic digging machines which met in the middle and were then abandoned because it was too expensive to extricate them. Here is the iconic shot of 50,000 soil-caked Brazilian gold miners spiralling up the sheer sides of an open pit, carrying the treasure of a financial system whose real currency today is no more than virtual pulses.

Add to these, from Selgado's second volume, *Migrants* (2000), portraits of the nomad labour crossing from one wage zone to another, seeking survival, often finding death, travelling on the tops of trains, in overcrowded boats watching the storms approach, trekking through deserts, scaling fences, running the borders. And here, in the photographs of Edward Burtynsky (2003), are the environments these proletarians traverse: the deserts filled with towering oil derricks and blazing wells; the Appalachian mountain decapitated and hollowed out by mining companies; China's mega-factories, big as small cities; the ship-breaking sites of India where vast hulks are dismantled; the piled hills of circuit boards in e-waste dumps, and the giant craters filled with car tyres from global automobile production; the twisting patterns of endless highways knotted into gigantic loops and cloverleaves like messages traced in the earth to be read by an alien civilization. And here are Burtynsky's more recent images, contributed to a collection by the photographer Robert Leslie, *Stormbelt* (2014), documenting a journey across the US from Florida to California through the Sunbelt at the height of the post-crash recession: 'Repossessed homes and men with "will do anything for money" signs told the tale', but, 'as the journey progressed, the impact of hurricanes, forest fires and drought became increasingly apparent'. This is the world of the global proletarians.

Where today are the images of the cybernetic systems which this proletariat labours to build, and with which it is being replaced? Perhaps we will find them in Luisa Whitton's (2013) photographs of Japan's humanoid androids or in Adam Curtis' cinematic essay on the legacy of cybernetics *Watched Over by Machines of Loving Grace* (2011). More important, however, is that soon such images may not be created by humans at all.

More than half a century ago, Jacques Lacan, in his cybernetics-influenced attempt at 'a materialist definition of the phenomenon of consciousness', suggested that consciousness be understood as a process of reflection, like the image in the mirror. He then hypothesised a moment when 'all living beings have disappeared. There are only waterfalls and springs left – lightning and thunder too.' In this situation, Lacan asks if 'the image in the mirror, the image in the lake – do they still exist?' And he answers that it's 'quite obvious they still exist':

> For one very simple reason – at the high point of civilisation we have attained, which far surpasses our illusions about consciousness, we

have manufactured instruments which, without in any way being audacious, we can imagine to be sufficiently complicated to develop films themselves, put them away in little boxes, and store them in the fridge. Despite all living beings having disappeared, the camera can nonetheless record the image of the mountain in the lake, or that of the Café de Flore crumbling away in total solitude. (Lacan 1991: 46)

Today we do not have to imagine such machines: robo-photography supplants humans for snapping wild life, Olympic athletes, even wedding shots, while Dronestagram compiles aerial shots across the planet, piggy-backing on the un-process-able flow of images generated by Google and the Pentagon. Perhaps today's Café de Flore – historically, the hang-out of France's existential philosophers – crumbles away not just by the passage of time, but because a military drone first photographed, then destroyed it.

Whirlwind of Dissolution

The nihilist philosopher, Nick Land – no friend of Marxists, but an astute reader of Marx – revives *The Communist Manifesto*'s famous 'melt into air' image when he describes capital as acting like a cyclone that periodically strikes a coastline, leaving 'a shock wave in the silt' and throwing up 'evanescent islands' which populations inhabit and cultivate, only to be destroyed 'when the cyclone returns and instantaneously consumes the tenuous residues of its previous ravages':

> Once the commodity system is established ... [c]apital [becomes] a runaway whirlwind of dissolution, whose hub is the virtual zero of impersonal accumulation. At the peak of its productive process the human animal is hurled into a new nakedness, as everything stable is progressively liquidated in the storm. (1992: 106)

For Marx, the vortex culminates in a destructive but liberating vaporization of the fetishistic illusions of capital, an emancipation in which humans take control of their own social destiny. In Land's vision what is liquidated is nothing less than the human itself, whose 'new nakedness' discloses only its inevitable supersession by the a-human machinic processes of a system that 'can't be bargained with, can't be reasoned with, doesn't show pity or remorse or fear and it absolutely will not stop, ever', for 'what appears to humanity as the history of capitalism is an invasion from the future by an artificial intelligent space that must assemble itself entirely from its enemy's resources' (2011: 338).

Mark Fisher (2010) has criticized Land for succumbing to the seductive sheen of media techno-fantasies, ignoring the reality of capital's mundane inefficiencies and low-wage labour that belie the somehow alluring threat of invincible AIs. For all its extremity, however, Land's account is only a dark-side re-write of doctrines currently percolated through the very core of the capitalist class by assorted trans-humanists and extropians populating the research centres of high-technology industries – the doctrine of what we can call 'singularity capitalism'. By this creed, continuing exponential growth in computing power will soon break through the barriers posed to accumulation posed by the very form of the human. Its ideologists range from Hans Moravec (1999), patriarch for uploaded 'mind children'; Kevin Kelly (2010), celebrant of a self-determining 'technium'; Hugo de Garis (2005), who looks forward to an end-time conflict between humans and 'artilects' (short for 'artificial intellects'), and, most famously, Ray Kurzweil (2005), proselytizer of human-AI fusion, whose doctrines are espoused by the owners of Google, and inform the extension of their interests from web-crawlers to self-directed cars, computerized vision and cutting-edge robotics. Promoted in the name of increasing individual capacity and convenience, this is a project of species self-supersession, in which the very distinction between machine and human is undone by the creating of ever more life-like machines and increasingly intensely machine-infiltrated workers.

A Marxist premise has been that the reproduction of capital requires reproduction of a working class: the social relations that generate value must be human relations, however inhumanly organized. This, however, is the assumption cybernetics confounded at its origin, by insisting on the transposability of different types of 'information engines' as 'automata' whether 'in the metal or in the flesh' (Wiener 1948: 42), and which contemporary computing seeks to abolish by eliminating the annoying 'variability' of the human in favour of entities – robotic or cyborg – 'fixed' and 'constant' in their subjugation to capital. Singularity theory removes the humanist confidence that such a capitalist system would, by annihilating the basis of value, destroy itself; instead it leaves the possibility that it would create, in successively larger incremental iterations, a surplus humanity on a ruined planet unfit for all but machine habitation.

Even if this prospect requires science fictional speculation, it now deserves consideration. In a discussion of the organic composition of capital and the profit rate, Andrew Kliman (2012) has recently suggested that capital accumulation could proceed without a large consumer goods section: in principle corporations can continually profit by producing means of production for other corporations. And in a remarkable essay Atle Kjøsen (2013b) has theorized that automata – androids – might be in effect 'proletarianized' by dependence on energy supplies controlled by capital. Synthesizing these observations, one can extrapolate a world in which automated corporate entities produce commodities (including means for yet better automation) for one another in a fully cybernetic value-circuit. There are certainly major technical obstacles to this project, though they are pushed back by each development in artificial intelligence, neuroscience and nanotechnology. But the possibilities that cybernetics' original automata fascination might eventually culminate in forms of autonomous artificial intelligence are receiving attention both from computing science (Bostrom 2014) and serious investigative journalists (Barrat 2013). There is no teleological necessity why such an outcome, in so many ways the logical destination of a mode of production with a bias to machinic development, might not be achieved by a system moving relentlessly towards a destination the young Marx glimpsed in the *Economic and Philosophic Manuscripts* of 1844: 'in the end, an inhuman power rules over everything' (1964: 156).

Accelerationism and Anarchism

As Jasper Bernes reminds (2013) us in his discussion of cybernetic logistic systems, there is a long-running left debate on the question of whether the forces of production developed by capital can be adopted by a communist project. Lenin's famous 'soviets plus electricity' formula proposes precisely such a reappropriation, but a more heterodox line suggests the technologies of capital subsumption are a poisoned chalice, implanted with the very logics of abstraction and command that require revolutionary abolition. In this debate, *operaismo* and autonomist thinkers have stood on both sides, with Raniero Panzieri (1980) representing the resolute view that the machine embodies capital's plan, and Negri, once a proponent of refusal and sabotage, now the most eloquent champion of digital reappropriation.

These issues are at stake in the recent emergence of 'acceleration-ism', a proposal for an explicitly left appropriation of Land's 'Kybernetics'. Accelerationism's *Manifesto* rejects tendencies within the current cycle of struggles towards a 'neo-primitivist localism' – 'a folk politics of localism, direct action, and relentless horizontalism'. It also, however, rejects Land's prophecy that 'the human can eventually be discarded as mere drag to abstract planetary intelligence'. Instead it declares for an explicitly 'Promethean' left politics, 'at ease with a modernity of abstraction, complexity, globality, and technology'. It seeks 'to preserve the gains of late capitalism while going further than its value system, governance structures, and mass pathologies will allow', finding a 'speed' that is not just unidirectional – 'a brain dead onrush' – but 'navigational', moving towards a high-technology communism (Williams and Srnicek 2013).

This programme takes inspiration from early left cybernetic experiments such as 'Project Cybersyn'. This was an attempt in the 1970s by the socialist government of President Allende in Chile, with the help of the left-wing cyberneticist Stafford Beer, to construct a computerized economic coordination system (Medina 2011). The experiment was truncated by the murderous military coup of General Pinochet. Its example, however, suggests to accelerationists that 'while much of the current global platform is biased towards capitalist social relations' this is not an inevitable necessity: 'These material platforms of production, finance, logistics, and consumption can and will be reprogrammed and reformatted towards post-capitalist ends' (Williams and Srnicek 2013).

Accelerationism's ringing slogan – 'The command of The Plan must be married to the improvised order of The Network' – has been humorously synopsized by supporters as 'a Communist Skynet', alluding to the networked artificial intelligence system featured in James Cameron's *Terminator* films. Certainly some of the best prospectii are science-fiction such as Ken Macleod's *The Star Fraction* (1994) or Ian Banks *Culture* series. The main techno-social possibilities accelerationism anticipates are directing automation to create free time for individual and social development, and the use of digital networks for sophisticated and democratic planning, especially to address major crises such as chaotic climate change: 'What accelerationism pushes towards is a future that is more modern – an alternative modernity that neoliberalism is inherently unable to generate' (Williams and Srnicek 2013).

Accelerationism has attracted considerable interest (Mackay and Avanessian 2014), including from some of the best of the post-*operaismo* thinkers. In some ways it can be seen as a logical outcome of this school's optimism about the possibilities of re-appropriation. Negri (2014) wrote a generally approving commentary on the *Accelerationist Manifesto*, and Tiziana Terranova's (2014) paper 'Red Stack Attack' makes adventurous contributions to the perspective, including discussion of virtual currencies as a potential harbinger of post-capitalism. Some of my own work is in an accelerationist mode, taking as its point of departure Francis Spufford's novel *Red Plenty* (2010) about early Soviet cybernetic efforts at economic planning and exploring its possible update into a new concept of a highly automated, network-planned but radically democratized communism in which not just social media but software agents play a part (Dyer-Witheford 2014b).

It is, however, important to consider this direction in the light of a critique which, though it precedes the *Accelerationist Manifesto*, aims directly at its assumption – that of the anarchist collective Tiqqun in its famous essay 'The Cybernetic Hypothesis' (2001), an essay recently given a timely revalidation by Alexander Galloway (2014). For this paper is not only a trenchant analysis of the 'cybernetic offensive' with which capital decomposed class resistance from the 1970s, but also an acerbic criticism of tendencies from the left to adopt these same cybernetic concepts and technologies.

For Tiqqun, cybernetics is a theory of adjustment of individuals to system requirements, of an incessant shaping through feedback loops to the internalized constraints of social programmes, which are then experienced as the autonomous conditions of subjectivity. However benign those constraints and modulations, the more efficient and totalizing they are more they raise the issue of what they would remain of the 'free development of all' promised by Marx as aim of communism. All social orders both create and limit the forms of subjective autonomy that are possible within them; but this doesn't mean that questions of scale and comprehensiveness of such systems, and the intensity of the technological controls through which socialization is effected, are irrelevant. The Tiqqun critique raises the issue of whether the creation of very large-scale communist cybernetic systems would not recreate similar alienations to the capitalist version:

> The reappropriation by the critical cyberneticians of the category of autonomy/self-rule – along with the ideas deriving from it,

self-organization, auto-poïesis, self-reference, self-production, self-valorization, etc. – is ... the central ideological maneuver of the last twenty years. Through the cybernetic prism, giving oneself one's own laws, producing subjectivities, in no way contradict the production of the system and its regulation. (2001)

Forms of weak and even internally contradictory systematization – multiple 'plans' rather than 'the Plan' – might be preferable to the very strong ones, which Accelerationism, with its pointed rejection of localisms, seems to envisage. Would it really be better to be governed by red AIs than neoliberal ones?

Neither accelerationist embrace nor anarchist rejection seems adequate to the challenge posed to the communist imagination by cybernetics. Communism is not an acceleration of capital's tendencies, any more than it is just a stop, a pulling of 'the emergency break' (Benjamin 2003: 402). It is a swerve, a departure in a different direction from that of capital. The argument of this book has been that contemporary capital increasingly subordinates the reproduction of variable capital (humans) to that of the fixed capital (machines) of which the capitalist class is the personified representative. This is an accelerating movement that proceeds by intermediate cyborg or symbiant stages towards even higher levels of automation. In this process, the creation of surplus populations, appearing in various forms of precarity, informal work, unemployment and destitution in differentiated global zones becomes the characteristic form of proletarianization. Struggles against this trajectory necessarily start from the current state of the vortex, within a cybernetic context, but must also move in a transverse, diagonal direction – that is, towards the dissolution of the capital relation, and with it of the domination of fixed or dead labour over living labour.

Communism will give primacy to the expanded reproduction (in the sense of the fulfilment and development of needs) of the human, not of capital. It should not therefore be identified with the development of technologies. The revolutionary process may appropriate technologies or develop new ones, but it may also free people from technological dependences. Such a position is neither cyborg nor Luddite; it does not imply a reactionary essentialism, a return to some supposedly extra-technological human authenticity. But it does insist that communist transformations of human 'species-becoming' will move at different paces and in different directions from those dictated by capital (Dyer-Witheford 2004). In the face of capital's cybernetic assault, it is necessary not only to uphold the most fundamental activities of proletarian reproduction – safe birth, loving care, provisions of food, water, environmental safety, collectivity and education – but also to affirm that these are matters of corporeality, of flesh, and not, for communists, indifferently transferable to automata of metal (or silicon), as they are for cybernetics and capital.

The issue of how much cybernetics communism needs cannot be purely theoretically resolved. Pro-cybernetic accelerationism and anti-cybernetic localisms may interact in a way neither would welcome. The most likely result of the acceleration of capital's current technological tendencies is an involuntary localism brought about by social, geopolitical and ecological disasters that disintegrates the subsuming processes of globalization. Such crises would generate barbaric results, but could also, given adequate prior organization, allow the creation of new communal forms that will, through a process of experimentation, have to determine their fit with re-purposed cybernetic systems. These experiments will unfold only as 'communist measures' (de Mattis 2014) undertaken in struggle, dependent on the conditions faced by movements as they endeavour to cross the river of fire separating capital from whatever comes after it.

General Crisis

In the 'Fragment on Machines' Marx observes that 'Forces of production and social relations – two different sides of the development of the social individual – appear to capital as mere means, and are merely means for it to produce on its limited foundation. In fact, however, they are the material conditions to blow this foundation sky-high' (1973: 705). The Fragment suggested that the development of techno-science would, in eliminating the need for wage labour, create such an explosive situation. As we argued in the previous chapter, it seems that today capital is gambling on its capacity to control this process sufficiently to sustain a prolonged project of machine intensification, containing and marginalizing surplus populations, and integrating a precarious workforce which has effectively been converted to a component of fixed capital – the 'conscious links' in a predominantly cybernetic system.

This gamble is, however, fraught with crisis possibilities. Schematically, we can say that cybernetic capital faces problems of *employment*, *ecology*, *enmity* and *entities*. The *employment* problem is that detailed in this book, as cybernetic production generates rising inequalities and surplus populations. The *ecological* problem is recorded pre-eminently in the readouts from meteorological supercomputers and satellite tracking stations of rising atmospheric CO_2, but also in a host of other indicators of biospheric wear-down. It is the consequence of the vast long-term expansion in the circulation of commodities, an expansion which for the last several decades has been intensified and speeded up by cybernetic supply chains. The *enmity* problem is the re-emergence of war, occasioned first by the overreach of the United States, and then by its abrupt weakening in the 2008 financial crisis, creating a situation in which insurgents and rival capitalist contenders take to the field, increasingly armed with the cybernetic weaponry that the imperial hegemon previously monopolized. The *entity* problem, already discussed in this chapter, is the tendency for management of all the preceding problems to be entrusted to semi-autonomous automated systems – those of the financial system and of the military being the most notable – whose long-term consequences are unknown. It is not fanciful – indeed, it is the starkest realism – to think of these tendencies interacting to produce a multi-factorial 'general crisis' akin to that which historians now perceive as having assailed the globe from England to China in the wars, ecological disasters and civil tumults of the seventeenth century, though potentially with even more calamitous outcomes (Parker 2013).

In such a crisis there will be proletarian resistance – revolts of the 'conscious linkages'. Such resistance will be varied, because singularity capitalism builds on, and is simultaneous with, earlier capitalist phases. Even while futuristic accumulation empties out the factories and offices of North America and Europe, primitive accumulation, long completed in the old core of the world system, continues in the land grabs of its new expansion areas, and the migrant proletariat this sets in motion pours into the new metropolii of Asia, Africa and the Americas, to become workers for a new cycle of expanded reproduction. But these processes are altered by the conditions of automation, globalization and financialization characteristic of futuristic accumulation. Primitive accumulation is reshaped by high-speed trading as food prices oscillate wildly; new working classes are barely formed before their robot replacements are brought on line: strata of professional and technical workers developing cybernetic systems initially expand explosively, then are eroded by the very systems they build. Each moment interferes with the next: the stages pile up on one another.

Because the dispossession of primitive accumulation overlaps the exploitation of expanded reproduction and the universal human dismissal of futuristic accumulation, the struggles of the global proletariat will not be the same as that of previous eras, but rather combine in strange permutations. Above all, they will not be a repetition of the same because the resources out of which the vortex forms itself are no longer those of a pre-industrial planet but rather of an exhausted, emission-filled biosphere, whose accelerated depletion the cybernetic vortex must now replace from its internal processes in increasingly hubristic projects of synthetic biology and geo-engineering.

There are no guarantees for the outcome of the cycle begun in 2011, only a likelihood that it will be waged in conditions of fresh financial catastrophe, wars and surrogate wars between rising and declining capitalist states, and continuing ecological degradation. The struggles that emerge in this vortex-world of global proletarians will not be nicely aligned or neatly supportive of one another, but rather an untidy and self-contradictory concatenation of flow separators, reverse spins and backwards eddies and upheavals, filled with atavistic as well as progressive elements, and shot through by as many mutual antagonisms as alliances.

One of the lessons of this century's cycle of struggles so far is that of the ambivalence *within* proletarian uprisings, which can manifest both in reactionary forms of fundamentalism and ethno-politics, desiring a return to some mythic time *before* capital, as well as in progressive aspirations to go *beyond* capital (Worth 2013). Advanced capital is already in the midst of a protracted war against reactionary but proletarian-supported movements of a theocratic anti-modernity, movements summoned into being in Afghanistan, Iraq, Syria, Somalia, Nigeria and around the world by the devastation of futuristic accumulation. These regressive movements display determination, military skill and, as Retort (2006) has observed, network sophistication. The challenge for contemporary communists is to find an equivalent that involves not the suicide bomb, but the strike, the riot, the occupation and the hack. This is the only potential 'no' to the no-future of capital's futuristic accumulation of job-loss, debt, eviction, foreclosure, storm-evacuation, acidified oceans and civilizational heat-death.

Five Indicators for a Human Front

Reviewing the history of the *operaismo* tendency from which he eventually diverged, Mario Tronti wrote: 'Workers' struggles determine the course of capitalist development; but capitalist development will use those struggles for its own ends if no organized revolutionary process opens up, capable of changing that balance of forces' (2012: 128). What might an 'organized revolutionary process' look like today? In the convulsions of the last century, communist organizing at points proceeded on the basis of Popular Fronts connecting social forces allied against fascism. Today, the scale of the global crisis generated by cybernetic capital calls for a 'Human Front' (Macleod 2003) crossing the segmentations of proletarianized and re-proletarianized populations, and of threatened intermediate strata, and aligning them against an oncoming wave of catastrophe.

To speak of a 'Front' is to do so in a double sense: meteorological, as a current within the cybernetic vortex capable of reversing and collapsing its destructive momentum; but also military, as a connected linkage of, in the broadest sense, fighting operations. It is also to adopt the term with some of the connotations given it by Ernst Bloch, who used it to signify a line of advance, towards the 'Nova' of new human possibilities. The Front for Bloch is informed by a spirit of 'militant optimism', set against the spurious 'false optimism' of a 'banal, automatic belief in progress', determined to make 'the countermove of freedom against so-called destiny'. 'The countermove against all the deadly manifestations from the family of Nothing and against the circulation of Nothing ... the countermove against all the pervasive ruin of pure negation (war, advent of barbarism)' (Bloch 1986: 199). The Front is the move against the 'death-statics' of capital, a project of 'fear, being armed, confidence' (Bloch 1986: 200). Such a Front would advance an agenda for human development against all national, ethnic and gendered exclusions, and opposed to capital's potential machinic subsumption of the species. Without pretending to anything as schematic or comprehensive as a programme or manifesto, here are five organizational indicators or orientations for such a Human Front relating to the cybernetic dynamics examined in this book.

1) *Bodies.* In its historical origins 'proletariat' refers to the reproduction of the species – to those who have lost everything except that reproductive capacity. Bodily, sensuous, fleshly and feeling human existence was taken by Marx as the basis for all his writing on proletarian existence, exploitation and revolt, as a given. It is today this given that is being taken away by a capitalism that orients itself increasingly towards the reproduction of its fixed, not variable, forms – to the reproduction of machines by machines. In this context, Franco Berardi (2012) is altogether correct when he suggests, in what can be read as a tacit criticism of the algorithmic and immaterialist preoccupations of *post-operaismo* and accelerationist theory, that the primary project for contemporary struggle is to recover the corporeality that the 'general intellect' is annihilating, and to counter the 'digital-financial hyper-abstraction that is liquidating the living body of the planet, and the social body'. Berardi, however, articulates this project more in aesthetic than in political terms; but poetry is not enough – the recovery of the body needs organizational form.

2) *Syndicates.* The cyber-proletariat we have described, the proletariat of the era of capital's machinic supersession of the human, is defined by the existence of large surplus populations, outside the scope of formal employment, a condition then refracted through various gradations of informal and precarious employment, and the intimidation of permanent workers and intermediate strata facing re-proletarianization. The result is a segmented proletariat, commonly subordinated to capital, but divided in many ways. In such a situation there is every likelihood of internecine conflict, with, on the one hand, defence by privileged sections, a category that now includes most of those who have permanent jobs, against gains by the precarious and pauperized, and, on the other, a 'negative solidarity' of resentment against those sections that have won any ground against capital, in a destructive dynamic running at multiple scales – local, regional and global.

To counter this, new, cross-segmentary struggle organizations are urgently needed: without invoking too much left-historical baggage, let us call these 'syndicates'. Some principles that should inform such organizations are: a) alliances of the working, workless, and precariously employed; b) taking responsibility for the social reproduction of the destitute and crisis-struck, without becoming a voluntarist substitute for a destroyed social safety net, but instead maintaining a fighting front; c) adopting a stance of 'raising from the bottom up', prioritizing the needs of the most precarious and pauperized workers in a racialized and feminized workforce. These new types of organization may emerge from within the perpetual struggle to remake labour unions into cross-segmentary organizations – a project consonant with what Immanuel Ness (2014) calls 'the syndicalist and autonomist restoration of class-struggle unionism'. It may also, however, come from the stronger entry into issues of work and worklessness by other radical currents (migrant rights, anti-racist and autonomist or anarchist organizers), as recently suggested by Chris Dixon (2014). More broadly, there is a space for new forms of syndicalism that aim to cross the boundaries of the four types of actions that have characterized the recent cycle of struggles – riots, wage struggles, occupations and hacktivism – each with their characteristic class compositions, so that these learn from and interpenetrate one another in a new organizational synthesis.

3) *Networks.* The 2011 cycle of struggles contributed to a renewed discussion of the 'communist horizon' (Dean 2012), and also some revived advocacy for the Leninist party. Yet the strongly horizontal tendency of contemporary struggles makes it unlikely any vanguard group will hegemonize their myriad molecular components under some molar organization.

This horizontalism is strongly associated with network practices. We agree with Rodrigo Nunes (2014) that any kind of contemporary 'party' organization would have to emerge from within the network setting. This setting is very unlikely to generate or be hegemonized by classic vanguardism. What may be feasible is a 'becoming party' of multiplicitous movements which learn, in the course of struggle, an increasing self-discipline, prioritizing objectives and coordinating operations around gradually developed common goals. As Nunes suggests, the real dynamics of such complex network systems is far from being strictly horizontal, always in actuality involving leadership forms – hubs of communication and influence that move to the fore and recede in particular times and contexts in a sort of rotating vanguardism which is also a divestment of the claim by any single organization to totalize the revolutionary project. However, as was discussed in Chapter 7, the accelerated, de-contextualized and surveilled nature of digital communication means that this networked process cannot be solely a form of cyber-activism, but has to be accompanied by slower, localized and secure processes of solidarity formation, negotiation and planning. In this sense, and in this sense only, we might say that while in the era of the mass worker the party constructed the cells, in that of the global proletariat the networked cells must create the party, an organization as far from Leninism as contemporary military organization, with its all-round battle-spaces and mobile fronts, is from vanguards.

4) *Transitions*. To make future crises occasions for communist breakthroughs rather than capitalist ones, proletarian movements should develop transitional plans, 'plan C's' (Plan C 2013) that counter both capital's mainlines of advance and its back-strategies. There are evident problems with post-*operaismo*'s tendency to reformist proposals, such as basic income schemes, which would shrink to 'dwarfish form' within capital. However, communisation theory's insistence on 'nothing but' an immediate communism that it can describe only in the most abstract terms is also implausible; we can't share its faith – the 'wager' – that this outcome will arrive without some premeditation. Planning for transitions to a post-capitalist communism is necessary, providing these plans are kept transitive, mobile and multiple, constantly subject to discussion within the movement and always understood not as fetishized programmes but as means to heightened struggle and full-out appropriations against capital.

The best models are those that push towards the dis-aggregation of capitalist globalization, even if this is understood as opening a way to new forms of internationalism or planetism. Along these lines, Roth, at the height of the Wall Street crash, suggested forms of trade union and social movement association that, as a short-term goal, would 'impose and sharpen' reformist programmes to overcome the crisis, pushing 'anti-cyclical' Keynesianism beyond its intended limits, promoting workers' control in recovered industries, and through progressive taxation and re-appropriation effecting a 'massive top down redistribution of wealth' (Roth 2010: 229). Longer-term goals would include radical reductions in working time, and the democratization of municipal governance, with local and regional socialization of resources gradually connecting in federated structures.

Other crises will require other plans, but this type of forward thinking could help synchronize erratic struggle cascades into a torrential force. What is likely to remain constant is Roth's emphasis on 'mass co-ordinated action' linked with 'world-wide information campaigns' and 'mass learning processes'. Noting the critical role of new scientific-technological labour in such activity, he calls for a 'globally linked association' that would not be a 'cadre organization claiming to be a vanguard' but a 'free and democratic association of people who have criticized, corrected, revised, expanded and subsequently appropriated ... concept[s] to test [their] usefulness in dialogue with the proletarian multiverse' (2010: 230).

5) *Readiness.* Concluding her major study of world labour activism in the twentieth century, Beverly Silver noted that one major reason for the relative quiescence in proletarian movements at the beginning of the twenty-first century was that the 'global political-military context contrasts sharply with ... that [which] produced radicalized and explosive labour unrest in the first half of the twentieth century' (2003: 176). In other respects, the capitalist offensive of restructuring, globalization and financialization, with 'growing structural unemployment, escalating inequalities and major disruptions', repeated the crisis patterns of previous eras. The missing condition was armed conflict. Since Silver wrote, this condition has reappeared, and, terrifyingly, seems likely to do so with increasing frequency and force; future proletarian struggles should adequate themselves to wartime.

Cybernetics was from its start the creation of war. It continued to develop in the context of war and impending war. It has been shaped not just by the Cold War, but by the ongoing attempts of the United States to adopt and adapt forms of network-empowered 'soft revolutions' in the former Soviet territories of Central and Eastern Europe which mimicked alter-globalist cyber-activism (Morozov 2011). Herrera (2014) suggests a similar play may have been involved, and gone wildly out of control, in Egyptian digital activism against Mubarak, which US cyber-warriors fostered as a grassroots 'modernizing' movement to fend off Islamic fundamentalism. Above all, since 2001 the cybernetic environment has been shaped – in ways of which the omni-surveillance revealed by Snowden is only the most obvious – by the 'war on terror'.

In the wake of 2011, and the wars following the uprisings in Ukraine and Syria, it is impossible to ignore the probability that a future communist movement will emerge in a more or less directly wartime context, with all this implies not only for civil divisions and foreign interventions, but, in terms of cybernetics, for media blackouts and blockades, censorship, viral mis- and dis-information saturation, potentially deadly information monitoring and abrupt communication disruptions. They should prepare accordingly to understand anonymization, encryption and verification techniques, carefully distinguishing public and covert operations, and laying the groundwork for organization when the nets go down.

In a collection appropriately named *In the Middle of a Whirlwind*, Kidd (2010) reminds us how the radical English working-class historian E. P. Thompson wrote of the difficulty of formulating any politics that could 'prepare us for a time when both capitalist and state communist needs and expectations may decompose, and human nature be made into a new form. This is perhaps to whistle into a typhoon' (1991: 11). We are surely in that typhoon now. But despite – or because of – such conditions, we can pit against Land's cyber-punk Terminator-futurology of exterminatory cybernetic capital an unlikely counter-narrative: *The Wizard of Oz*. Dorothy, our female proletarian protagonist, is plucked off the land in a tornado and swept to a domain under the spell of a malign force that enslaves entire populations with its bio-drone flying monkeys. Somehow these fractioned and uncertain forces assemble a coalition capable of dispelling the mystifications and fetishism to which they have been subjected, recapturing their world and extricating themselves from the terrifying system that has engulfed them. The contested ruby slippers, with their capacities for leaping over space and time, stand in nicely for the cybernetic means of production and communication.

This invocation may betray radical theory's debt to mythic trope. But the story is more complicated than just that. For *The Wizard of Oz* is, at least in its most widely received version, a fairy-tale informed by militant theory. There is critical disagreement about the political origins of Frank Baum's original novel; however, the songwriter for the great 1939 film, Yip Harburg, was a communist sympathiser, who in the midst of the Great Depression created in its lyrics an expression of popular front resistance to capital. This was strikingly recalled when, following the death of Margaret Thatcher, the BBC temporarily banned broadcasts of 'Ding Dong, the Wicked Witch is Dead' (Tucker 2013). Today, an annihilatory cybernetic vortex demands nothing less than a resistant human front made up of all those who are small in relation to the gigantism of cybernetic capital, of beings compounded with straw and tin, yet animal in nature, capable of care for one another and for the world. A first step along this brick road is, however, for communists to acknowledge the new conditions of class composition and unflinchingly observe: 'Toto, I've a feeling we're not in Kansas anymore.'

Bibliography

(All internet documents accessed 4–5 December 2014)

Achtenberg, Emily (2010) 'Bolivia's Lithium Challenge', *NACLA*, 15 April, https://nacla.org/news/bolivia%E2%80%99s-lithium-challenge

Adler, Jerry (2012) 'Raging Bulls: How Wall Street Got Addicted to Light-Speed Trading', *Wired*, 8 March, http://www.wired.com/2012/08/ff_wallstreet_trading/all

Aker, Jenny C. and Mbiti, Isaac M. (2010) 'Mobile Phones and Economic Development in Africa', *Journal of Economic Perspectives*, 24(3): 207–32.

Alarcón, Rafael Medina (2014) 'Peasant Warriors in an Electronic Social-Formation: From rural communities to transnational circuits of dependence in postwar El Salvador', *Convergence: International Journal of Research in New Media*, http://con.sagepub.com/content/early/2014/07/25/1354856514544085

Alpert, Daniel (2013) *The Age of Oversupply: The Greatest Challenge to the Global Economy*. London: Penguin.

Alquati, Romano (1974) 'The Network of Struggles in Italy', http://libcom.org/library/network-of-struggles-italy-romano-alquati

Alquati, Romano (2013) [1961] 'Organic Composition of Capital and Labor-Power at Olivetti', *Viewpoint Magazine*, 27 September, http://viewpointmag.com/2013/09/27/organic-composition-of-capital-and-labor-power-at-olivetti-1961

Amin, Samir (2010) *The Law of Worldwide Value*. New York: Monthly Review.

Anandan, Tanya (2013) 'The End of Separation: Man and Robot as Collaborative Coworkers on the Factory Floor', *Robotics Online*, 6 June, http://preview.tinyurl.com/ktk2025

Anderson, Nate (2010) 'Riots Lead Mozambique to Ban Cell Phone Anonymity', *Arstechnica*, 28 October, http://arstechnica.com/tech-policy/2010/10/riots-lead-mozambique-to-ban-cell-phone-anonymity

Andrejevic, Mark (2009) 'Exploiting YouTube: Contradictions of User-Generated Labour', in Snickers, Pelle and Vondreau, Patrick (eds.) *The YouTube Reader*, Stockholm: National Library of Sweden, 406–23.

Andrejevic, Mark (2015) 'The Droning of Experience', *Fiberculture*, forthcoming.

Aneesh, A. (2006) *Virtual Migration: The Programming of Globalization*. Durham: Duke University Press.

Antunes, Ricardo (2013) *The Meanings of Work: Essay on the Affirmation and Negation of Work*. Boston: Brill.

Aouragh, Miryam and Alexander, Anne (2011) 'The Egyptian Experience: Sense and Nonsense of the Internet Revolution', *International Journal of Communication*, 5: 1344–58.

AP (Associated Press) (2010) 'Mozambique Food Riots Spark Fears Worldwide', *CBC News*, 3 September, http://www.cbc.ca/news/mozambique-food-riots-spark-fears-worldwide-1.950178

AP (Associated Press) (2014) 'Poverty, Disparity Grow Along with Prosperity in Silicon Valley's Boom', *Fox News*, http://www.foxnews.com/tech/2014/03/06/poverty-disparity-grow-along-with-prosperity-in-silicon-valley-boom

Aronowitz, Stanley (1994) *The Jobless Future: Sci-Tech and the Dogma of Work*. Minneapolis: University of Minnesota Press.

Arria, Michael (2012) 'Beyond Clicktivism: Jodi Dean on the Limits of Technology in the Occupy Movement', *Motherboard*, 18 November, http://motherboard.vice.com/en_ca/blog/beyond-clicktivism-jodi-dean-on-the-limits-of-technology-in-the-occupy-movement

Arthur, Brian (2011) 'The Second Economy', McKinsey Institute, http://www.mckinsey.com/insights/strategy/the_second_economy

Arthur, Charles (2011) 'Developers Express Concern Over Pirated Games on Android Market', *Guardian Technology Blog*, 17 March, http://www.guardian.co.uk/technology/blog/2011/mar/17/android-market-pirated-games-concerns

Ashby, W. R. (1948) 'Design for Brain', *Electronic Engineering*, 20: 379–83.

Aspray, William, Mayadas, Frank and Vardi, Moshe Y. (2006) 'Globalization and the Offshoring of Software: A Report of the ACM Job Migration Task Force. Association for Computing Machinery', http://www.acm.org/globalizationreport/pdf/fullfinal.pdf

Assange, Julian (2012) *CypherPunks: Freedom and the Future of the Internet*. New York: O/R Books.

Atkinson, Robert D. and Stewart, Luke A. (2013) 'Just the Facts: The Benefits of Information and Communications Technology', *Information Technology and Innovation Foundation*, http://www.itif.org/publications/just-facts-benefits-information-and-communications-technology

Auden W. H. (1950) 'Oxford', *Collected Shorter Poems, 1930–1944*. London: Faber & Faber.

Baca, Marie (2010) 'Toxic-Waste Sites Haunt Silicon Valley', *Wall Street Journal*, July 15, http://online.wsj.com/news/articles/SB10001424052748704111704575355212354653420

Bacon, David (2011) 'Up Against the Open Shop: The Hidden Story of Silicon Valley's High-Tech Workers', *Truthout*, 4 March, http://preview.tinyurl.com/m72dnpa

Balakrishnan, Gopal (ed.) (2003) *Debating Empire*. New York: Verso.

Baldwin, Richard (2011) 'Trade and Industrialization After Globalisation's 2nd Unbundling: How Building and Joining a Supply Chain Are Different and Why it Matters', National Bureau of Economic Research, Working Paper 17716, http://www.nber.org/papers/w17716

Ball, James (2011) 'Social Media Has its Own Class Divide', *Guardian*, 8 December, http://www.theguardian.com/commentisfree/2011/dec/08/social-media-blackberry-messenger

Ballard, J. G. (1966) *The Crystal World*. New York: Farrar, Straus & Giroux.

Barajas, Adolfo, Chami, Ralph, Fullenkamp, Connel, Gapen, Michael and Montiel, Peter (2009) 'Do Workers' Remittances Promote Economic Growth?', International Monetary Fund Working Paper 09/153, https://www.imf.org/external/pubs/ft/wp/2009/wp09153.pdf

Barbrook, Richard (2000) 'Cyber-Communism: How the Americans are Superseding Capitalism in Cyberspace', *Science as Culture*, 9(1): 5–40.

Barbrook, Richard and Cameron, Andy (1996) 'The Californian Ideology', *Science as Culture*, 26: 44–72.

Barrat, James (2013) *Our Final Invention: Artificial Intelligence and the End of the Human Era*. New York: Thomas Dunne.

BBC (2011) 'Foxconn "mulls $12bn Brazil move" as it seeks expansion', 13 April, http://www.bbc.co.uk/news/business-13058866

BBC (2013a) 'US employee "outsourced job to China"', 16 January, http://www.bbc.com/news/technology-21043693

BBC (2013b) 'Amazon workers face "increased risk of mental illness"', 24 November, http://www.bbc.com/news/business-25034598

BBC (2013c) 'Amazon testing drones for deliveries', 2 December, http://www.bbc.com/news/technology-25180906

BBC (2014) 'Algorithm appointed board director', 16 May, http://www.bbc.com/news/technology-27426942

Beja, Jean Phillipe (2012) 'The New Working Class Renews the Repertoire of Social Conflict', *China Perspectives*, 2: 3–7.

Bell, Daniel (1973) *The Coming of Post-Industrial Society*. New York: Basic.

Bell, Peter and Cleaver, Harry (1982) 'Marx's Crisis Theory as a Theory of Class Struggle', *Research in Political Economy*, 5: 189–261.

Benjamin, Walter (1969) 'Theses on the Philosophy of History', in his *Illuminations*, New York: Schoken Press, 253-264.

Benjamin, Walter (2003) *Selected Writings, Volume 4: 1938–40*. Cambridge, MA: Belknap Press.

Berardi, Franco (2012) 'Cognitarian Subjectivation', *e-flux*, 20, http://www.e-flux.com/journal/cognitarian-subjectivation

Bergvall-Karebon, Birgitta and Howcraft, Debra (2011) 'Mobile Applications Development on Apple and Google Platforms', *Communications of the Association for Information Systems*, 29(1): 565–80.

Berman, Marshall (1982) *All That is Solid Melts Into Air: The Experience of Modernity*. New York: Simon & Schuster.

Bernes, Jasper (2013) 'Logistics, Counterlogistics and the Communist Prospect', *Endnotes 3*: 172–201.

Bey, Hakim (1991) *TAZ: The Temporary Autonomous Zone*. New York: Semiotext(e).

Bhavnani, Asheeta, Won-Wai Chiu, Rowena, Janakiram, Subramaniam and Silarszky, Peter (2008) *The Role of Mobile Phones in Sustainable Rural Poverty Reduction.* World Bank: ICT Policy, http://preview.tinyurl.com/62680x

Biao, Xiang (2007) *Global "Body Shopping": An Indian Labour System in the Information Technology Industry.* Princeton: Princeton University Press.

Bloch, Ernst (1986) *The Principle of Hope.* Vol. 1. Oxford: Blackwell.

Böhm, Steffen, Land, Chris and Beverungen, Armin (2012) 'The Value of Marx: Free Labour, Rent and "Primitive" Accumulation in Facebook', Working Paper, University of Essex, https://www.academia.edu/1571230/The_Value_of_Marx_Free_Labour_Rent_and_Primitive_Accumulation_in_Facebook

Bolaño, Roberto (2004) *2666.* New York: Farrar, Strauss and Giroux.

Bonacich, Edna and Wilson, Jake B. (2009) *Getting the Goods: Ports, Labor, and the Logistics Revolution.* Ithaca, NY: Cornell University Press.

Bonefeld, Werner and Holloway, John (1995) *Global Capital, National State and the Politics of Money.* London: Palgrave Macmillan.

Bonta, Mark and Protevi, John (2004) *Deleuze and Geophilosophy: A Guide and Glossary.* Edinburgh: Edinburgh University Press.

Bostrom, Nick (2014) *Superintelligence: Paths, Dangers, Strategies.* Oxford: Oxford University Press.

Bousquet, Marc (2008) *How the University Works: Higher Education and the Low-Wage Nation.* New York: New York University Press.

Boutang, Yann Moulier (2011) *Cognitive Capitalism.* Polity: Cambridge.

Bowley, Graham (2010) 'Ex-Physicist Leads Flash Crash Inquiry', *New York Times*, 20 September, http://www.nytimes.com/2010/09/21/business/economy/21flash.html

Bratton, Benjamin (2014) 'On Apps and Elementary Forms of Interfacial Life: Object, Image, Superimposition', in Miller, Paul and Matviyenko, Svitlana (eds.) *The Imaginary App*, Cambridge, MA: MIT Press, 1–16.

Braverman, Harry (1974) *Labour and Monopoly Capitalism: The Degradation of Work in the Twentieth Century.* New York: Monthly Review Press.

Brophy, Enda and de Peuter, Greig (2014) 'Labours of Mobility: Communicative Capitalism and the Smartphone Cybertariat', in Herman, Andrew, Hadlaw, Jan and Swiss, Thomas (eds.) *Theories of the Mobile Internet: Materialities and Imaginaries*, New York: Routledge.

Brown, Brian A. (2013) 'Primitive Digital Accumulation: Privacy, Social Networks and Biopolitical Exploitation', *Rethinking Marxism*, 25(3): 385–403.

Bryan, Dick and Rafferty, Michael (2006) *Capitalism with Derivatives: A Political Economy of Financial Derivatives, Capital and Class.* New York: Palgrave.

Brynjolfsson, Eric and McAfee, Andrew (2014) *The Second Machine Age: Work, Progress, and Prosperity in a Time of Brilliant Technologies.* New York: Norton.

Buchanan, Mark (2013) *Forecast: What Physics, Meteorology and the Natural Sciences Can Teach Us About Economics.* London: Bloomsbury.

Burrell, Jenna (2010) 'Evaluating Shared Access: Social Equality and the Circulation of Mobile Phones in Rural Uganda', *Journal of Computer-Mediated Communication*, 15: 230–50.

Burtynsky, Edward (2003) *Manufactured Landscapes: The Photographs of Edward Burtynsky*. New Haven, CT: Yale University Press.

Caffentzis, George (2013) *In Letters of Blood and Fire: Work, Machines, and Value in the Bad Infinity of Capitalism*. New York: PM Press.

Camfield, David (2007) 'The Multitude and the Kangaroo: A Critique of Hardt and Negri's Theory of Immaterial Labour', *Historical Materialism*, 15: 21–52.

Carchedi, Guglielmo (1977) *On the Economic Identification of Social Classes*. London: Routledge and Kegan Paul.

Carchedi, Guglielmo (1997) 'High-Tech Hype: Promises and Realities of Technology in the Twenty-First Century', in J. Davis, Hirschl, Thomas and Michael Stack (eds.), *Cutting Edge: Technology, Information, Capitalism and Social Revolution*, London: Verso, 73–86.

Carmody, Pádraig (2012) 'The Informationalization of Poverty in Africa? Mobile Phones and Economic Structure', *Information Technology and International Development*, 3: 1–17.

Castells, Manuel (2002) *The Internet Galaxy*. Oxford: Oxford University Press.

Castells, Manuel (2012) *Networks of Outrage and Hope: Social Movements in the Internet Age*. Cambridge: Polity.

Chakraborty, Indranil (2014) 'Digital Capitalism and the Informal Economy: The Case of Support Service Workers in the Indian IT Sector', Dissertation in progress, Faculty of Information and Media Studies, University of Western Ontario.

Chan, Jenny and Ngai, Pun (2010) 'Suicide as Protest for the New Generation of Chinese Migrant Workers: Foxconn, Global Capital, and the State', *The Asia-Pacific Journal*, 37(2), http://www.japanfocus.org/-Ngai-Pun/3408

Chan, Jenny, Ngai, Pun and Selden, Mark (2013) 'The Politics of Global Production: Apple, Foxconn and China's New Working Class', *New Technology, Work and Employment*, 28(2): 100–15.

Chang, Shenlin (2006) *The Global Silicon Valley Home: Lives and Landscapes within Taiwanese-American Trans-Pacific Culture*. Stanford: Stanford University Press.

Chang, Shenlin, Chiu, Hua-Mei and Tu, Wen-Ling (2006) 'Breaking the Silicon Silence: Voicing Health and Environmental Impacts within Taiwan's Hsinchu Science Park', in Smith, T., Sonnenfeld, D. A. and Pellow, D. N. (eds.) *Challenging the Chip*. Philadelphia: Temple University Press, 170–80.

Chen, Adrian (2014) 'The Laborers Who Keep Dick Pics and Beheadings Out of Your Facebook Feed', *Wired*, 23 October, http://www.wired.com/2014/10/content-moderation

Chen, Brian X. (2011) *Always On: How the iPhone Unlocked the Anything-Anytime-Anywhere Future – and Locked Us In*. New York: Da Capo.

CIO (Chief Information Officer) (2007) 'When Bad Things Happen to Good Projects', 2 April, http://www.cio.com/article/2439385/project-management/when-bad-things-happen-to-good-projects.html

Clark, Matthew (2007) 'Unserved by Banks, Poor Kenyans Now Just Use a Cellphone', *Christian Science Monitor*, 12 October, http://www.csmonitor.com/2007/1012/p01s03-woaf.html

Cleaver, Harry (1979) *Reading Capital Politically*. Brighton, Harvester.

Cleaver, Harry (1995) 'The Zapatistas and the Electronic Fabric of Struggle', https://webspace.utexas.edu/ hcleaver/www/zaps.html

Clemens, Paul (2011) *Punching Out: One Year in a Closing Auto Plant*. New York: Doubleday.

Clifton, Jon and Ryan, Ben (2014) 'Only 1.3 Billion Worldwide Employed Full Time for Employer', *The World at Work*, http://www.gallup.com/poll/174791/billion-worldwide-employed-full-time-employer.aspx

Cockburn, Cynthia (1983) *Brothers: Male Dominance and Technological Change*. London: Pluto.

Cockburn, Cynthia (1985) *Machinery of Dominance: Women, Men and Technical Know-How*. London: Pluto.

Cockshott, Paul, Cottrell, Alan, Michaelson, Gregory, Wright, Ian P. and Yakovenko, Victor M. (2009) *Classical Econophysics*. London: Routledge.

Colatrella, Steven (2011) 'A Worldwide Strike Wave, Austerity and the Political Crisis of Global Governance', Libcom.org, http://libcom.org/library/worldwide-strike-wave-austerity-political-crisis-global-governance-steven-colatrella

Collins, Greg (2009) 'Connected: Exploring the Extraordinary Demand for Telecoms Services in Post-collapse Somalia', *Mobilities*, 4(2): 203–23.

Conway, Flo and Siegelman, Jim (2005) *Dark Hero of the Information Age: In Search of Norbert Wiener, the Father of Cybernetics*. New York: Basic Books.

Cooper, Melinda (2010) 'Turbulent Worlds: Financial Markets and Environmental Crisis', *Theory, Culture & Society*, 27(2/3): 167–90.

Cope, Zak (2012) *Divided World Divided Class: Global Political Economy and the Stratification of Labour Under Capitalism*. Kersplebedeb Pub.

Cortada, James W. (2004) *The Digital Hand: How Computers Changed the Work of American Manufacturing, Transportation and Retail Industries*. Oxford: Oxford University Press.

Coté, Mark and Pybus, Jennifer (2007) 'Learning to Immaterial Labour 2.0: MySpace and Social Networks', *Ephemera: theory and politics in organization*, 7(1): 88–106.

Cowen, Deborah (2014) *The Deadly Life of Logistics: Mapping Violence in Global Trade*. Minneapolis: University of Minnesota.

Cunningham, John (2009) 'Invisible Politics – An Introduction to Contemporary Communisation', *Mute*, 14, http://www.metamute.org/editorial/articles/invisible-politics-introduction-to-contemporary-communisation

Curtis, Adam (2011) *Watched Over by Machines of Loving Grace*. BBC.

Credit Suisse, *Global Wealth Report 2011*, https://publications.credit-suisse.com/tasks/render/file/index.cfm?fileid=88E41853-83E8-EB92-9D5895A42B9499B1

Dalla Costa, Mariarosa and James, Selma (1972) *The Power of Women and the Subversion of the Community*. Bristol: Falling Wall Press.

D'Angelo, Massimo (2010) 'The Production of Commons and the "Explosion" of the Middle Class', *Antipode*, 42(4): 954–77.

Dassbach, Carl H. A. (1986) 'Industrial Robots in the American Automobile Industry', *Critical Sociology*, 13(53): 53–61.

Davidson, Helen (2014) 'Carlos Slim calls for three-day working week to improve quality of life', *Guardian*, 21 July, http://www.theguardian.com/business/2014/jul/21/carlos-slim-calls-for-three-day-working-week-to-improve-quality-of-life

Davis, Mike (1986) *Prisoners of the American Dream*. New York: Verso.

Davis, Mike (2007) *Planet of Slums*. New York: Verso.

Davis, Mike (2011) 'Spring Confronts Winter', *New Left Review*, 72: 5–15.

D'Costa, Anthony P. (2003) 'Uneven and Combined Development: Understanding India's Software Exports', *World Development*, 31(1): 211–26.

Dean, Jodi (2009) *Democracy and other Neoliberal Fantasies: Communicative Capitalism and Left Politics*. Durham, NC: Duke University Press.

Dean, Jodi (2012) *The Communist Horizon*. London: Verso.

Dean, Jodi and Passavant, Paul (eds.) (2003) *Empire's New Clothes: Reading Hardt and Negri*. New York: Routledge.

de Garis, Hugo (2005) 'The Artilect War: Cosmists Vs. Terrans: A Bitter Controversy Concerning Whether Humanity Should Build Godlike Massively Intelligent Machines', http://agi-conf.org/2008/artilectwar.pdf

DeLanda, Manuel (2011) *Philosophy and Simulation: The Emergence of Synthetic Reason*. New York: Continuum.

de Mattis, Léon (2014) 'Communist Measures: Thinking a Communist Horizon', *SIC International Journal of Communisation*, 2, http://www.sicjournal.org/en/communist-measures

Denning, Michael (2010) 'Wageless Life', *New Left Review*, 66: 79–85.

DeParle, Jason (2010) 'Global Migration: A World Ever More on the Move', *New York Times*, 27 June, http://preview.tinyurl.com/ohweg5q

Deterritorial Support Group (2012) 'All the Memes of Production', *New Left Project*, http://www.newleftproject.org/index.php/site/article_comments/all_the_memes_of_production

Dixon, Chris (2014) *Another Politics: Talking Across Today's Transformative Movements*. Oakland: University of California.

Dobbs, Richard et al. (2012) 'The World at Work: Jobs, Pay, and Skills for 3.5 Billion People', McKinsey Global Institute, http://www.mckinsey.com/insights/employment_and_growth/the_world_at_work.

Dohse, Knuth, Jurgens, Ulrich and Nialsch, Thomas (1985) 'From "Fordism" to "Toyotism"? The Social Organization of the Labor Process in the Japanese Automobile Industry', *Politics & Society*, 14: 115–46.

Dossani, Rafiq and Kenney, Martin (2003) 'Went for Cost, Stayed for Quality?: Moving the Back Office to India', *Berkeley Roundtable on the International Economy*, http://escholarship.org/uc/item/0b7764

Draper, Hal (1978) *Karl Marx's Theory of Revolution*, Vol. II. New York: Monthly Review.

Duncan, Richard (2012) *The New Depression: The Breakdown of the Paper Money Economy*. Singapore: John Wiley & Sons.

Durfee, Don (2012) 'China's Turn Toward More Machines', *New York Times*, 5 June, http://www.nytimes.com/2012/06/05/business/global/chinas-turn-toward-more-machines.html?pagewanted=all&_r=0

Dyer-Witheford, Nick (1999) *Cyber-Marx: Cycles and Circuits of Struggle in High-Technology Capitalism*. Urbana: University of Illinois Press.

Dyer-Witheford, Nick (2001) 'Empire, Immaterial Labor, the New Combinations, and the Global Worker', *Rethinking Marxism*, 13(3/4): 61–9.

Dyer-Witheford, Nick (2002) 'E-Capital and the Many-Headed Hydra', in Elmer G. (ed.) *Critical Perspectives on the Internet*, Rowman & Littlefield, 129–64.

Dyer-Witheford, Nick (2004) '1844/2004/2044: The Return of Species-Being', *Historical Materialism*, 12(4): 3–25.

Dyer-Witheford, Nick (2005) 'Cyber-Negri: General Intellect and Immaterial Labor', in Murphy T. and Mustapha, Abdul-Karim, *The Philosophy of Antonio Negri: Resistance in Practice*. London: Pluto, 136–62.

Dyer-Witheford, Nick (2008) 'For a Compositional Analysis of the Multitude', Bonefeld, W. (ed.) *Subverting the Present, Imagining the Future*. New York: Autonomedia, 247–65.

Dyer-Witheford, Nick (2014a) 'App Worker', in Miller, Paul and Matviyenko, Svitlana (eds.), *The Imaginary App*, Cambridge, MA: MIT Press, 125–44.

Dyer-Witheford, Nick (2014b) 'Red Plenty Platforms', *Culture Machine*, 13, 1–26.

Dyer-Witheford, Nick and de Peuter, Greig (2009) *Games of Empire: Global Capitalism and Videogames*. Minneapolis: University of Minnesota Press.

Dymski, Gary A. (2009) 'Racial Exclusion and the Political Economy of the Subprime Crisis', *Historical Materialism*, 17: 149–79.

Dyson, George (2012) *Turing's Cathedral: The Origins of the Digital Universe*. New York: Pantheon.

Economist (2001) 'The Internet: Easy.com, easy.go', *The Economist*, 12 April, http://www.economist.com/node/569835

Economist (2009a) 'The Semiconductor Industry: Under New Management', *The Economist*, 2 April, http://www.economist.com/node/13405279

Economist (2009b) 'Telecoms in Emerging Markets: Mobile Marvels', *The Economist*, 24 September, http://www.economist.com/node/14483896

Economist (2010) 'Riots in Mozambique: The Angry Poor', *The Economist*, 9 September, http://www.economist.com/node/16996835

Economist (2011a) 'Labour Market Trends: Winners and Losers', *The Economist*, 10 September, http://www.economist.com/node/21528434

Economist (2011b) 'Foxconn: Robot's Don't Complain', *The Economist*, 6 August, http://www.economist.com/node/21525432

Economist (2012) 'A Fall to Cheer: For the First Time Ever, the Number of Poor People is Declining Everywhere', *The Economist*, http://www.economist.com/node/21548963

Economist (2013a) 'Derivatives Markets Regulation: Back to the Futures?', *The Economist*, 4 February, http://www.economist.com/blogs/freeexchange/2013/02/derivatives-markets-regulation

Economist (2013b) 'The March of Protest', 29 June, http://www.economist.com/news/leaders/21580143-wave-anger-sweeping-cities-world-politicians-beware-march-protest

Economist (2013c) 'Why Does Kenya Lead the World in Mobile Money?', *The Economist*, 27 May, http://www.economist.com/blogs/economist-explains/2013/05/economist-explains-18

Economist (2014) 'The Future of Jobs: The Onrushing Wave', *The Economist*, 18 January, http://www.economist.com/news/briefing/21594264-previous-technological-innovation-has-always-delivered-more-long-run-employment-not-less

Eden, David (2012) *Autonomy: Capitalism, Class and Politics*. Farnham: Ashgate.

Edu-Factory Collective (ed.) (2009) *Toward a Global Autonomous University: Cognitive Labor, The Production of Knowledge, and Exodus from the Education Factory*. New York: Autonomedia.

Edwards, Paul N. (1997) *The Closed World: Computers and the Politics of Discourse in Cold War America*. Cambridge, MA: MIT Press.

Elder, Sara and Schmidt, Dorothea (2004) 'Global Employment Trends for Women, 2004', ILO Employment Trends Unit, http://ilo.org/wcmsp5/groups/public/---ed_emp/---emp_elm/documents/publication/wcms_114325.pdf

Empire Logistics (2014) 'Toyota Workers in India Continue Strike', Libcom.org, http://libcom.org/blog/toyota-workers-india-continue-strike-31032014

Endnotes (2008) *Endnotes 1: Bring Out Your Dead*, http://endnotes.org.uk/issues/1

Endnotes (2010) *Endnotes 2: Misery and the Value Form*, http://endnotes.org.uk/issues/2

Endnotes (2013) *Endnotes 3: Gender, Race, Class and Other Misfortunes*, http://endnotes.org.uk/issues/3

Eudy, Jan (2003) 'Human Contamination', *Cintas Cleanroom Resources*, 2 April, http://www.cintas.com/PDF/CleanroomResources/CintasApr03.pdf

Fabrega, J. and Paredes, P. (2013) 'Social Contagion and Cascade Behaviors on Twitter', *Information*, 4(2), 171–81.

Fadli (2013) 'Batam, Alleged Transshipment Point for Ivory from Africa', *The Jakarta Post: Batam*, 10 March, http://www.thejakartapost.com/news/2013/03/10/batam-alleged-transshipment-point-ivory-africa.html

Faris, David M. (2013) *Dissent and Revolution in a Digital Age: Social Media, Blogging and Activism in Egypt*. New York: I. B. Taurus.

Federici, Silvia (2012) *Revolution at Point Zero: Housework, Reproduction and Feminist Struggle*. Oakland: PM Press.

Ferguson, Niall (2008) *The Ascent of Money: A Financial History of the World*. New York: Penguin Press.

Fernández Kelly, M. Patricia (1983) *For We Are Sold, I and My People: Women and Industry in Mexico's Frontier*. Albany, NY: SUNY Press.

Fiegerman, Seth (2014) 'Google Founders Talk About Ending the 40-Hour Work Week', *Mashable*, 7 June, http://mashable.com/2014/07/07/google-founders-interview-khosla

Fischer, Florian (2013) 'Cascades of Collective Action? Analyzing the Impact of Protest History and Social Media on Regime Change in the Context of the 2011 Uprisings in Egypt and Syria', CGP Working Papers, http://www.global-politics.org/publications/working-papers/cgp-wp-01-2013/CGP_Cascades_of_Collective_Action_Florian_Fischer.pdf

Fisher, Mark (2009) *Capitalist Realism: Is There No Alternative?* Winchester, UK: Zero Works.

Fisher, Mark (2010) 'Terminator vs. Avatar: Notes on Accelerationism', *Mark Fisher Reblog*, http://markfisherreblog.tumblr.com/post/32522465887/terminator-vs-avatar-notes-on-accelerationism

Florida, Richard (2002) *The Rise Of The Creative Class: And How It's Transforming Work, Leisure, Community And Everyday Life*. New York: Basic Books.

Florida, Richard (2013) 'Why San Francisco May Be the New Silicon Valley', http://www.citylab.com/work/2013/08/why-san-francisco-may-be-new-silicon-valley/6295

Fontaine, Jessica (2014) 'Aging Analytics UK Launches VITAL, a Predictive Investment Tool For the Regenerative Medicine Sector', *Cadogan Consulting Group*, 13 May, http://www.thecorporatecounsel.net/nonMember/docs/05_14_AgingAnalytics.pdf

Ford, Michele and Lenore Lyons (2008) 'Living Like Kings', *Inside Indonesia*, January–March, http://www.insideindonesia.org/feature-editions/living-like-kings

Fortunati, Leopoldina (1995) *The Arcana of Reproduction: Housework, Prostitution, Labor and Capital*. New York: Autonomedia.

Foster, Christopher and Heeks, Richard (2011) 'Employment and the Mobile Sector in Developing Countries', *Background Paper for UNCTAD Information Economy Report*, http://infomediation.files.wordpress.com/2013/12/foster_heeks_2011_employment-and-the-mobile-sector-in-developing-countries.pdf

Foster, John Bellamy, McChesney, Robert W. and Jonna, R. Jamil (2011) 'The Global Reserve Army of Labor and the New Imperialism', *Monthly Review*, 63(6), http://monthlyreview.org/2011/11/01/the-global-reserve-army-of-labor-and-the-new-imperialism

Frank, Andre Gunder (1966) *The Development of Underdevelopment*. New York: Monthly Review Press.

Freeland, Chrystia (2012) *Plutocrats: The Rise of the New Global Super-Rich and the Fall of Everyone Else*. New York: Penguin.

Friedman, Thomas (2005) *The World Is Flat: A Brief History of the Twenty-first Century*. New York: Farrar, Straus and Giroux.

Friends of Gongchao (2013a) '10 Paragraphs Against 1 Rotten Apple – iSlavery at Foxconn', http://www.gongchao.org/en/islaves-struggles/10-paragraphs-against-1-rotten-apple

Friends of Gongchao (2013b) 'Against the Fetish of Representation: Class Struggle in China Beyond the Leftist Grand Narrative', http://www.gongchao.org/en/texts/2013/against-the-fetish-of-representation#sdfootnote11sym

Friends of Kolinko and GurgaonWorkersNews (2012) 'Burn-out in the Global Call Centre', *Mute*, 30 December, http://www.metamute.org/editorial/articles/burn-out-global-call-centre

Fuchs, Christian (2008) 'Deconstructive Class Analysis: Theoretical Foundations and Empirical Examples', *ICT & S Centre Research Paper*, http://icts.sbg.ac.at/media/pdf/pdf1666.pdf

Fuchs, Christian (2011) 'A Contribution to the Critique of the Political Economy of Google', *Fast Capitalism*, 8(1), http://www.uta.edu/huma/agger/fastcapitalism/8_1/fuchs8_1.html

Fuchs, Christian (2012) 'Social Media, Riots, and Revolutions', *Capital and Class*, 36(3): 383–91.

Fuchs, Christian (2014a) *Digital Labour and Karl Marx*. New York: Routledge.

Fuchs, Christian (2014b) *Social Media: A Critical Introduction*. Los Angeles: Sage.

Fumagalli, Andrea (2007) *Bioeconomia e Capitalismo Cognitivo: Vesro un Nuovo Paradigma di Accumulazione*. Rome: Carocci.

Gabriel, Anita (2012) 'Indonesia's Batam Losing Its Economic Luster', *Jakarta Globe*, 30 March, http://www.thejakartaglobe.com/archive/indonesias-batam-losing-its-economic-luster

Gallagher, James (2014) 'Recession "led to 10,000 suicides"', *BBC News*, 11 June, http://www.bbc.com/news/health-27796628

Galloway, Alexander R. (2014) 'The Cybernetic Hypothesis', *differences*, 25(1): 107–31.

Gambino, Ferruccio and Sacchetto, Devi (2014) 'The Shifting Maelstrom: From Plantations to Assembly-Lines', in Roth, Karl Heinz and van der Linden, Marc (eds.) *Beyond Marx: Theorising the Global Labour Relations of the Twenty-First Century*, Leiden: Brill, 89–120.

Garnham, Nicholas (1990) *Capitalism and Communication: Global Culture and the Economics of Information*. London: Sage.

Gaspar de Alba, Alicia and Guzmán, Georgina (eds.) (2010) *Making a Killing: Femicide, Free Trade, and La Frontera*. Austin, TX: University of Texas Press.

Gates, Bill (1995) *The Road Ahead*. London: Penguin.

Georgakas, Dan (1975) *Detroit, I Do Mind Dying: A Study in Urban Revolution*. New York: St. Martin's Press.

Gerbaudo, Paolo (2012) *Tweets and the Streets: Social Media and Contemporary Activism*. London: Pluto.

Gereffi, Gary and Korzeniewicz, Miguel (eds.) (1994) *Commodity Chains and Global Capitalism*. Westport: Greenwood.

Gershenfeld, Neil, Krikorian, Raffi and Cohen, Danny (2004) 'The Internet of Things', *Scientific American*, 291: 76–81.

Gibbs, Samuel (2013) 'What is Boston Dynamics and Why Does Google Want Robots?', *Guardian*, 17 December, http://www.theguardian.com/technology/2013/dec/17/google-boston-dynamics-robots-atlas-bigdog-cheetah

Glaberman, Martin (1952) *Punching Out*. Libcom.org, https://libcom.org/library/punching-out-martin-glaberman

Global Times (2010) 'New Strike Affects Parts Supplier to Toyota and Honda', 2 June.

Gómez, Ignacio (2012) 'Colombia's Black-market Coltan Tied to Drug Traffickers, Paramilitaries', *International Consortium of Investigative Journalists*, 4 March, http://www.icij.org/projects/coltan/colombias-black-market-coltan-tied-drug-traffickers-paramilitaries

Goode, Eric and Miller, Claire Cain (2013) 'Backlash by the Bay: Tech Riches Alter a City', *New York Times*, 24 November, http://www.nytimes.com/2013/11/25/us/backlash-by-the-bay-tech-riches-alter-a-city.html?_r=0

Grant, Tavia (2014) 'Meet the New Middle Class: Robots', *Globe & Mail*, 20 April, http://www.theglobeandmail.com/report-on-business/meet-the-new-middle-class-robots/article18074074

Greeley, Brendan (2013) 'Kenyans Find the Unintended Consequences of Mobile Money', *Bloomberg Businessweek Magazine*, 23 May, http://www.businessweek.com/articles/2013-05-23/kenyans-find-the-unintended-consequences-of-mobile-money

Greenberg, Andy (2012) *This Machine Kills Secrets: How Wikileakers, Cypherpunks and Hacktivists Aim to Free the World's Information*. New York: Dutton.

Greenspan, Alan (2008) *The Age of Turbulence: Adventures in a New World*. New York: Penguin.

Grossman, Elizabeth (2011) 'Toxics in the "Clean Rooms": Are Samsung Workers at Risk?' *Environment 360*, 9 June, http://e360.yale.edu/feature/toxics_in_the_clean_rooms_are_samsung_workers_at_risk/2414

GurgaonWorkersNews (2010a) 'Developing Unrest: New Struggles in Miserable Boom-Town Gurgaon', *GurgaonWorkersNews*, 25, http://gurgaonworkersnews.wordpress.com/content-list-of-published-newsletters

GurgaonWorkersNews (2010b) 'Local Automobile Workers: Electronic Flow Regime Combining Welding Robots and Slum Production', *GurgaonWorkersNews*, 33, http://gurgaonworkersnews.wordpress.com/gurgaonworkersnews-no-933/#fn1

Hafner, Katie (1998) *Where Wizards Stay Up late: The Origins of the Internet*. New York: Simon & Schuster.

Haiven, Max and Stoneman, Scott (2009) 'Wal-Mart: The Panopticon of Time', *Globalization Working Papers*, http://www.academia.edu/1474872/Wal-Mart_The_ panopticon_of_time

Haley, Melinda (2010) 'The Industrial Machine and the Exploitation of Women: The Case of Ciudad Juárez', *The Forum on Public Policy*, http://forumonpublicpolicy. com/vol2010no5/archivevol2010no5/haley.pdf

Hall-Jones, Peter (2010) 'Strike Wave Signals Global Shift', *New Unionism Blog*, 21 October, http://newunionism.wordpress.com/2010/10/21/strikes

Hamlin, Kevin, Gridneff, Ilya and Davison, William (2014) 'Ethiopia Becomes China's China in Global Search for Cheap Labor', *Bloomberg Businessweek Magazine*, July 22, http://www.bloomberg.com/news/2014-07-22/ethiopia-becomes-china-s-china-in-search-for-cheap-labor.html

Han, Jiwon, Liem, Wol-san and Lee, Yoomi (2013) 'In the Belly of the Beast: Samsung Electronics Domestic Supply Chain and Workforce in South Korea', *Asian Labour Update*, 82, http://www.amrc.org.hk/text/node/1340

Haraway, Donna (1985) 'A Manifesto for Cyborgs: Science, Technology, and Socialist Feminism in the 1980s', *Socialist Review*, 80: 65–108.

Hardt, Michael and Negri, Antonio (2000) *Empire*. Boston: Harvard University Press.

Hardt, Michael and Negri, Antonio (2004) *Multitude: War and Democracy in an Age of Empire*. New York: Penguin.

Hardt, Michael and Negri, Antonio (2011) *Commonwealth*. Cambridge, MA: Belknap Press.

Hardt, Michael and Negri, Antonio (2012) 'Declaration', http://antonionegriinenglish. files.wordpress.com/2012/05/93152857-hardt-negri-declaration-2012.pdf

Hart-Landsberg, Martin (2013) *Capitalist Globalization: Consequences, Resistance and Alternatives*. Monthly Review Press: New York.

Hawksley, Humphrey (2014) 'Why India's Brick Kiln Workers "live like slaves"', http://www.bbc.com/news/world-asia-india-25556965

Hayes, Dennis (1989) *Behind the Silicon Curtain: The Seductions of Work in a Lonely Area*. Boston: South End Press.

Hayles, Katherine N. (1999) *How We Became Posthuman: Virtual Bodies in Cybernetics, Literature, and Informatics*. Chicago: University of Chicago Press.

Head, Simon (2014) *Mindless: Why Smarter Machines are Making Dumber Humans*. New York: Basic Books.

Heinrich, Michael (2012) *An Introduction to the Three Volumes of Karl Marx's Capital*. New York: Monthly Review Press.

Henderson, J., Dickens, P., Hess. M., Coe. N. and Yeung, H. (2002) 'Global Production Networks and the Analysis of Economic Development', *Review of International Political Economy*, 9: 436–64.

Heron, Gil Scott (1971) 'The Revolution Will Not Be Televised'. Flying Dutchman/ RCA.

Herrera, Linda (2014) *Revolution in the Age of Social Media: The Egyptian Popular Insurrection and the Internet*. London: Verso.

Herszenhorn, David M., Hulse, Carl and Stolberg, Sheryl Gay (2008) 'Talks Implode During a Day of Chaos; Fate of Bailout Plan Remains Unresolved', *New York Times*, 25 September, http://www.nytimes.com/2008/09/26/business/26bailout.html?_r=2&pagewanted=1&hp

Hesmondhalgh, David (2010) 'User-Generated Content, Free Labour and the Cultural Industries', *Ephemera: theory and politics in organization*, 3/4, http://www.ephemerajournal.org/sites/default/files/10-3hesmondhalgh.pdf

Hirsch, Afua (2013) 'This is Not a Good Place to Live: Inside Ghana's Dump for Electronic Waste', *Guardian*, 13 December, http://www.theguardian.com/world/2013/dec/14/ghana-dump-electronic-waste-not-good-place-live

Hooks, Christopher (2014) 'Q&A with Molly Molloy: The Story of the Juarez Femicides is a "Myth"', *Observer*, 9 January, http://www.texasobserver.org/qa-molly-molloy-story-juarez-femicides-myth

Hong, Yu (2010) 'Will Chinese ICT Workers Unite?: New Signs of Change in the Aftermath of the Global Economic Crisis', *Work Organisation, Labour and Globalisation*, 4(2): 60–79.

Horst, Heather and Miller, Daniel (2006) *The Cell Phone: An Anthropology of Communication*. Berg: New York.

Howard, Philip N. and Hussain, Muzammil M. (2013) *Democracy's Fourth Wave? Digital Media and the Arab Spring*. Oxford: Oxford University Press.

Howe, John (2013) 'Prototype Boulevard', *New Left Review*, 82: 85–96.

Huws, Ursula (2003) *The Making of a Cybertariat: Virtual Work in a Real World*. New York: Monthly Review.

Huws, Ursula (2014) *Labor in the Global Digital Economy: The Cybertariat Comes of Age*. New York: Monthly Review.

IFR (International Federation of Robotics) (2012) 'History of Industrial Robots', http://www.ifr.org/uploads/media/History_of_Industrial_Robots_online_brochure_by_IFR_2012.pdf

IFR (International Federation of Robotics) (2014) 'Service Robots', http://www.ifr.org/service-robots

Ilavarasan, Vigneswara (2007) 'Is Indian Software Workforce a Case of Uneven and Combined Development?', *Equal Opportunity International*, 26(8): 802–22.

ILO (2011) 'Key Indicators of the Labour Market', 7th Edition. Geneva: International Labour Organization. *Information*, 4(2): 171–81.

ILO (2012) 'Global Employment Trends for Women 2012: Labour Market Gender gap: Two Steps Forward, One Step Back', http://www.ilo.org/global/about-the-ilo/newsroom/news/WCMS_195445/lang--en/index.htm

Ischenko, Volodymyr (2014) 'Ukraine's Fractures', *New Left Review*, 87: 7–33.

ITU (International Telecommunications Union) (2012) 'Why Mobile Phones Drive Economic Growth in the Developing World', *ICT Statistics Newslog*, 16 March, http://www.itu.int/ITU-D/ict/newslog/Why+Mobile+Phones+Drive+Economic+Growth+In+The+Developing+World.aspx

ITU (International Telecommunications Union) (2013) 'Key ICT Indicators for Developed and Developing Countries and the World (Totals and Penetration Rates)', www.itu.int/en/ITU-D/.../ITU_Key_2005-2013_ICT_data.xls

Jain, Rahul (2014) 'First IT Jobs Went Offshore, Now They're Being Automated', *The Outsource Blog*, 13 September, http://www.theoutsourceblog.com/2014/09/first-it-jobs-went-offshore-now-theyre-being-automated

Jamaa, Abdullahi (2011) 'Somali Pirates Tap into Sophisticated Navigation', *Onislam*, http://www.onislam.net/english/health-and-science/technology/452729-somali-pirates-tap-into-sophisticated-navigation.html

Jamieson, Dave (2014) 'Meet the Real Amazon Drones', *Huffington Post*, 24 April, http://www.huffingtonpost.com/2014/04/24/amazon-delivery-lasership_n_5193956.html

Johnston, John (2008) *The Allure of Machinic Life: Cybernetics, Artificial Life and the New AI*. Cambridge, MA: MIT Press.

Jordan, Tim (2008) *Hacking Digital Media and Technological Activism*. Cambridge: Polity.

Jung, E. Alex (2014) 'Wages for Facebook', *Dissent Magazine*, http://www.dissentmagazine.org/article/wages-for-facebook

Jünger, Ernst (2000) [1957] *The Glass Bees*. New York: New York Review of Books.

Jünger, Ernst (2004) [1924] *Storm of Steel*. New York: Penguin.

Jurgens, Ulrich, Maisch, Thomas and Dohse, Knuth (1993) *Breaking from Taylorism: Changing Forms of Work in the Automobile Industry*. Cambridge: Cambridge University Press.

Kaiman, Jonathan (2014) 'Rare Earth Mining in China: The Bleak Social and Environmental Costs', *Guardian*, 20 March, http://www.theguardian.com/sustainable-business/rare-earth-mining-china-social-environmental-costs

Kan, Michael (2013) 'Foxconn to Speed Up "Robot Army" Deployment', *IT World*, 26 June, http://www.itworld.com/362706/foxconn-speed-robot-army-deployment-20000-robots-already-its-factories

Kelly, Kevin (2009) 'The New Socialism: Global Collectivist Society is Coming Online', *Wired* 17(6).

Kelly, Kevin (2010) *What Technology Wants*. New York: Viking.

Kenny, Charles and Sandefur, Justin (2013) 'Can Silicon Valley Change the World?', *Foreign Policy*, 24 June, http://www.foreignpolicy.com/articles/2013/06/24/can_silicon_valley_save_the_world

Kidd, Dorothy (2010) 'Whistling Into the Typhoon: A Radical Inquiry into Autonomous Media', in T. C. Collective (ed.), *In the Middle of a Whirlwind*. Oakland: AK Press.

Kidd, Dorothy (2012a) 'Occupy in San Francisco Bay', Cities are Us Conference, June, Coimbra, Portugal, https://www.academia.edu/1941154/_Occupy_in_the_San_Francisco_Bay

Kidd, Dorothy (2012b) 'How Long Will Our Fingers Extend? Critical Praxis, and Chinese Working Class Contentious Politics', *Academia*, https://www.academia.edu/2100900/How_Long_Will_Our_Fingers_Extend_Critical_Praxis_and_Chinese_Working_Class_Contentious_Politics

Kjøsen, Atle Mikkola (2013a) 'Human Material in the Communication of Capital,' *communication +1*, 2(3), http://scholarworks.umass.edu/cpo/vol2/iss1/3

Kjøsen, Atle Mikkola (2013b) 'Do Androids Dream of Surplus Value?', Conference paper, Mediations 2.5, London, Ontario, 18 January, http://www.academia.edu/2455476/Do_Androids_Dream_of_Surplus_Value

Kliman, Andrew (2012) *The Failure of Capitalist Production: Underlying Causes of the Great Recession*. London: Pluto.

Knutson, Ryan and Day, Liz (2012) 'In Race For Better Cell Service, Men Who Climb Towers Pay With Their Lives', *ProPublica: Journalism in the Public Interest*, 22 May, http://www.propublica.org/article/cell-tower-fatalities

Kolinko (2002) 'hotlines – call centre |inquiry | communism' http://www.nadir.org/nadir/initiativ/kolinko/lebuk/e_lebuk.htm

Kurzweil, Ray (2005) *The Singularity is Near: When Humans Transcend Biology*. New York: Viking.

Lacan, Jacques (1991) *The Seminar of Jacques Lacan. Book II: The Ego in Freud's Theory and in the Technique of Psychoanalysis 1954–1955*. New York: Norton.

Land, Nick (1992) *The Thirst for Annihilation: George Bataille and Virulent Nihilism (An Essay in Atheistic Religion)*. London: Routledge.

Land, Nick (2011) *Fanged Noumena: Collected Writings 1987–2007*. Falmouth: Urbanomics.

Lapavitsas, Costas (2013) *Profiting Without Producing: How Finance Exploits Us All*. London: Verso.

Lazzarato, Maurizio (2004) *Les Revolutions du Capitalisme*. Paris: Le Seuil.

Leach, Dirk (1986) *Technik*. Paris: Gris Banal.

Lebowitz, Michael (2009) 'Marx's Falling Rate of Profit: A Dialectical View', in *Following Marx: Method, Critique and Crisis*. Chicago: Haymarket Books.

Leech, Garry (2014) 'How Billionaires Talk in Davos: Distorting Poverty to Promote Capitalism', *Counter-Punch*, 29 January, http://www.counterpunch.org/2014/01/29/distorting-poverty-to-promote-capitalism

Leslie, Robert and Burtynsky, Edward (2014) *Stormbelt*. New York: Dewi Lewis.

Lessard, Bill and Baldwin, Steve (2000) *NetSlaves: True Tales of Working the Web*. New York: McGraw Hill.

Leung, Linda (2007) 'Mobility and Displacement: Refugees' Mobile Media Practices in Immigration Detention', *Media/Culture*, 1, http://journal.media-culture.org.au/0703/10-leung.php

Levy, David L. (2008) 'Political Contestation in Global Production Networks', *Academy of Management Review*, 33(4): 943–63.

Levy, Steven (1984) *Hackers: Heroes of the Computer Revolution*. New York: Doubleday.

Lewis, Michael (2014) *Flash Boys: A Wall Street Revolt*. New York: Norton.

Lewis, Paul et al. (2011) *Reading the Riots: Investigating England's Summer of Disorder*. London: Guardian Books.

Licklider, J. R. (1960) 'Man-Computer Symbiosis', *IRE Transactions on Human Factors in Electronics* HFE-1 (March): 4–11, http://groups.csail.mit.edu/medg/people/psz/Licklider.html

Licklider, J. R. (1968) 'The Computer as a Communication Device', *Science and Technology* (April), http://www.utexas.edu/lbj/archive/news/images/file/20_20_03_licklider-taylor-1.pdf

Liddle, Steve (2014) 'Somalia's Other Pirates – The Telecom Companies', Gulfnews.com, 16 January, http://gulfnews.com/news/region/somalia/somalia-s-other-pirates-the-telecom-companies-1.1278269

Linden, Marcel van der (2008) *Workers of the World: Essays Toward a Global Labor History*. Boston: Brill.

Linden, Marcel van der and Roth, Karl Heinz (eds.) (2014) *Beyond Marx: Theorising the Global Labour Relations of the Twenty-First Century*. Leiden: Brill.

Lipietz, Alain (1987) *Mirages and Miracles: The Crisis of Global Fordism*. London: Verso.

Lipton, Michael (1977) *Why Poor People Stay Poor: Urban Bias in World Development*. New York: Maurice Temple Smith.

Lohmann, S. (1994) 'The Dynamics of Informational Cascades: The Monday Demonstrations in Leipzig, East Germany, 1989–1991', *World Politics*, 47(1): 42–101.

Lohmann, S. (2000) 'Collective Action Cascades: An Informational Rationale for the Power in Numbers', *Journal of Economic Surveys*, 14(5): 654–84.

Lucca-Negro, O. and O'Doherty, T. (2001) 'Vortex Breakdown: A Review', *Progress in Energy and Combustion Science*, 27: 431–81.

Lugt, Hans J. (1983) *Vortex Flow in Nature and Technology*. New York: John Wiley.

Lüthje, B., Hürtgen, S., Pawlicki P. and Sproll, M. (2013) *From Silicon Valley to Shenzhen: Global Production and Work in the IT Industry*. Boulder, CO: Rowman and Littlefield.

Lynn, Barry C. (2005) *End of the Line: The Rise and Coming Fall of the Global Corporation*. New York: Doubleday.

Mackay, Robin and Avanessian, Armen (eds.). (2014) *#Accelerate#*. Falmouth: Urbanomics.

Macleod, Ken (1994) *The Star Fraction*. London: Orbis.

Macleod, Ken (2003) *The Human Front*. London: Gollancz.

Macmillan, Douglas, Burrows, Peter and Ante, Spencer E. (2009) 'Inside the App Economy', *Business Week*, 22 October, http://www.businessweek.com/magazine/content/09_44/b4153044881892.htm

McNally, David (2011) *Global Slump: The Economics and Politics of Crisis and Resistance*. Oakland, CA: PM Press.

Madrigal, Alexis C. (2013) 'Not Even Silicon Valley Escapes History', *The Atlantic*, 23 July, http://www.theatlantic.com/technology/archive/2013/07/not-even-silicon-valley-escapes-history/277824

Maher, Stephen (2011) 'The Political Economy of the Egyptian Uprising', *Monthly Review*, 6, http://monthlyreview.org/2011/11/01/the-political-economy-of-the-egyptian-uprising

Mandel, Michael (2012) *Where the Jobs Are: The App Economy*. South Mountain Economics, LLC, http://www.technet.org/wp-content/uploads/2012/02/TechNet-App-Economy-Jobs-Study.pdf

Mandelbrot, Benoit B. and Hudson, Richard L. (2004) *The (Mis)Behaviour of Markets: A Fractal View of Risk, Ruin and Reward*. New York: Basic.

Mann, Eric (1987) *Taking on General Motors*. Los Angeles: Institute of Labor Relations, University of California.

Manzerolle, Vincent R. and Kjøsen, Atle Mikkola (2012) 'The Communication of Capital: Digital Media and the Logic of Acceleration', *triple C: Cognition, Communication, Co-operation*, 10(2): 214–29.

Manzerolle, Vincent and Kjøsen, Atle Mikkola (2014) '*Dare et Capere*: Virtuous Mesh and a Targeting Diagram: A Capitalist Love Story', in Miller, Paul D. and Matviyenko, Svitlana (eds.) *The Imaginary App*. Cambridge, MA: MIT Press, 252–80.

Marazzi, Christian (2010) *The Violence of Financial Capitalism*. New York: Semiotext(e).

Markoff, John (2012) 'Skilled Work, Without the Worker', *New York Times*, 18 August, http://preview.tinyurl.com/k7rg2m8

Markoff, John (2013) 'Google Puts Money on Robots, Using the Man Behind Android', *New York Times*, 4 December, http://www.nytimes.com/2013/12/04/technology/google-puts-money-on-robots-using-the-man-behind-android.html?pagewanted=all&_r=2&

Marks, Brian (2012) 'Autonomist Marxist Theory and Practice in the Current Crisis', *ACME: An International E-Journal for Critical Geographies*, 11(3): 467–91, http://www.acme-journal.org/vol11/Marks2012.pdf

Marsh, Allison (2004) 'Tracking the PUMA', IEEE Global History Network, http://www.ieeeghn.org/wiki/images/b/bf/Marsh.pdf

Martin, Randy (2002) *Financialization of Daily Life*. Philadelphia: Temple University Press.

Marx, Karl (1964) [1844] *The Economic and Philosophical Manuscripts of 1844*. New York: International Publishers.

Marx, Karl (1970) *A Contribution to the Critique of Political Economy*. New York; International Publishers.

Marx, Karl (1973) [1857] *Grundrisse*. Harmondsworth: Penguin.

Marx, Karl (1977) [1867] *Capital: Volume 1*. Vintage: New York.

Marx, Karl (1981a) [1884] *Capital: Volume 2*. Vintage: New York.

Marx, Karl (1981b) [1894] *Capital: Volume 3*. Vintage: New York.

Marx, Karl (2000) *Theories of Surplus Value*. New York: Prometheus Books.

Marx, Karl and Engels, Friedrich (1964) [1848] *The Communist Manifesto*. Washington: Washington Square Press.

Mason, Paul (2007) *Live Working or Die Fighting: How the Working Class Went Global*. London: Harvill Secker.

Mason, Paul (2012) *Why It's Kicking Off Everywhere: The New Global Revolutions*. London: Verso.

Matviyenko, Svitlana (2014) 'Liquid Categories for Augmented Revolutions', *The Exceptional and the Everyday: 144 Hours in Kiev*, http://www.the-everyday.net

Medina, Eden (2011) *Cybernetic Revolutionaries: Technology and Politics in Allende's Chile*. Cambridge, MA: MIT Press.

Mendoza, Martha (2013) 'Silicon Valley Poverty is Often Ignored by the Tech Hub's Elite', *Huffington Post*, 3 October, http://www.huffingtonpost.com/2013/03/10/silicon-valley-poverty_n_2849285.html

Mezzadra, Sandro and Neilson, Brett (2013) *Border as Method, or, the Multiplication of Labor*. Durham, NC: Duke University Press.

Midnight Notes Collective (2009) *Promissory Notes: From Crisis to Commons*, http://www.midnightnotes.org/Promissory%20Notes.pdf

Milanović, Branko (2011a) 'Global Inequality: From Class to Location, from Proletarians to Migrants', World Bank Policy Research Working Paper No. 5820, http://elibrary.worldbank.org/doi/pdf/10.1596/1813-9450-5820

Milanović, Branko (2011b) *The Haves and the Have-Nots: A Brief and Idiosyncratic History of Global Inequality*. New York: Basic.

Mindell, David A. (2002) *Between Human and Machine: Feedback, Control, and Computing*. Baltimore: Johns Hopkins University Press.

Mirowski, Philip (2013) *Never Let a Serious Crisis go to Waste: How Neoliberalism Survived the Financial Meltdown*. London: Verso.

Mitra, Sramana (2008) 'The Coming Death Of Indian Outsourcing', Forbes.com, http://www.forbes.com/2008/02/29/mitra-india-outsourcing-tech-enter-cx_sm_0229outsource.html

Mohun, Simon (1983) 'Organic Composition of Capital', in Bottomore, T. (ed.) *A Dictionary of Marxist Thought*, Cambridge, MA: Harvard University Press, 356–7.

Moody, Kim (1988) *An Injury to All: The Decline of American Unionism*. New York: Verso.

Moravec, Hans P. (1999) *Robot: Mere Machine to Transcendent Mind*. New York: Oxford University Press.

Morozov, Evgeny (2011) *The Net Delusion: The Dark Side of Internet Freedom*. New York: Public Affairs.

Morris-Suzuki, Tessa (1997) 'Robots and Capitalism', in Davis, Jim, Hirschl, Thomas and Stack, Michael (eds.) *Cutting Edge: Technology, Information Capitalism and Social Revolution*. London: Verso.

Morton, Tim (2013) *Hyperobjects: Philosophy and Ecology after the End of the World*. Minneapolis: University of Minnesota.

Mosco, Vincent and Wasko, Janet (eds.) (1988) *The Political Economy of Information*. Madison: University of Wisconsin Press.

Mumo, Muthoki (2014) 'Safaricom Profit Hits Sh23bn as M-Pesa Powers its Growth', *Daily Nation*, 13 May, http://mobile.nation.co.ke/news/Safaricom-profit-hits-Sh23bn/-/1950946/2312386/-/format/xhtml/-/15pik9gz/-/index.html

Murphy, James T., Carmody, Pádraig and Surborgc, Björn (2014) 'Industrial Transformation or Business as Usual? Information and Communication Technologies and Africa's Place in the Global Information Economy', *Review of African Political Economy*, 41(140): 264–83.

Murray, Fergus (1983) 'The Decentralisation of Production: The Decline of the Mass-Collective Worker?', *Capital and Class*, 7(1): 74–99.

Myoung-Hee, Kim, Hyunjoo, Kim and Domyung, Paek (2014) 'The Health Impacts of Semiconductor Production: An Epidemiologic Review', *International Journal of Occupational and Environmental Health*, 20: 95–114.

Nadeem, Shehzad (2011) *Dead Ringers: How Outsourcing is Changing the Way Indians Understand Themselves*. Princeton: Princeton University Press.

Negri, Antonio (2014) 'Some Reflections on the #ACCELERATE MANIFESTO', http://criticallegalthinking.com/2014/02/26/reflections-accelerate-manifesto

Nenni, Daniel (2010) 'TSMC GigaFab Tour!', Semi.Wiki.com, 10 January, http://www.semiwiki.com/forum/content/417-tsmc-gigafab-tour.html

Ness, Immanuel (ed.) (2014) *New Forms of Worker Organization: The Syndicalist and Autonomist Restoration of Class-Struggle Unionism*. Oakland: PM Press.

Ngai, Pun (2005) *Made in China: Women Factory Workers in a Global Workplace*. Durham, NC: Duke University Press.

Nicolaus, Martin (1967) 'Proletariat and Middle Class in Marx: Hegelian Choreography and the Capitalist Dialectic', *Studies on the Left*, 7: 22–49.

Noble, David (1984) *Forces of Production: A Social History of Industrial Automation*. New York: Alfred Knopf.

Noys, Benjamin (ed.) (2011) *Communization and its Discontents: Contestation, Critique and Contemporary Struggles*. New York: Autonomedia.

Noys, Benjamin (2010) *The Persistence of the Negative: A Critique of Contemporary Theory*. Edinburgh: Edinburgh University Press.

NSB (National Science Board) (2012) 'Science and Engineering Indicators 2012', http://www.nsf.gov/statistics/seind12/c6/c6s1.htm

Null, Christopher and Caulfield, Brian (2003) 'Fade To Black', *Business 2.0*, 1 June, http://money.cnn.com/magazines/business2/business2_archive/2003/06/01/343371/index.htm

Nunes, Rodrigo (2008) 'Learning From Porcupines: Analytic War Machines and an Ethics of Intervention', *Transversal*, 6 June, http://transform.eipcp.net/correspondence/1213798160

Nunes, Rodrigo (2014) *Organisation of the Organisationless: Collective Action After Neworks*. London and Luneberg: Mute and Post-Media Lab.

OECD (2011) 'Size of the ICT Sector', in *OECD Factbook 2011–2012: Economic, Environmental and Social Statistics*. OECD Publishing, http://dx.doi.org/10.1787/factbook-2011-72-en

OECD (2011) *Divided We Stand: Why Inequality Keeps Rising*. OECD Publishing.

OECD (2012) *OECD Factbook 2013: Economic, Environmental and Social Statistics*, http://www.oecd-ilibrary.org/sites/factbook-2013-en/08/02/02/index.html

OECD (2013a) *OECD Factbook 2013: Economic, Environmental and Social Statistics*, 'Investment in ICT', http://tinyurl.com/majepu2

OECD (2013b) 'Crisis Squeezes Income and Puts Pressure on Inequality and Poverty', http://www.oecd.org/els/soc/OECD2013-Inequality-and-Poverty-8p.pdf

Ohno, Taiichi (1988) *Toyota Production System: Beyond Large-Scale Production*. Cambridge, MA: Productivity Press.

OICA (Organisation Internationale des Constructeurs d'Automobiles) (2013) *Economic Contributions*, http://www.oica.net/category/economic-contributions/auto-jobs

Oxfam (2014) *Working for the Few: Political Capture and Economic Inequality*. London: Oxfam.

Packer, George (2013) 'Change the World: Silicon Valley Transfers its Slogans – and its Money – to the Realm of Politics', *The New Yorker*, 27 May, http://www.newyorker.com/magazine/2013/05/27/change-the-world

Panzieri, Raniero (1980) [1961] 'The Capitalist Use of Machinery: Marx Versus the Objectivists', in Slater P. (ed.) *Outlines of a Critique of Technology*. Highlands: Humanities Press, 44–69.

Parker, Geoffrey (2013) *Global Crisis: War, Climate Change and Catastrophe in the Seventeenth Century*. New Haven: Yale University Press.

Pasquinelli, Matteo (2014a) 'Italian Operaismo and the Information Machine', *Theory, Culture & Society*, published online before print, 2 February, http://preview.tinyurl.com/lqkqdjt

Pasquinelli, Matteo (2014b) 'The Labour of Abstraction: Seven Transitional Theses on Marxism and Accelerationism', 9 June, http://matteopasquinelli.com/labour-of-abstraction-theses

Paterson, Kent (2010), 'Temping Down Labor Rights: The Manpowerization of Mexico', *CorpWatch*, 6 January, http://www.corpwatch.org/article.php?id=15496

Patterson, Scott (2010) *The Quants: How a New Breed of Math Whizzes Conquered Wall Street and Nearly Destroyed It*. New York: Crown Business.

Pellow, David Naguib and Park, Lisa Sun-Hee (2002) *The Silicon Valley of Dreams: Environmental Injustice, Immigrant Workers and the High-Tech Global Economy*. New York: New York University Press.

Perez, Carlotta (2009) 'The Double Bubble at the Turn of the Century: Technological Roots and Structural Implications', *Cambridge Journal of Economics*, 33(4): 779–805.

Peters, Michael A., Britiz, Roderigo and Bulut, Ergin (2009) 'Cybernetic Capitalism, Informationalism and Cognitive Labour', *Geopolitics, History, and International Relations*, 1(2): 11–40.

Pew Research Centre (2012) 'Global Digital Communication: Texting, Social Networking Popular Worldwide Usage', http://www.pewglobal.org/2011/12/20/global-digital-communication-texting-social-networking-popular-worldwide

Pickering, Andrew (2010) *The Cybernetic Brain: Sketches of Another Future*. Chicago: University of Chicago Press.

Pietrzyk, Kamilla (2010) 'Activism in the Fast Lane: Social Movements and the Neglect of Time', *Fast Capitalism*, 1, http://www.uta.edu/huma/agger/fastcapitalism/7_1/pietrzyk7_1.html

Plan C (2013) *What We Need is a Plan C*, 24 October, http://www.weareplanc.org/c-is-for-plan-c/#.VH4aya9ozIU

Pollak, Joel (2014) 'Are Silicon Valley's High-paid Techies the New Proletariat?', *Breitbart*, 20 April, http://www.breitbart.com/Breitbart-California/2014/04/29/Are-Silicon-Valley-s-High-Paid-Techies-the-New-Proletariat

Porter, M. E. (1985) *Competitive Advantage: Creating and Sustaining Superior Performance*. New York: Free Press.

Poster, Winifred R. (2011) 'Emotion Detectors, Answering Machines, and E-Unions: Multi-Surveillances in the Global Interactive Service Industry', *American Behavioral Scientist*, 55(7): 868–901.

Poulantzas, Nicos (1973) 'On Social Classes', *New Left Review*, 78: 54–27.

PrivCo (2013) 'Yesterday's Big Payday for the IRS; 1600 Twitter Employees Now Millionaires', *PrivCo: Private Company Financial Intelligence*, 8 November, http://www.privco.com/the-twitter-mafia-and-yesterdays-big-irs-payday

Prunier, Gerard (2011) *Africa's World War: Congo, the Rwandan Genocide, and the Making of a Continental Catastrophe*. Oxford: Oxford University Press.

Przeworski, Adam (1977) 'Proletariat into a Class: The Process of Class Formation from Karl Kautsky's *The Class Struggle* to Recent Controversies', *Politics & Society*, 7(4): 343–401.

Ptak, Laurel (2013) 'Wages for Facebook', 21 December, http://laurelptak.com/post/42794613329/wagesforfacebook

Qiu, Jack Linchuan (2009) *Working-Class Network Society: Communication Technology and the Information Have-Less in Urban China*, Cambridge, MA: MIT Press.

Radynski, Oleksiy (2014a) 'Maidan and Beyond, Part I', *e-flux*, http://www.e-flux.com/journal/maidan-and-beyond-part-i

Radynski, Oleksiy (2014b) 'Maidan and Beyond, Part II: The Cacophony of Donbas', *e-flux*, http://www.e-flux.com/journal/maidan-and-beyond-part-ii-the-cacophony-of-donbas

Ramtin, Ramin (1991) *Capitalism and Automation: Revolution in Technology and Capitalist Breakdown*. London: Pluto.

Reguly, Eric (2014) 'Is WhatsApp and its Ilk Killing Jobs?', *Globe & Mail*, 27 March, http://www.theglobeandmail.com/report-on-business/rob-magazine/jobs-optional/article17666903

Reich, Robert (1992) *The Work of Nations: Preparing Ourselves for 21st Century Capitalism*. New York: Vintage.

Reiss, Bob (2001) *The Coming Storm: Extreme Weather and Our Terrifying Future*. New York: Hyperion.

Retort (2006) *Afflicted Powers: Capital and Spectacle in a New Age of War*. New York: Verso.

Rice, Andrew (2011) 'Life on the Line', *New York Times*, 28 July, http://www.nytimes.com/2011/07/31/magazine/life-on-the-line-between-el-paso-and-juarez.html?pagewanted=all&_r=0

Rifkin, Jeremy (1995) *The End of Work: The Decline of the Global Labor Force and the Dawn of the Post-Market Era*. New York: Putnam.

Rivera, Amaad, Cotto-Escalera, Brenda, Desai, Anisha, Huezo, Jeannette and Muhammad, Dedrick (2008) *Foreclosed: State of the Dream 2008*. Institute for Policy Studies.

Robbins, Martin (2012) 'The Missing Millions of Kibera', *Guardian*, 1 August, http://www.theguardian.com/science/the-lay-scientist/2012/aug/01/africa-propaganda-kibera

Roberts, Sarah T. (2015) *Behind the Screen: Digitally Laboring in Social Media's Shadow World*. Forthcoming.

Robins, Kevin and Webster, Frank (1988) 'Cybernetic Capitalism: Information, Technology, Everyday Life', in Mosco, Vincent and Wasko, Janet (eds.) *The Political Economy of Information*, Madison: University of Wisconsin Press, 44–75.

Rocamadur (2014) 'The Feral Underclass Hits the Streets: On the English Riots and Other Ordeals', *SIC: International Journal of Communisation*, 2, http://sicjournal.org/files/PDF/sic-2-07-the-feral-underclass-hits-the-streets.pdf

Rodríguez, Sergio González (2013) *The Femicide Machine*. New York: Semiotext(e).

Ross, Andrew (ed.) (1997) *No Sweat: Fashion, Free Trade, and the Rights of Garment Workers*. New York: Verso.

Ross, Andrew (2006) *Fast Boat to China: Corporate Flight and the Consequences of Free Trade. Lessons from Shanghai*. New York: Pantheon.

Roth, Karl Heinz (2010) 'Global Crisis – Global Proletarianization – Counter-perspectives', in Fumagalli, A. (ed) *Crisis in the Global Economy: Financial Markets, Social Struggles, and New Political Scenarios*. Los Angeles: Semiotext(e), 197–237.

Rotman, David (2013) 'How Technology is Destroying Jobs', *MIT Technology Review*, 12 June, http://www.technologyreview.com/featuredstory/515926/how-technology-is-destroying-jobs

Rulison, Larry (2011) 'Fab 8 Edges Away From the Human Touch', *Times Union*, 20 October, http://www.timesunion.com/business/article/Fab-8-edges-away-from-the-human-touch-2228842.php

RW (Revolutionary Worker) (2000) 'Living on the Bottom of Silicon Valley: Proletarians in California's High Tech Zone', *Revolutionary Worker Online*, 14 May, http://www.revcom.us/a/v22/1052-059/1054/silicon.htm

Saad-Filho, Alfredo and Morais, Lecio (2014) 'Mass Protests: Brazilian Spring or Brazilian Malaise?' in Panitch, Leo et al. (eds.) *Socialist Register 50: Registering Class*. London: Merlin.

Saffer, Dan (2014) 'Why We Need to Tame Our Algorithms Like Dogs', *Wired*, http://www.wired.com/2014/06/algorithms-humans-bffs

Sampedro, Victor and Sánchez Duarte, Jose (2011). 'La red era la plaza' (The net was the square), http://www.ciberdemocracia.es/articulos/RedPlaza.pdf

Sanhati (2010) 'Do 600 Million Cellphone Accounts Make India a Rich Country? A Lesson in Economics for Mr. Chidambaram', *Sanhati*, http://sanhati.com/excerpted/2388

Saraswati, Jyoti (2012) *Dot.compradors: Power and Policy in the Development of the Indian Software Industry*. London: Pluto.

Saul, Heather (2014) 'Turkey Coal Mine Explosion: Protester Attacked by Adviser to Turkish PM Recep Tayyip Erdogan "was relative of dead miner"', *Independent*, 15 May, http://www.independent.co.uk/news/world/europe/turkey-coal-mine-explosion-turkish-pms-advisor-yusuf-yerkel-caught-kicking-protester-9374732.html

Scaruffi, Piero (2010) 'A History of Silicon Valley', http://www.scaruffi.com/politics/sv.html

Schifferers, Steve (2007) 'The Decline of Detroit', BBC News, 19 February, http://news.bbc.co.uk/2/hi/business/6346299.stm

Schiller, Dan (1999) *Digital Capitalism: Networking the Global Market System*. Cambridge, MA: MIT Press.

Schiller, Dan (2012) 'Digital Depression: The Crisis of Global Capitalism', Television Studies Conference, University of Oregon, Portland.

Schlosser, Eric (2013) *Command and Control: Nuclear Weapons, the Damascus Accident, and the Illusion of Safety*. New York: Penguin.

Schumpeter, Joseph A. (1942) *Capitalism, Socialism and Democracy*. London: Routledge.

Schwartz, Peter, Leyden, Peter, and Hyatt, Joel (2000) *The Long Boom: A Vision For The Coming Age Of Prosperity*. New York: Basic Books.

Schwarz, A. G., Sagris, Tasos and Void Network (eds.) (2010) *We Are an Image From the Future: The Greek Revolt of December 2008*. Oakland: AK Press.

Selgado, Sebastiano (1993) *Workers: An Archeology of the Industrial Work*. New York: Aperture.

Selgado, Sebastiano (2000) *Migrations*. New York: Aperture.

Selwyn, Benjamin (2014a) *The Global Development Crisis*. Oxford: Polity.

Selwyn, Benjamin (2014b) 'Beyond 2015: Is Another Development Possible?' *The Bullet*, 1040, www.socialistproject.ca/bullet

Shaiken, Harley (1984) *Work Transformed: Automation and Labor in the Computer Age.* New York: Holt, Rinehart and Winston.

Shannon, Claude E. and Weaver, Warren (1949) *The Mathematical Theory of Communication.* Urbana: University of Illinois Press.

Sharpe, Richard (2013) 'The ICT Value Chain: Perpetuating Inequalities', in Cudworth, T., Senker, Peter and Walker, Kathy (eds.) *Technology, Society and Inequality: New Horizons and Contested Futures.* New York: Peter Lang, 33–46.

Shirky, Clay (2008) *Here Comes Everybody: The Power of Organizing Without Organizations.* New York: Penguin.

Shirky, Clay (2011) 'The Political Power of Social Media: Technology, the Public Sphere, and Political Change', *Foreign Affairs*, January/February, http://www.foreignaffairs.com/articles/67038/clay-shirky/the-political-power-of-social-media

Siegel, Lenny and Markoff, John (1985) *The High Cost of High Tech: The Dark Side of the Chip.* Harper & Row: New York.

Silver, Beverly (2003) *Forces of Labor: Workers' Movements and Globalization since 1870.* Cambridge: Cambridge University Press.

Silver, Beverly and Zhang, Lu (2009) 'China as an Emerging Epicenter of World Labor Unrest', in Hung, Ho-fung (ed.) *China and the Transformation of Global Capitalism,* Baltimore: Johns Hopkins University Press, 174–87.

Simon, Roland (2011) 'The Concept of the Cycle of Struggles', Libcom.org, https://libcom.org/library/concept-cycle-struggles-roland-simon

Simonite, Tom (2012) 'What Facebook Knows', *MIT Technology Review*, 13 June, http://www.technologyreview.com/featuredstory/428150/what-facebook-knows

Singer, Andre (2014) 'Rebellion in Brazil', *New Left Review*, 85.

Singer, P. W. (2009) *Wired for War: The Robotics Revolution and Conflict in the Twenty-First Century.* New York: Penguin Press.

Singh, Sarina et al. (2003) *India.* Melbourne: Lonely Planet.

Sithigh, D. M. (2013). 'App Law Within: Rights and Regulation in the Smartphone Age', *International Journal of Law and Information Technology*, 21(2): 154–86.

Sivy, Michael (2013) 'Why Derivatives May Be the Biggest Risk for the Global Economy', *Time*, 27 March, http://business.time.com/2013/03/27/why-derivatives-may-be-the-biggest-risk-for-the-global-economy

Smith, Ted, Sonnenfeld, D. A. and Pellow, D. N. (eds.) (2006) *Challenging the Chip: Labor Rights and Environmental Justice in the Global Electronics Industry.* Philadelphia: Temple University Press.

Snyder, Michael (2014) 'The Size of the Derivatives Bubble Hanging Over the Global Economy Hits a Record High', *Global Research*, 27 March, http://www.globalresearch.ca/the-size-of-the-derivatives-bubble-hanging-over-the-global-economy-hits-a-record-high/5384096

Solimano, Andrés and Watts, Nathalie (2005) 'International Migration, Capital Flows and the Global Economy: A Long Run View', http://www.cepal.org/en/publications/international-migration-capital-flows-and-global-economy-long-run-view

Solnit, Rebecca (2013) 'Diary', *London Review of Books*, 35(3): 34–5.

Sonderman, Jeff (2014) 'How the Huffington Post Handles 70+ Million Comments a year', *Poynter*, 5 August, http://www.poynter.org/news/mediawire/190492/how-the-huffington-post-handles-70-million-comments-a-year

Spufford, Francis (2010) *Red Plenty*. London: Faber and Faber.

Stanford, Jim (2010) 'The Geography of Auto Globalization and the Politics of Auto Bailouts', *Cambridge Journal of Regions, Economics and Society*, 3: 383–405.

Steiner, Christopher (2012) *Automate This: How Algorithms Came to Rule Our World*. New York: Penguin.

Stevens, Chris (2011) *Appillionaires: Secrets From Developers Who Struck it Rich on the App Store*. New York: Wiley.

Streitfied, David (2012) 'As Boom Lures App Creators, Tough Part is Making a Living', *New York Times*, 17 November, http://preview.tinyurl.com/mrz563l

Streitfeld, David and Mallia Wollan (2014) 'Tech Rides are Focus of Hostility in Bay Area', *New York Times*, 31 January, http://www.nytimes.com/2014/02/01/technology/tech-rides-are-focus-of-hostility-in-bay-area.html?_r=0

Stross, Randall (2010) 'When the Assembly Line Moves Online', *New York Times*, 30 October, http://www.nytimes.com/2010/10/31/business/31digi.html

Struna, Jason (2009) 'Toward a Theory of Global Proletarian Fractions', *Perspectives on Global Development and Technology*, 82/3): 230–60.

Sturgeon, Timothy, van Biesebroeck, Johannes and Gereffi, Gary (2008) 'Value Chains, Networks and Clusters: Reframing the Global Automotive Industry', *Journal of Economic Geography*, 8(3): 297–321.

Sullivan, Andrew (2009) 'The Revolution Will be Twittered', *The Atlantic*, 13 June, http://www.theatlantic.com/daily-dish/archive/2009/06/the-revolution-will-be-twittered/200478

Taylor, J. D. (2014) 'Spent? Capitalism's Growing Problems with Anxiety', *Roar Magazine: Reflections on a Revolution*, 14 March, http://roarmag.org/2014/03/neoliberal-capitalism-anxiety-depression-insecurity

Terranova, Tiziana (2000) 'Free Labor: Producing Culture For the Digital Economy', *Social Text*, 18(2): 33–58.

Terranova, Tiziana (2004) *Network Culture: Politics for the Information Age*. London: Pluto.

Terranova, Tiziana (2010) 'New Economy, Financialization and Social Production in the Web 2.0', in Fumagalli, A. (ed.) *Crisis in the Global Economy: Financial Markets, Social Struggles, and New Political Scenarios*. Los Angeles: Semiotext(e), 153–70.

Terranova, Tiziana (2014) 'Red Stack Attack! Algorithms, Capital and the Automation of the Common', *EuroNomade*, http://www.euronomade.info/?p=1708

Theorie Communiste (2011) 'The Present Moment', Libcom.org, 15 May, https://libcom.org/library/present-moment-theorie-communiste

Therborn, Göran (2012) 'Class in the 21st Century', *New Left Review*, 78: 5–29.

Therborn, Göran (2014) 'New Masses? Social Bases of Resistance', *New Left Review*, 85: 7–16.

Thibodeau, Patrick (2012) 'In a Symbolic Shift, IBM's India Workforce Likely Exceeds U.S.', *Computerworld*, 29 November, http://preview.tinyurl.com/msopu5x

Thompson, E. P. (1991) *Customs in Common*. New York: The New Press.

Thorburn, Elise (2014) 'Social Media, Subjectivity, and Surveillance: Moving on From Occupy, the Rise of Live Streaming Video', *Communication and Critical/Cultural Studies*, 11(1): 52–63.

Thorburn, Elise (2015) *Technology, Bodies, Assemblages and the Recuperation of Social Reproduction in the Assembly Movements of 2011–12*, PhD Dissertation, Faculty of Information and Media Studies, University of Western Ontario.

Tiqqun (2001) 'The Cybernetic Hypothesis', *Tiqqun* 2, http://cybernet.jottit.com

Toffler, Alvin (1980) *The Third Wave*. New York: Morrow.

Tronti, Mario (2012) 'Our Operaismo', *New Left Review*, 73: 119–39.

Trott, Ben (2013) 'Reading the 2011 Riots: England's Urban Uprising – An Interview with Paul Lewis', *South Atlantic Quarterly*, 112(3): 541–9.

Tsing, Anna (2009) 'Supply Chains and the Human Condition', *Rethinking Marxism*, 12(2): 148–76.

TSMC (2010) 'TSMC Begins Construction on GigafabTM in Central Taiwan', 16 July, http://www.tsmc.com/tsmcdotcom/PRListingNewsAction.do?action=detail&language=E&newsid=5041

Tucker, Noah (2013) 'Yip Harburg: The Man Behind the Munchkins', *Socialist Unity*, 16 April, http://socialistunity.com/yip-harburg-the-man-behind-the-munchkins

United Nations (2013) 'National Accounts Main Aggregate Database. GDP/Breakdown at Constant 2005 Prices in US Dollars (all regions)', December, http://unstats.un.org/unsd/snaama/dnlList.asp

United Nations Statistics Division (2014) 'Population Below National Poverty Line, Total, Percentage', https://data.un.org/Data.aspx?d=MDG&f=seriesRowID%3A581

US Census Bureau (2003–2011) 'Information & Communication Technology Survey', https://www.census.gov/econ/ict

US Department of Labor, Bureau of Labor Statistics (2011) 'International Labor Comparisons: Manufacturing in China', http://www.bls.gov/fls/china.htm

US Department of Labor, Bureau of Labor Statistics (2013) 'Employment by Major Industry Sector', http://www.bls.gov/emp/ep_table_201.htm

Valladares, Rodriguez Maria (2014) 'Derivatives Markets Growing Again, With Few New Protections', *New York Times*, 13 May, http://dealbook.nytimes.com/2014/05/13/derivatives-markets-growing-again-with-few-new-protections/?_php=true&_type=blogs&_r=0#

Vance, Ashlee (2010) 'Merely Human? That's So Yesterday', *New York Times*, 12 June, http://www.nytimes.com/2010/06/13/business/13sing.html?pagewanted=all&_r=0

Vercellone, Carlo (ed.) (2006) *Capitalismo cognitivo*. Roma: Manifestolibri.

Vidal, Jon (2013) 'Toxic "e-waste" Dumped in Poor Nations, says United Nations', *Guardian*, 14 December, http://www.theguardian.com/global-development/2013/dec/14/toxic-ewaste-illegal-dumping-developing-countries

Virno, Paolo (1996) 'Notes on General Intellect', in Makdisi, Saree, Casarino, Cesare and Karl, Rebecca (eds.) *Marxism Beyond Marxism*, London: Routledge, 265–72.

Virno, Paolo (2004) *A Grammar of the Multitude*. New York: Semiotext(e).

von Neumann, John (1966) *Theory of Self-Reproducing Automata*. Urbana: University of Illinois Press.

Wallis, Cara (2011) 'Mobile Phones Without Guarantees: The Promises of Technology and the Contingencies of Culture', *New Media & Society*, 13(3): 471–85.

Wang, Vincent (2014) 'TSMC Reaffirms IoT is The Next Big Thing at Technology Symposium', *CTimes*, 29 May, http://en.ctimes.com.tw/DispNews.asp?O=HJY5TAYDFVMSAA00N6

Wark, McKenzie (2004) *A Hacker Manifesto*. Cambridge, MA: Harvard University Press.

Warren, Elizabeth (2014) 'The Vanishing Middle Class', in Johnston, D. K. (ed.) *Divided*, New York: New Press.

Watson, Sara (2012) 'I Didn't Tell Facebook I'm Engaged, So Why is it Asking About my Fiancé?', *The Atlantic*, 14 March, http://www.theatlantic.com/technology/archive/2012/03/i-didnt-tell-facebook-im-engaged-so-why-is-it-asking-about-my-fianc/254479

Webster, Frank and Robins, Kevin (1986) *Information Technology: A Luddite Analysis*. London: Praeger.

Weis, Tony (2007) *The Global Food Economy: The Battle for the Future of Farming*. New York: Zed Books.

Welland, Michael (2009) '"Sand to Chips" – What's the Real Story?' *Through the Sand Glass*, 9 August, http://throughthesandglass.typepad.com/through_the_sandglass/2009/08/sand-to-chips---whats-the-real-story.html

Weller, Ken (1973) 'The Lordstown Struggle and the Real Crisis in Production', Libcom.org, http://libcom.org/library/lordstown-struggle-ken-weller

Wheatley, Alan (2013) 'What About Workers' Share of Income?' *Globe & Mail*, July 23, http://www.theglobeandmail.com/report-on-business/international-business/what-about-workers-share-of-income/article13361857

White, Jerry (2010) 'UAW Membership Continues to Plummet', *World Socialist Web Site*, 1 April, http://www.wsws.org/en/articles/2010/04/uawm-a01.html

Whitton, Luisa (2013). *What About the Heart*, http://luisawhitton.com/Projects/WhatAboutTheHeart

WHO (World Health Organization) (2010) 'Urban Population Growth', *Global Health Observatory*, http://www.who.int/gho/urban_health/situation_trends/urban_population_growth_text/en

Wiener, Norbert (1948) *Cybernetics, or, Control and Communication in the Animal and the Machine*. New York: John Wiley.

Wiener, Norbert (1949) 'Letter to UAW President Walter Reuther', Libcom.org, http://libcom.org/history/father-cybernetics-norbert-wieners-letter-uaw-president-walter-reuther

Wiener, Norbert (1950) *Human Use of Human Beings: Cybernetics and Society*. Boston: Houghton Mifflin.

Wildcat (2008) 'Beyond the Peasant International', *Wildcat*, 82, http://www.wildcat-www.de/en/wildcat/82/w82_bauern_en.html

Wildcat (2007/8) 'Faces of Migration', *Wildcat* ('Unrest in China', at #80), http://www.infoshop.org/node/5253

Wildcat (2013) 'Umschlagspunkte: Thesis on "New Proletariat" and Re-concentration', *Wildcat*, 94, http://www.wildcat-www.de/en/wildcat/94/e_w94_umschlagspunkte.html

Wille, Rob (2014) 'A Venture Capital Firm Just Named an Algorithm to its Board of Directors – Here's What it Actually Does', *Business Insider*, 13 May, http://www.businessinsider.com/vital-named-to-board-2014-5#ixzz3BPiyoiGy

Williams, Alex and Srnicek, Nick (2013) '#Accelerate: Manifesto for an Accelerationist Politics', *Critical Legal Thinking*, 14 May, http://criticallegalthinking.com/2013/05/14/accelerate-manifesto-for-an-accelerationist-politics

Wójcik, Dariusz (2011) *The Global Stock Market: Issuers, Investors, and Intermediaries in an Uneven World*. Oxford: Oxford University Press.

Woland/Blaumachen (2014) 'From Sweden to Turkey: The Uneven Dynamics of the Era of Riots', *SIC International Journal of Communisation*, 2: 7–13.

Wolfram, Stephen (2002) *A New Kind of Science*. Champaign, IL: Wolfram Media.

Wolfson, Todd (2014) *Digital Rebellion: The Birth of the Cyber Left*. Urbana: University of Illinois Press.

Womack, James P., Jones, Daniel T. and Roos, Danile (1990) *That Machine that Changed the World*. New York: Macmillan.

World Bank (2013a) *The Little Data Book on Information and Communication Technology*. Washington DC: International Bank for Reconstruction and Development/The World Bank.

World Bank (2013b) *World Development Report 2013: Jobs*. Washington DC: World Bank.

World Bank (2014a) 'GDP Per Capita (Current US$)', http://data.worldbank.org/indicator/NY.GDP.PCAP.CD

World Bank (2014b) 'Household Final Consumption Expenditure Per Capita (Constant 2005 US$)', http://data.worldbank.org/indicator/NE.CON.PRVT.PC.KD

World Robotics (2014) 'Global Robotics Industry: Record Beats Record', *World Robotics*, http://www.worldrobotics.org/index.php?id=home&news_id=273

Worth, Owen (2013) *Resistance in the Age of Austerity: Nationalism, the Failure of the Left and the Return of God*. London: Zed Books.

Wright, Erik Olin (1978) *Class, Crises, and the State*. London, Verso.

Wright, Melissa (2006) *Disposable Women and Other Myths of Global Capitalism*. New York: Routledge.

Wright, Melissa (2007) 'Femicide, Mother Activism and the Geography of Protest in Northern Mexico', *Urban Geography*, 28(5): 401–25.

Wright, Steve (2002) *Storming Heaven: Class Composition and Struggle in Italian Autonomist Marxism*, London: Pluto Press.

Wulandari, Sri (2011) 'The Global Supply Chain is our God?', *Asian Labour Update*, 78: 27–31.

Wyly, Evlin, Moos, Markus, Hammel, Daniel and Kabahizii, Manuel (2009) 'Cartographies of Race and Class: Mapping the Class-Monopoly Rents of American Subprime Mortgage Capital', *International Journal of Urban and Regional Research*, 33(2): 332–54.

Xuena, Li (2013) 'Why Foxconn's Switch to Robots Hasn't Been Automatic', Caixin. com, 14 May, http://english.caixin.com/2013-05-14/100527915.html

Zaloom, Caitlin (2006) *Out of the Pits: Traders and Technology from Chicago to London*. Chicago: University of Chicago Press.

Zerowork Collective (1975) 'Introduction to *Zerowork I*', https://libcom.org/library/introduction-zerowork-i

Žižek, Slavoj (2012) *The Year of Living Dangerously*. New York: Verso.

Index

Compiled by Sue Carlton

CPSIA information can be obtained
at www.ICGtesting.com
Printed in the USA
FFHW02n0200251018
48961689-53209FF